GW00467503

# PERFECT UNION

# PERFECT
# UNION

## MICHAEL BLUCHER

MACMILLAN
Pan Macmillan Australia

First published 1995 in Macmillan by Pan Macmillan Australia Pty Limited
St Martins Tower, 31 Market Street, Sydney

Copyright © Michael Blucher, Goomong
Pty Limited and Jason Little Pty Limited 1995

All rights reserved. No part of this book may be reproduced or
transmitted in any form or by any means, electronic or mechanical,
including photocopying, recording or by any information storage and
retrieval system, without prior permission in writing from the publisher.

National Library of Australia
cataloguing-in-publication data:

Blucher, Michael.
Perfect union: the parallel lives of Wallaby centres Tim Horan
and Jason Little.
Includes index.
ISBN 0 7329 0814 0.
1. Horan, Tim. 2. Little, Jason. 3. Rugby Union
football players — Australia — Biography. I. Title.
796.333092294

Front cover photograph by Action Photographics
Back cover photograph by Patrick Hamilton
Author photograph by Stewart Riley

Typeset in Bembo 12/15pt by DOCUPRO, Sydney
Printed in Australia by McPherson's Printing Group

*To my family and friends, one of the largest and most enthusiastic
proofreading teams in the history of publishing.*

# Acknowledgments

The author wishes to acknowledge the following people for their support and assistance: Tania Hudson, Terry Doyle, Peter FitzSimons, Jack Gibson, Karen Grassie, Greg Growden, Katrina Horan, Alan Hornsby, Dick McGruther, Bob Templeton, Jim Tucker, the Wallaby players and management and the McLeod family.

# Contents

# Foreword

## by Will Carling

*England World Cup captain and centre.*

I was very honoured when asked to write the foreword for this book as well as being slightly surprised. A Pom writing the foreword for two great Australian sportsmen!

I remember when I first became aware of the Little-Horan centre partnership back in 1989 against France. Very few players have made such a dramatic impact on international rugby. The French, known for their flair and brilliance, came up against a largely restructured Australian XV after its defeats by the British Lions. Very few people, including myself, expected anything but a comfortable French victory, especially considering their vastly superior experience in the three-quarter line. How wrong we were, and how Horan and Little have continued to confound older, more experienced players around the world.

As a fellow centre, I have analysed their play as closely as most, if not closer! And unfortunately I have to say as an Englishman that I can not find too many weaknesses.

It is fair to say that they had a great start in international life playing outside Farr-Jones and Lynagh—at the time quite easily the best half-back partnership in world rugby. They also had the experience and charisma of Campese hovering on the wing to deflect the attention of defences away from them. Nevertheless, their contribution was, and still is immense, not only in attack but also defence.

For me, Philippe Sella was the first of the 'complete' centres. He had pace as well as fast hands, but his defence was similar to that of a flanker, as were his mauling and rucking skills. There have been many great attacking centres, carving gaping holes in opponents' defences and many less celebrated defensive experts in the same position, but until Horan and Little I do not believe there were any who married the two skills so completely. Added on to this is their ability to chase and retrieve high kicks, a skill so few three-quarters acquire and yet one that has produced tries at regular intervals for both Horan and Little.

I could write and write about their skills and exploits as great centres, but not only would it depress me, it would be held against me for ever more by the England squad! More importantly, however, is that I do not believe it is just their rugby skills that set Little and Horan apart. I have been lucky enough to play against some great players, but rarely have I come across two such unassuming men, whose humility off the field is in direct proportion to their brilliance on it.

Having lost the 1991 World Cup final, the England team were faced with having to attend the formal dinner. Not a thrilling prospect at the best of times, but after such a defeat, enthusiasm was running at an all-time low. My memories of that evening were not only of the pain of losing the game, but of the behaviour of the Australian team. There was obvious pride, but also such a lack of arrogance, as expected by many English players, that the evening passed almost painlessly. Within that, Tim Horan and Jason Little played a great part, and much as I respected them as players, much more did I respect them as people after the dinner.

I feel a fraud writing this foreword as most of my mind is telling me that I do not deserve the chance. That being said, I would not pass on the opportunity to wish Tim a very quick and full recovery from his knee injury and I really do hope to see him back playing to his full potential.

To them both, I hope I do not retard sales with these few words and hopefully we might get the chance to compete against one another in the World Cup. *Perfect Union* is a fascinating read and a great story and I hope it is appreciated for how remarkable it is.

Will Carling, February 1995

# Introduction

It is not altogether common for two sportsmen to have their lives lumped together in one biography. In the case of Tim Horan and Jason Little, it was clearly the logical path to travel.

Since their arrival on the international rugby scene in 1989, the pair have almost become a single entity. Like salt and pepper, fish and chips, horse and cart, it seems almost improper to talk about one without the other.

Yet oddly enough, for all the extraordinary parallels in their lives, all the common bonds they share, they remain two distinctly different characters. Almost chalk and cheese!

One is a happily married family man, who has trodden a clearly defined career path since the day he left school. In nautical terms, he could be likened to a motor launch—powerful, noisy, totally driven. His best mate is the racing yacht, the free spirit, destined to go places in style but in no hurry to get there. But however different their outlooks and priorities, their friendship remains as firm as it was the day their paths first crossed.

By little co-incidence, Tim and Jason were together when I first met them back in 1989. I had just started work in a media and public relations role at Queensland Rugby Union. They had not yet arrived on the representative rugby scene, though clearly it was only a matter of time before they did.

Over the ensuing six years, I would get to know both of them very well, through touring with the Queensland team, working constantly with them at Ballymore, and seeing them both quite regularly on a social basis.

Quickly they became the focus of the Queensland Rugby Union marketing thrust—the media and the public demanded to know more. And it was my job to facilitate that process whenever and wherever possible.

I never really stopped to think how familiar I had become with the pair of them until April 29 1993, the day I organised a press conference in recognition of Jason's 50th game for Queensland. Halfway through the conference, *Sun* newspapers reporter Mark Oberhardt asked Jason to nominate his five favourite memories of playing rugby for Queensland.

Somewhat reluctantly, Jason looked across to me and asked: 'Blooch, what are my five favourite memories?!'

It was just another one of Little's quirky throw-away lines, but it helped crystallise something in my mind. Not long after, the three of us sat down for the first time and bounced around the idea of writing a book.

As anyone who has ever undertaken such a project will attest, compiling a work of non-fiction is an all-consuming task. It requires total commitment and dedication on so many different fronts, and complete co-operation on countless others.

In that regard, I have been enormously fortunate. Tim and Jason, or 'Helmet' and 'Pooch' as they were listed in the computer files, could not have been more co-operative, offering all the assistance and support I needed, without for a moment forfeiting their trademark sense of humour. To their unending credit, the pair of them remain as natural and un-affected as the day they first walked through the Ballymore gates.

The two families, in particular Pat and Ray Little and Mike and Helen Horan, were just as accommodating. No matter how tedious or repetitive the questioning became they were cheerful and co-operative. Nothing was ever a chore.

It should be noted, in fact, that of the 107 people I spoke to—from the Grade 3 class-mate, through to the most cele-brated rugby international—co-operation was never once a problem. This can only reflect the esteem in which the pair are held.

I guess the pitfall in any project of such magnitude is to become so personally involved that objectivity is misplaced. But I feel very fortunate to have been working with such a rich topic, and just as honoured to have been entrusted with chronicling the lives of two people I hold in such high regard.

Michael Blucher, 1995.

# Chapter One

## Twickers to Gundi

*'Champions aren't made in gyms. Champions are made from something they have deep inside them—a desire, a dream, a vision.'*

MUHAMMAD ALI

Even Woody was wearing a tie. Twenty-eight years he'd been turning up to functions at Goondiwindi, and not once had he buttoned up his collar. But this was different. The World Cup was in town.

Rugby Union's Holy Grail, the William Webb Ellis Trophy, had been dispatched to the Australian outback for the gratification of Australia's rank and file. And Woody, lover of both the game and his country, wasn't about to let the occasion pass without an appropriate gesture of respect.

'See this tie,' he told the gathering in Gundi's Railway Hotel. 'It's being worn today, but then it's going back in the cupboard, and staying there 'til we win the cup again!' Woody wandered off to charge his glass and toast the victorious Australian Wallabies, for perhaps the 20th time that afternoon.

One table across, a small cluster of men were engaged in some serious male bonding. The debate was spirited. 'Do you reckon it's the real one?' the first one asked.

1

'Not a chance,' piped his mate. 'They wouldn't bring the Cup out here.'

'No, Horan assured me it was the fair dinkum World Cup,' the third bloke said assertively, his haughty name effectively ending the need for further discussion.

It was true. All 39cm, 102oz and $25,000 worth of the gold plated Cup was in Goondiwindi, 12,000-odd miles and two lifetimes away from the hallowed halls of London's stuffy East India Club, home of Rugby's powerbrokers. And it was in the keeping of two young sportsmen who enjoyed a special affinity with these sun-drenched cotton fields of south-west Queensland.

Tim Horan and Jason Little grew up together on the Darling Downs. They played together as juniors—in rugby league teams, in cricket teams and, ultimately, in rugby union teams. They excelled together, and on November 2, 1991, they walked up on the podium at Twickenham, in front of the Queen, to hold aloft the Webb Ellis Trophy. Naturally enough, together.

With the pomp and ceremony having settled, and the confetti of Sydney's World Cup ticker-tape parade long since swept away, Horan and Little headed back to the state's south-west corner—their old stomping ground—to show the rural folk Rugby Union's most coveted possession. They had just four days. The Willian Webb Ellis Trophy—or 'Bill' as the Wallabies called it—had a schedule at the time no less hectic than the Australian Prime Minister. Brisbane shopping centre one day, Sydney school the next, Tasmanian rugby club the day after that. Not since the America's Cup in 1983, or perhaps the Ashes series win in 1989, had there been an Australian *team* sporting achievement which pumped more blood to the hearts of the country's population. Everybody involved in rugby—and many who'd never heard of the game—wanted to lay eyes on the trophy.

The people of the Darling Downs, however, were being treated to a private viewing by Horan and Little. And the Railway Hotel, home of Gundi's infamous Trotting Ducks rugby union club, was the launching pad of the Horan and Little show. According to legend, a bemused Englishman granted the club its name in honour of the Emu—which, to the Englishman's sadly uneducated eye, could be mistaken for a large duck.

History aside, a large gaggle of 'Ducks', given ample warning of the World Cup Screening waddled into the Railway to greet Horan and Little, envoys of the all-conquering Wallaby squad. As far as the 'Ducks' were concerned, there was symmetry which simply couldn't be ignored. Not only did the Trotting Ducks wear a gold jersey, just like the Wallabies, but in 1991 they too were Cup winners.

While Tim, Jason, Nick, and the boys were slogging it out in Wales, Dublin and Twickenham; Prickle, Webby and Mudguts were also waging war, in Warwick, Dalby and Toowoomba. Fate determined that both native species emerged triumphant—the Wallabies securing the Webb Ellis trophy in London, the Trotting Ducks the Risdon Cup in Toowoomba.

And here, 12,541 miles from Twickenham (there's a sign in the centre of town which tells you), sat the respective spoils, side by side in front of a giant banner bonding the two most distant parameters of rugby's world-wide spectrum. The ornate Webb Ellis Trophy, gleaming gold on the left, and on the right the Risdon, just back from the local panel beater's shop. (Grand final celebrations in these parts can get a little boisterous.)

Gundi's Top Duck, president Geoff Cairns' feared the 'dual display' may have appeared a little irreverent. 'No problems,' Horan assured him. 'Go for your life.'

While country custom isn't exactly formal, propriety does have its place. The formalities included a brief welcome from the Mayor of Goondiwindi, Tom Sullivan, who'd rushed to the Railway from the opening of a new weir in Boggabilla, the sister town just the other side of the New South Wales border. A new weir and the Webb Ellis Trophy in the space of three hours—it's doubtful there'd been a bigger day in Gundi since the town's most famous export, the legendary racehorse Gunsynd, ran third to Piping Lane in the 1972 Melbourne Cup.

Alderman Tom somewhat bashfully admitted his son played for the local league team, but all the same, he stressed he liked union and had watched all the Wallabies' matches on television. Tim looked across at Jason and smiled. It was reassuring to know that politicians were the same flexible souls no matter where you were in the world.

A few more speeches, a few small presentations, and the formalities were complete. Jeff Makin, another of the Duck's pioneers, but a man better known for having the most lethal handshake in south-west Queensland, signed off by calling three cheers for Horan and Little.

Instamatic cameras worked overtime, capturing on film the moment many, in years to come, would proudly relate to the grandchildren . . .'And here's one of me with Tim Horan and Jason Little . . . you wouldn't remember them son, but they were the best centre pairing in world rugby . . .' They lined up in droves to have their photographs taken . . . with the Cup, with Tim, with Jason, and combinations of all three.

John 'Prickle' Thorn, a grazier with a property just on the outskirts of town, asked his son, Stuart 'Prickle' Thorn, if he was going to have his photo taken holding the Cup aloft, a la Farr-Jones, at Twickenham.

Stuart went to school with Jason at Toowoomba Grammar. A gangly 193 cm, he was a pretty handy addition to Queensland Country's lineout in his day, but he politely declined the offer. 'Naah, Dad, I'm going to wait until I win it,' he said. Not five minutes later, there he was in a throng of people, hoisting the Cup proudly above his head. 'Yeah well

. . . on second thoughts,' he told his father, 'I mightn't ever get another chance—I thought I'd better do it now.'

There was an eager Englishman among the gaggle, a man by the name of David Sharp. 'Sharpie' was the man most commonly accredited with bringing rugby union—and the Trotting Ducks—to Goondiwindi. He had cried tears of blood on November 2, 1991, after the Aussies had held his countrymen at bay to take the final 12–6. But today he was as Aussie as a XXXX stubbie in the back of a Holden ute.

'You know, I'm probably the only Englishman ever to touch this Cup,' he mused. 'At least I'm one ahead of Will Carling and his boys!' He marched off in search of his beer jug.

As the afternoon wore on, the tales came thick and fast, as the locals rummaged through history to find the smallest vestige of association with rugby union's centres of attention. 'You probably won't remember me Tim, but you used to walk to East State School with my son . . .'

'Sorry to bother you Jason, but do you remember this photo . . . here we are together in Townsville, in the Under 12 Queensland track and field team . . .'

In another place, at another time, the behaviour might have been construed as boorish. But here, in the heart of the Darling Downs, the overriding factor was that Horan and Little shared a genuine affinity with these people. Horan did remember the boy—not his name—but walking to school with him. And Jason could recall the photo, even the day it was taken. What touched him more though, was the fact that the track and field girl, having heard on the radio that Little was coming to town, had driven more than 60 kilometres to show him the picture.

She confessed it had taken her 30 minutes to garner the necessary courage, before she fronted her old athletics teammate in the carpark, only minutes before he was about to drive off.

'Amazing,' said Little, after the girl wandered away, her heart fluttering. 'I haven't seen her since Grade 6. I can't believe she went to so much trouble. I've probably still got the same photo at home.'

In a day or two, Little would have time to check. The World Cup roadshow was going right past his family's pig farm, a sprawling 400 hectare property at Jimbour, 27 kilometres from Dalby.

Perhaps while Jason was rummaging through old photo albums, Tim could go down to the Littles' piggery and torment the piglets, just as he did when he was growing up. Perhaps not. Horan these days is a little more circumspect about the pigs. He has been ever since the day Ray Little, Jason's father, agreed to let the boys give a new litter of piglets their iodine injection.

A determined 11-year-old, Tim was holding the wriggling, slippery little beasts, while Jason implanted the needle in their necks. Everything was going according to plan, until one little piglet unleashed itself just as Jason was about to administer the injection.

*Yoooouch!* The needle plunged straight into Tim's hand, causing it to swell to twice its normal size. Maybe he'd stay in the living room this time around.

But Dalby, Jimbour, the photos, the piggery, were still days away. There were a couple of stops to make in the interim.

The closest was Surat, population 600, and proud winner of the Queensland Tidy Town Award for 1991, but much more importantly the hometown of Tim's childhood sweetheart, now wife, Katrina Ferris. Katrina's dad, Rob, still lived there, and his life wouldn't be worth living if he let his son-in-law, World Cup hero, trophy in hand, speed through town without stopping in at the local store for pikelets and steaming hot coffee.

Cousins, friends, townsfolk, council workers with muddy boots, traipsed into the kitchen at the back of the general store, to shake the hands of the celebrated duo, and to cast a discerning eye over the small but magnificent trophy. The visit lasted no more than an hour but was a resounding success. And for organising it, Rob Ferris was almost as big a legend as his son-in-law.

Some 45 minutes up the road was Roma, a renowned rugby league stronghold of 8000 people. On this particular afternoon, it didn't matter—rugby league, rugby union, rugby tiddly-winks—there were a couple of world champions in their midst, and world champions don't find their way into Roma that often. They would be welcomed with open arms.

A brief visit to the local high school preceded a hastily convened lunch for 150. All were eager to hear 'How'd you do it? How'd you win the Cup?' Little and Horan told them, as best they could. Horan even delved into the nuances of scrummaging, a wonderfully bold bluff given that he knew absolutely nothing about forward play.

The pair then steeled themselves for the impending photo session: 'Take one of me with the Cup, and me with Jason, and what about . . .' The enthusiasm was infectious, although once again the scepticism surrounding the Cup's authenticity was rife. 'It's not the real one though . . . is it?' one middle-aged lady asked, half in statement of fact, half in polite enquiry.

'The real one would be locked up in a box in London somewhere.'

Her male friend piped up: 'Yeah, they wouldn't bring the *real* one out here.' Horan offered the assurance, as he'd done perhaps 50 times before in the past 48 hours. 'No this is it. The real Bill Webb Ellis. The one and only.'

The function was drawing to a close. As a parting gesture, Roma's rugby club, the Echidnas (one of the victims of the all-conquering 1991 Trotting Ducks), presented Horan and Little with a ball signed by the team, in sheer mockery of their own remoteness. A vinyl football, with 20 or so anonymous names and a hastily scrawled illustration of an Echidna—hardly a prize item in a sports memorabilia auction, but Horan quickly entered into the spirit. 'You're kidding, a ball signed by the Echidnas. I've *ALWAYS* wanted one of these.'

The goods and chattels had been packed away, and the roadshow was about to resume when a small, fragile looking old lady appeared outside Roma's Commonwealth Hotel.

She was standing there nervously, clutching what might have been her last five dollar note. It wasn't. It was something much more valuable—a souvenir program from the 1937 match between Toowoomba and the touring Springboks.

Mrs Hannay heard 'on the wireless' that the World Cup was coming to town, and she just wanted to see it, as well as show the boys her program. She was too nervous to touch the Cup—she just wanted to look at it. She recalled Toowoomba on that day in 1937, the match played on a fine but icy winter's afternoon. And meeting the Springbok captain, 'a fine man by the name of Danie Craven'. Later, in the town hall, she would dance the night away with Gerry Brand. 'I think he played fullback that day—I know he kicked the goals,' she regaled.

Then, suddenly, the trip down memory lane came to an abrupt halt. It was time to go. The World Cup—it may make Woody wear a tie, and 'Sharpie' cry tears of blood, but nobody, not even William Webb Ellis, makes Joyce Hannay late for her bridge game.

# Chapter Two

## Life on the Farm

*'I never felt that football built character. That is done by parents . . . you give us a boy with character and we'll give you back a man.'*
AMERICAN FOOTBALL COACH JOHN McKAY

The rickety old school bus groaned to a halt on the narrow dirt road, right in the heart of the Jimbour plain.

The driver, a burly man by the name of Jack Keen, peered expectantly out the window, as the bony blond-haired youngster, heavily laden with school port and lunch-box, galloped down his family driveway, as fast as five-year-old legs would take him.

Gazing across the cotton fields, and sorghum paddocks to the west, the kid could see the bus coming for miles. He could time his run to perfection, but he couldn't afford to be late. Jack Keen waited for no-one. He had too many other stops to make.

Still puffing, Jason Little climbed aboard the small yellow bus and took his seat, at the same time checking that the contents of his school port—and more importantly, his lunch-box—hadn't been sprayed all over the driveway amidst the frenzy of arms and legs.

Mr Keen, in customary silence, clunked the bus back into gear, wrenched the wheel to the right, and the old diesel chugged up the road towards the Jimbour State School, leaving a cloud of dust in its wake.

Some 210km north-east, another blond-haired kid stood at the entrance to his family's dairy farm at Kandanga, in the lush Mary Valley, outside Gympie on Queensland's Sunshine Coast.

It was 8.27am. He had also learned to time his arrival at the front gate to perfection. Arrive a little too early, and he would be assigned a small chore in the dairy just to fill in time. But too late, he'd miss the bus, and that carried a mandatory punishment of cleaning out the dairy when he got home from school. 8.26 to 8.27 was perfect.

He dunked a cup into a fresh bucket of milk, stirred in a couple of heaped spoonfuls of Milo from a tin kept just inside the entrance to the cow shed, and gulped the drink down.

While Goomong Road was a little too windy for Tim Horan to be able to see the bus coming, he could always hear the engine echoing through the valley.

Right on the dot of 8.30, the small vehicle pulled up. He climbed up the steps and took his usual seat among the four Pickersgills sisters. They were rough girls, all a little older than he, but just as good as anyone in the neighbourhood to play footy with.

The door slid shut, the driver, Mrs Tiplady, revved the engine, and the bus resumed its journey across to Kandanga State School, some 25 minutes away.

There was something very special about growing up in the country.

The fresh frosty mornings, the wide open spaces, the animals, creeks to swim, trees to climb—for kids, life on the farm was just one big banquet waiting to be feasted upon.

And if there was such a thing as rural pedigree, Jason Little would have been a blue ribbon winner. His father, Ray, was born and bred on the farm. So too Ray's mum and dad, and Ray's mum and dad's mum and dad . . . all in a space of 240 square kilometres, some three and a half hours west of Brisbane.

Much the same can be said of Jason's mother, born Patricia Mary Bacon, eldest daughter of Frederick and Mary Bacon, dairy and grain farmers from nearby Bowenville, population 215—a few less on weekends.

The two families lived no more than 40–mile apart. (That's MILE—not miles. Nobody in the country ever uses the 's' when discussing distance.) Or 64 kilometres for those more used to metric.

It seemed only appropriate that a girl with a name like Patricia Bacon should finish up marrying a pig farmer from Jimbour. The two first met at a Debutante Ball at Oakey in 1952—there weren't many large social occasions in those days—and when there was one, you had to make the most of it.

Ray, then 18, resplendent in a white tuxedo, arrived with his cousin, Joy, but dumped her at the door and made a bee-line for the petite little blonde on the other side of the room. It may well have been the fastest Ray has ever moved in his life.

'She was the prettiest little girl I'd ever seen,' he harks. 'I couldn't take my eyes off her.'

It took a while—things tend to in the country—but the relationship gradually blossomed. Ray, the aggressor, Pat a little more circumspect, but no less enthusiastic.

Farming, dancing, tennis, friends, good old-fashioned family values—there was ample common ground upon which a solid relationship could be built.

So it came as very little surprise when the pair, having reached the 'suitable' ages of 22 and 21, were married at St Stephen's Church in Toowoomba in September of 1959.

In terms of lifestyle, in terms of friends, in terms of happiness, the pair were very wealthy. In terms of money, they were not. Pat and Ray were both products of honest, hardworking parents, who had been forced to strive for everything they made. On the land in the 1940s and 50s, there were no freeways to success. Just long, winding dirt roads. Pat and Ray grew up knowing full well the value of money.

Pat still remembers vividly her mother, quite a few years before, making her measure a piece of sticky tape before she cut it off. 'We didn't waste a thing—we saved everything we could. Even as a kid I got badly scolded once for making a mud pie out of an egg—it was the only egg the chooks had laid that morning. I never did it again.'

So the newlyweds, both well versed about the evils of waste, assembled their collective goods—a couple of uteloads—and moved in with Ray's parents on the 400-hectare property at Jimbour, until they could afford to build their own home.

In keeping with the trends of the time, Ray Little never had the benefit of a formal education. His solitary year at Toowoomba Grammar School was largely an unhappy one. He wasn't a bad student, and he certainly enjoyed the extra-curricular activities—the football and cricket. But unless you were in the top 10 percent academically, and intended to pursue a profession, you didn't stay at school—you went back to the land.

That's exactly what Ray did. In his 12 months in Toowoomba he missed the farm horribly, becoming so homesick at times he pleaded with his parents to come into 'the city' and fetch him. His parents reasoned there was little point in keeping him at school if his obsession in life was farming. He came home for Christmas in 1952, and never went back. His school uniform—grey pants, white shirt and blue and gold tie—were shuffled away in a cupboard, and replaced by what would become his uniform for life—khaki shorts, khaki shirt, workin' boots, and a straw hat.

Bugger maths, bugger English, bugger history, there was farming to be done, there was a living to be made.

Pat could well appreciate his thinking. She too, had been sent to boarding school—Fairholme College in Toowoomba —at the age of 14, to learn how to become a young lady. But after two years she was back in the dairy at Bowenville, milking the cows and feeding the pigs.

'I was going back the following year to start nursing,' she says. 'But Mum and Dad had just branched out into cows, so I stayed and helped them milk. The family always came first.'

Finances being what they were in those formative years, Ray had little option but to 'share farm' in his early married life. The concept of share farming was pretty straight forward. Somebody else owned the land. You worked like hell, and got a percentage of the profit—the owners got the balance. It was a very common practice in the late 60s, and early 70s.

Trigonometry, logarithms and subjective clauses mightn't have come that easily to Ray, but farming did. A quiet, deep thinking, practically minded man, he might well have been born on a tractor, with a tiny tobacco pipe sticking out of his mouth and a straw hat on his head. He was as much a part of the rural landscape at Jimbour as the fertile black soil which feeds the crops.

Ray worked tirelessly from dawn to dusk, even beyond during harvest season, when bags of grain—600 in a day—had to be sown and stacked. Pat was the invaluable assistant, the little cog which kept the bigger cogs turning. She'd be up with the sparrows every morning, in company with Ray's mother Gwen, preparing the mountain of food required to fuel a small army of farmers engaged in heavy manual labour.

She would take the troops morning tea, then head back to the house to prepare lunch. Then afternoon tea. Then dinner. If a tractor or another vital piece of farm machinery broke down, she or Gwen would drive into Dalby and pick up a replacement part. Every day was a long one.

Gradually, the financial rewards began to appear. Ray's inexhaustible propensity for work and indepth knowledge of all things agrarian was starting to pay dividends. With the tidy sum they had earned in the first year, the Littles were in a position to build their home at Glengarry, the property at Jimbour.

Pat had always been determined to have a large family. Herself one of five children, her thinking had also been strongly moulded by a childhood incident which, even today, she finds difficult to talk about.

At the age of eight, Pat, and her four-year-old sister Margaret, had been watching their father cut logs for the cow yard. The were sitting well clear of any danger, but one of the trees fell awkwardly. Their frantic father screamed for them both to run. Pat ran one way, Margaret the other. The giant tree landed on top of the toddler, killing her instantly.

The tragedy taught Pat untold lessons—not the least of which was just how fickle the world could be. What if that happened to one of her children. If she had two, the other would be left a single child. No. She wanted a big family.

Four to be precise—the first Stephen, just 18 months after the wedding. When Jason was born in the Dalby Hospital at 8.30am, on August 26, 1970, weighing a monstrous 9lb 9.5oz, and measuring 21 inches in length, she decided she'd had enough. 'I feared the next one might be bigger still!' Pat says. 'It was time to call it quits.'

As a toddler, Jason, ever curious, ever adventurous, was prone to the usual thrills and spills. Good fun kids' stuff, the type which gives parents ulcers . . . *Hmmm. Can I climb on to that bathroom basin? Sure I can. Up, up up . . . Ahh made it. Look at the view from . . . whooooooops. Splat. Whhhhhaaaaaaa!*

The odd stitch, a bit of iodine, some Band-Aids, but nothing too serious . . . until a family holiday at Coolangatta in the summer of 1975. Coming back from the beach with elder sister Janelle, who was 12 at the time, four-year-old Jason was crossing a busy road—the road which divides Queensland and New South Wales.

Standing by a first-floor kitchen window, Pat's attention was first caught by the sound of screeching tyres.

She looked up, just in time to see her youngest son airborne, high above the bonnet of a white Holden.

*Oh my God! The falling log!* The memories came flooding back. She tore down the stairs, her feet hardly touching the steps on the way.

Down on the footpath, Jason was wailing, but more out of shock than anything else—bar a few bumps and bruises, his body was pretty much in mint condition.

Janelle's memory is hazy: 'I can't even remember hearing the screech of the tyres. I just recall standing on the median strip—Jason was beside me, then without warning, he stepped off into the path of the car. It all happened in a split second, but it was amazing he wasn't badly injured. The car was travelling at quite a speed.'

Jason's recollection is just as foggy: 'All I can really remember was being carried upstairs—and mum reaching for a bottle of something.'

'Not something—anything,' Pat says. 'I was shaking like a leaf. I needed something to calm my nerves.'

The driver of the white Holden, himself badly shaken by the incident, nervously drove off, doubtlessly unaware what a huge impact he'd almost had on Australian sport.

The annual summer holiday was a good sign for the Little family. After the frugal times of their early married life, in which they had struggled to make ends meet, the financial belt had been let out a couple of notches by a succession of good seasons.

A man with a keen eye for development opportunities, Ray had continued to acquire property through the late 60s and early 70s by reinvesting the returns from the farm.

Ray had also diversified into pork, constructing a high tech piggery on the north-west corner of the property. The piggery required employing two fulltime staff to operate it, but it guaranteed the family a steady cash flow. With a succession of good seasons and inflated commodity prices, the money gradually started to roll in.

That didn't mean much to Jason who, at the time, was simply looking for playmates. Stephen and Janelle were at boarding school in Toowoomba by then, while Ashley was being carted off by Mr Keen in the school bus every morning to Jimbour State School. All that space to play in, and nobody to share it with.

Jason would spend hours following people—his dad on the tractor, uncle Garry through the cotton fields, farm hands Keith Kelly and Greg Taylor around the piggery, or on the odd occasion it was raining, his mother around the house.

'He was like a little puppy,' Keith Kelly remembers. 'One day, we were walking across this little bridge which led from the piggery, Jason wasn't really looking where he was going and "plop", down he went, straight into a giant pond of pig shit! I had to get the high pressure water hose and wash him down before Pat saw him. He stunk to high Heaven.'

One afternoon, in November, the heat of the early afternoon sun having got the better of him, Jason, aged five and a bit, retreated into the house to be greeted by the rather strange sight of his father sitting down in front of the television, watching a cricket Test match between Australia and the West Indies.

It was strange for two reasons. One, he hardly ever saw his father watching television, and two, NEVER did he watch it during the day.

Casting his mind back, Jason can still hear Norman May's commentary . . . 'So in he comes, Thomson, from the Stanley St end, bowling to Richards . . .'

The moment sticks in his mind as the first occasion he ever took any significant interest in sport.

'I thought to myself: "Gee, this cricket must be important if Dad is sitting here watching it during the day when he should be working. Maybe it's worth having a game".'

One game! Try 10! Try 20! Inside the next month there weren't enough daylight hours, nor people on the farm to send down the number of cricket balls this five-year-old wanted to belt.

Morning, noon and night, the requests came. When Ashley was at home, it was Ashley. When Ashley was at school, it was Dad. When Dad was too busy, it was uncle Garry, or Greg or Keith. When they weren't available, the last resort, Mum—complete with apron for shining the ball—was called upon to send a few down.

'Come on, Mum, just a few more.' *Whack!* 'Faster Mum . . .'

'He really did have an insatiable appetite for cricket,' Pat recalls. 'Christmas presents, birthday presents—cricket gear was all Jason ever wanted at that stage. He was fanatical, far more so than the other boys had been. We even put a golf ball in one of my old pairs of stockings and rigged it up to the clothes line, so he could play by himself. Jason would spend an hour at a time, hitting the golf ball with a cricket stump, when there was nobody around to bowl to him.'

When Ashley was at home, and not troubled by the asthma which incovenienced him as a child, the backyard Test matches—one of the great Australian traditions—would be played. They were always intensely competitive affairs. Before play commenced, the roller from the old clay tennis court would be used to iron out any bumps in the pitch. Ashley was older—so he always got to be the Australians—Jason was doomed to spend the morning as the Pakistanis, the West Indians, or Heaven forbid, the Poms.

The captains—normally Greg Chappell and Zaheer Abbas depending on who was touring that summer—could nominate nine trees as fieldsmen. Some were more useful than others, but neither skipper ever dared leave the oleander bush, at short leg, out of their starting line-up. He was very useful, particularly for that short rearing ball.

Both teams would bat right through the order, until a result was recorded. Just as many times as not, the competitive spirit would reach fever pitch . . . Lillee not given a wicket when he should have been, or Asif Iqbal given out when he wasn't . . . tempers would flare . . . push would come to shove . . .

'We had some horrible blues,' Ashley remembers. 'Mum would never know who started them, so she'd belt us both with the wooden spoon. Using that theory, she was certain to get the culprit.'

The boys got to know that wooden spoon pretty well. They knew where it was kept, and when it was going to be used.

A battle of wits gradually developed. Whenever Jason sensed major hostility in the air he would bolt out into the sorghum paddocks and hide, for up to two hours at a time. When he felt the heat was off, he'd return. Sometimes it worked, sometimes it didn't. But it was worth a try.

Tempers and egos weren't the only things left in tatters by the competitiveness of the backyard Test matches. In the duration of one summer, Jason and Ashley, with occasional assistance from Janelle's boyfriend, Guy Alexander, broke 11 windows of the house. It became a joke. The Olsen Hardware van wouldn't be 15 minutes out the front gate, and SMASH—another glorious cover drive, straight through Janelle's bedroom window.

By early January, Pat had come to know the Olsen Hardware telephone number off by heart. She conceded defeat, deciding to wait until the end of the cricket season, and get all of them fixed at once.

Two days later, Lillee bowls to Miandad . . . *Smash* . . . there goes another one!

'A good decision,' Pat thought to herself.


'Let it go Dad, let it run around for a bit . . .'

Mike Horan, tomahawk in hand, stood back, as the fowl ran around the yard like . . . well . . . like a chook with its head cut off.

Sharp left, sharp right, a backflip, a somersault, another backflip.

Five metres away, Tim and Matt Horan, laughing hysterically, were doing the same. Sharp right, sharp left, a backflip, a somersault . . . in near perfect timing with the distressed bird. The boys were three and four at the time. They got to thinking this life on the farm was a fair bit of fun.

However, there might not have been any chooks, or cows, had their father not spotted an advertisement in the farming and pastoral column of *The Sydney Morning Herald*, some 12 months earlier.

'Dairy Farm . . . 165 acres, 50 acres irrigated. Lush Mary Valley region, backing onto the Mary River. Property includes comfortable country style home. $38,000 . . .' It sounded perfect.

The Horan family was living in Sydney's north-west at the time, having moved south in the interests of Mike's fledgling football career. Four years prior, in 1968, he wanted to be a rugby league star—to make some real money. Now that he had a bit of money, he just wanted to be a farmer.

Exactly what attracted him to the farm in the first place, he can't really remember.

His only exposure to anything remotely rural was an annual visit to the Brisbane Exhibition Ground with Grandma Horan. The pair of them would sit in the John McDonald Stand from dawn to dusk, watching the dairy and beef cattle parade around the ring.

Otherwise zilch.

The son of a decorated Queensland policeman, Mike had grown up at Moorooka on Brisbane's southside. It was a traditional Irish Catholic upbringing—school at the local convent, footy or cricket on Saturday, mass on Sunday morning, then off to visit your grandparents on Sunday afternoon. Not a farm implement or an animal in sight.

He attended St Laurence's Christian Brothers College at Annerley, where he was clearly an outstanding contributor. First class student, 1st XV rugby player for three years, 1st XI cricketer for three years, 800m track champion and, in the whole scheme of things, a logical choice for school captain in 1962. He was expected to go onto university—all good students were. The thought of more study repulsed him, but he enrolled in Veterinary Science. At least it had some rural flavour, reminiscent of the days he enjoyed with Grandma Horan at the 'Ecca'.

First year out of school, he was hardly setting the world on fire with his studies, but the football was going well. From his deeds with University's Colts team, he'd been picked to captain the Queensland Under 19 team, which under his direction from five-eighth would go on to take out the national Under 19 championship.

The studies, meanwhile, waned. By the end of the year he'd failed two subjects, but topped the year in animal husbandry. Farming was definitely a passion. And he knew he would be good at it. Sometime in his life, he would give it a go.

Having dropped out of university midway through his second year, Mike Horan's life momentarily looked a little tangled, but the following year, it quickly unravelled with two consequential meetings. The first was with an attractive young nurse by the name of Helen Brannelly, who, four years later, would become his wife. The second, two weeks earlier, was with the drive-in bottle shop attendant at the Stone's Corner Hotel.

Horan stopped there one Friday night early in January, to pick up a few 'tallies' for the evening's festivities. As the attendant approached him, he recognised the face immediately—it was none other than Clive Churchill, the former rugby league great who, since his retirement, had moved to Queensland to coach Easts.

A conversation was struck up. 'You look like you play a bit of football, how would you like to come and have a game with Easts?'

Mike Horan was genuinely flattered. *Clive Churchill— Rugby League Legend—The Little Master—picked ME as a footballer! Where do I sign?*

He did, and three years later the impact of that chance meeting was still being felt, with Horan interrupting his honeymoon on the Hawkesbury River to trial for Parramatta against St George. He was a handy centre, without ever establishing himself as a permanent fixture in the Eels first-grade side.

It was a tough environment, very competitive people in a very competitive world. Horan played two seasons with Parramatta, but gradually priorities changed. He had a young wife, by that stage two young children, and a good job as a lab technician at the CSIRO.

Football was clearly on the outer. The young couple had achieved what they set out to do—come to Sydney, get enough money together to buy a farm, and return 'home'.

*'Dairy Farm..165 acres . . .'* That was it. The advertisement in *The Sydney Morning Herald* was their calling. The Horans

packed up their blue EH Holden—two small boys and two big dogs in the back—and drove back to Queensland.

Young Timothy was two and a half when he stepped on Queensland soil for the first time.

Born on May 18, 1970, he was obviously far too young to appreciate the gamble his parents were taking by starting afresh in a totally foreign lifestyle. All the same, he did like the look of his new home—the wide open spaces, the lush green grass, the animals . . . the tractor.

How he loved that tractor. He followed it everywhere. Mike remembers one morning driving up to the back of the farm to get the heifers in the top paddock—it was a decent journey—a couple of kilometres at least, up hill, down dale.

Having rounded them up, he went to get back on the tractor, and he saw Tim standing there. 'He was only about three at the time, but he'd gone through two creeks, and across a small dam to get there. It must have taken him about 40 minutes from the time he set off. He was a determined little bloke.'

The two boys, Tim and Matt, who was 14 months older, were put to work on the farm—at a ridiculously early age, Helen reflects today.

They rounded up the cows, shifted the irrigation pipes, pumped diesel down into the service tank, hosed out the dairy, even drove the tractor—all inside the first 12 months of moving to the farm.

'Looking back now, it seems a little strange, but they were very much like little men,' she says. 'They grew up very quickly with what they were asked to do.'

Kandanga was a very friendly, homely little environment, in stark contrast to their frantic lifestyle in Sydney, where they'd been two of 3.5 million. Here, they were two of 200. They were a lot more comfortable.

The Horans instantaneously involved themselves in the lo-cal community (as Mike would do years later as a member of State Parliament). He took on the role of secretary of the local dairy farmers' organisation, as well as helping to establish Mary Valley Apex club, the Wide Bay Artificial Breeders' Co-operative, and perhaps most significantly, the Mary Valley Junior Rugby League club.

The Tigers, as Mike decided to call them, had four teams, the youngest being under eight, which he coached. There was a shortage of farm kids in the area, so Tim, still two months short of his fourth birthday, used to go along and make up the numbers.

His father would station him back at fullback, just to make the field look a little busier, and the Tiger cubs look a little less vulnerable.

He wasn't allowed to tackle—he'd just stand at the back of the field, the tails of his jersey hanging out the bottom of his shorts, eating his 20c bag of lollies.

'Can't I play, Dad . . . can't I play?'

'No son . . . you're too small. You might get hurt.'

The following season, when his parents finally granted him permission to get involved, Tim was nothing short of dyna-mite. A hungry little monster had been let out of his cage.

Week after week, game after game, kids one and a half times his size, and almost twice his age, would charge at him. But he'd herd them towards the touchline, a bit like their dog 'Bluey' did with the cows—then WHACK—bury them into the ground.

'I probably sound like a braggart parent,' Mike admits. 'But even from the very earliest of ages, Tim seemed to have a good appreciation of where the touchline was. He knew in-stinctively where he had to stand, and where he had to run, in order to stop these bigger kids.'

Before too long, the local paper, *The Gympie Times*, had dubbed the mite 'Changa', after the famous St George rugby league fullback, Graeme 'Changa' Langlands. On June 18, 1975, they wrote: 'Pint-sized fullback Tim "Changa" Horan saved three certain tries, fearlessly tackling boys almost twice his size'.

Young Changa simply couldn't get enough football. He'd coax his older brother out into the backyard, to play with him. When it got too rough, Matt would retire inside to the sanctity of his bedroom, and a mystery novel. But the game would go on . . .

Helen would listen from the kitchen window, and giggle to herself at the sporting theatre below:

Toolshed door flies open . . . 'And here they come, led out by their captain, Tim Horan. What a season he's having.' The commentary would stop briefly, while Tim tossed with the opposing captain—the invisible kid standing just opposite the invisible referee. 'We'll run that way sir', which meant the Invisibles would be defending the outhouse end.

He'd hoof the ball down the yard, then run back and retrieve it . . . 'Horan, beats one, beats another, beats a third, great run from Horan, they won't stop him, he's going to go all the way. What a try!'

Before the conversion attempt—which oddly enough was always successful—came the action replay. Back he'd go, and do it all again. 'Horan, beats one, beats another . . .'

'He'd entertain himself for hours,' Helen recalls. 'He'd get dressed up in his little jersey, the matching shorts, socks; he always had a whale of a time.'

There were occasions when Dad had time to play, and the opposition became a little stiffer. The wily veteran would feign to pass one way, Tim would fall for it, and Mike would step around him and score, commentating, of course, as he touched the ball down between the water tank and the mandarin tree. 'Another try to Mike Horan . . . this man's on fire this afternoon . . .'

'Tim got so cranky whenever I dummied to him,' Mike says. 'But it certainly taught him a lesson. Right from his earliest competitive football, he refused to fall for a dummy. He'd tackle players on suspicion, rather than have them run past him.'

With Kandanga only 35 minutes drive from Noosa, it was not uncommon for the Horan family to duck off to the beach on the weekend. Milk the cows in the morning, a swim at Noosa, lunch on the Tewantin River, then back in time for the second milking session in the late afternoon.

In early 1975, they made one such excursion—it was probably the first time the family's new addition, Emma, born in October the previous year, had felt the sand between her toes.

While Helen had her hands full with the new toddler, Mike was paddling around in the Tewantin River with Tim and Matt, building up an appetite for lunch.

The 'DEEP WATER' sign, under some circumstances, might have sounded the alarm bells ringing, but under such close supervision, what could possibly go wrong . . .

'Dad, Tim's being silly,' Matt yelped.

Mike, who'd momentarily been distracted while fetching an inflatable duck for another small boy, looked over to where the boys had been standing in waist-deep water.

No Tim. WHERE THE HELL IS TIM?

Seconds later, Tim's head momentarily appeared—then disappeared again.

His desperate father ploughed through the murky water, dived down and plucked Tim, coughing and spluttering, from the river bed.

'Another five seconds, and who knows what would have happened,' Mike says. 'I reckon Tim was on his last breath. He couldn't swim—he was dog paddling. It was a miracle I found him so quickly—the water was so deep and visibility so poor. In fact an eight-year-old boy drowned in exactly the same spot about 10 days later. It was incredibly danger-ous.'

Who got the bigger fright out of the mishap—Tim or his frantic parents—is debatable. The four-year-old was back to his ebullient best 20 minutes later, but spoke about the in-cident for months on end.

Had he known him, Tim could have compared notes with another four-year-old boy, who just two weeks before had been through a similar ordeal, albeit with a car, at the other end of south-east Queensland's holiday strip.

Another day, in another life, and with a little less luck, neither Jason Little nor Tim Horan might have advanced beyond the age of four.

# Chapter Three

## When Two Worlds Collide

*'A friend? What is a friend? Just one with whom you dare to be yourself'*

Jason Little arrived at Jimbour State School in grade one with a clearly defined goal—he wanted to be the fastest runner in his class.

As he learned inside the space of an hour, it would not be that difficult. There were only eight other children in grade one, only one of whom was a boy. His name was also Jason. In a head to head battle, young Little would clearly be the faster Jason.

Still, the lack of competition was only a minor setback. He was just happy to be there. School meant a ready supply of playmates, and plenty of cricket in the lunch hour. He was going to have a good time, he was sure.

Jimbour State School was located right in the heart of town, directly across the road from the other two business concerns which made up the CBD—the butcher, and the general store.

That motorists had to slow down to 60km/h, as they passed through town, was a standing joke among the locals. They reasoned it must have been for tourism purposes. Any faster than 60km/h, and the motorists would not have seen it at all.

The school consisted of just two buildings—a double storey weatherboard classroom block and a hall—a pint-sized oval, covered in clover in winter and bindies in summer, a couple of large shady trees and some swings. Modest, but ample for the 35 children who strolled through the front gates in their grey uniforms, Monday to Friday.

There were just two teachers on staff—a Mrs Graham and a Mr Karate, the latter of whom arrived at school each day on a motor bike. Jason and the other kids thought that was pretty cool, but it didn't preclude them having a field day with his name. Quite frequently, when Mr Karate's back was turned, rulers were set up between desks, and snapped in two by fierce karate chops . . . *Miss-tahhhh . . . Kar-ateeeeee . . . Crack!*

In the eyes of the blond and spindly Little, school classes were OK, except they interfered with the major attraction—running around on the oval at lunchtime.

His mother each morning would pack him monstrous lunches—beetroot of course, meticulously wrapped separately to stop the sandwiches getting soggy—but three or four days a week, he'd wolf the lot down at 'little lunch' so he could spend more time on the oval at 'big lunch'.

And on the rare occasion he was given lines to write out—usually for talking to his cousin Amanda in class—he had the ingenuity to sticky-tape four pencils together, so it only took him a quarter of the time. Everything focussed on freeing up as much time as possible to play on the oval.

He was quite a competent student, although not as devoted or methodical as older brother Ashley, who in grade five was sufficiently moved to write a letter to God, asking him for assistance in passing a social studies test. His mother was never sure if Ashley posted the letter, or for that matter, where he sent it if he did.

By the time he reached grade three, Jason was already in the Jimbour cricket team, not through the weight of any great number of runs or wickets—merely on numbers. For a cricket team, you needed 11—and there were only 18 boys in the school. As far as sport went, it was all hands on deck. His chances of selection were good.

Batting as a tailender, and fielding at backstop, you're not likely to create a huge impression, but Tony Doyle, long serving coach of the Dalby Shell Shield team, was a man with an eagle eye, particularly when it came to cricketing talent.

He first spotted Jason in the nets at the Dalby State School. Jason was just eight at the time. He'd tagged along to cricket practice with older brother Ashley, whose aggressive batting had not only wrecked half a house but had also earned him a spot in the Dalby side in his final year of primary school.

Doyle stood watching, eyes agog, as this slightly built buck-toothed youngster dispatched the bowling of 12-year-old kids with consummate ease.

'I remember wandering over to the team manager, Peter Groom, and saying: "I've just been watching this kid bat—he must be all of eight years old and I reckon he's damn near as good as any player we've got here." I didn't even know who he was. I wondered what the hell he was doing at our training.'

Doyle soon found out who he was, and kept a keen eye on him. The kid was going to be good.

The following year, Doyle invited Jason back to the Darling Downs trials, disregarding the fact he was two years younger than all the other kids. After two days of Possibles v Probables, the rookie 10-year-old was an Essential—an automatic selection in the District side. In years to come, the moment would stand out in Jason's memory—it was the first representative sporting team he had been chosen in.

The Little sporting merry-go-round had started to spin. So too, the tyres of Ray and Pat's old white Ford. On Saturdays it would carry the three of them all over the south-east corner of the state—three hours to Redcliffe, two and a half hours to Brisbane, two hours to Ipswich, three hours to the Gold Coast—in search of Shell Shield runs, wickets and catches.

They had always been particularly supportive parents, but now, with Stephen back running the farm, Janelle at university, and Ashley at boarding school, they could devote all their spare time to Jason.

What time they didn't have, they made.

'They were remarkable people,' Doyle recalls. 'When we didn't have enough cars for transport, the Littles would offer to take two. When we didn't have enough billets, the Littles would offer to take more. They just couldn't do enough to help. I suspect they would have driven to the moon, if Jason had a game there.'

By the same token, the Littles were fortunate. Life on the farm was going very much according to plan. The family had continued to acquire land throughout the 70s, 80 hectares here, 150 hectares there. By the late 70s, the Littles were one of the bigger players in the local grain market, with more than 1600 hectares under harvest.

A piece of land Ray bought for $100,000 in 1974 had yielded $100,000 worth of crops in its first year, while the piggery, now one of the most technologically advanced in the region, was also proving very lucrative. Like all farmers, they had been through the turbulent times, but now they were riding the crest of the wave. The value of land had doubled between 1974 and 1978, and doubled again between 1978 and 1980. Interest rates were low, commodity prices were high—spirits were high. Life was good.

With the days getting shorter, and the nights cooler, the sporting focus at Glengarry gradually switched from cricket to football. The bat and ball went back in the cupboard, out came the old Steeden football, complete with pen markings around the end so the boys knew when they threw the perfect spiral pass.

Jason had been introduced to football by the Brimblecombe boys, who lived just 'five mile' away—the country equivalent of next door neighbours. There were four Brimblecombe brothers—which meant, at one stage, they accounted for almost a quarter of the male population at Jimbour State School. It also meant they had ample resources for a game of football in the backyard, and it was there, on the Brimblecombes' Wyalong property, Jason acquired the most fundamental of his skills—catching, running, passing . . . and ducking.

Craig Brimblecombe recalls: 'They were fairly torrid encounters—the odd head-high, but nothing too malicious—just typical schoolboy buffoonery. My most vivid memory of Jason was not so much his skills, or his fancy footwork, but his intensely competitive spirit. I wouldn't go as far as to say he was a bad sport, but he hated like hell to lose.'

For formal competition, the boisterous mob had to be driven to Jandowae, 27 kilometres away . . . just a quick spin of the Falcon's wheels. Jimbour managed to scrape together a school cricket team, but the extra two required for a rugby league side stretched resources beyond the limit. Jandowae Junior Rugby League club was the nearest, and most suitable alternative. Each Saturday Jandowae would play in a Zone 4 competition, against teams from neighbouring Roma, Murgon, Wandoan and Tara, as well as Ipswich and the Gold Coast.

Ross Clarke, now the principal of Moranbah East High School in central Queensland, helped establish the club back in the early 70s. The very mention of Jason Little's name these days triggers his memory of a 'little pest'. 'I mean that in the nicest possible way. But in the early days he was this little tike, who came up to your knee. He was always hanging around, just wanting to play. Finally we gave him a run in the Under 10s. He was only six at the time, we put him at hooker to keep him out of the way, but in a matter of weeks he'd developed into one of the best front-on tacklers I have ever seen in that age group. And that took a lot of courage, because the other kids were so much bigger and older than he was. His technique was amazing. His Dad, I'm sure, had a lot to do with Jason's early success. He was the perfect father—not at all pushy, but very supportive. Jason used to soak up information, and any advice his father offered.'

One of the many aspects of weekly football Jason did enjoy was the level of acceptance it offered among his peers. As somebody who was both younger and smaller than the bulk of his teammates, his early displays of courage generated enormous respect. He'd walk off the field, his chest puffed out, as proud as punch.

In one game, against Murgon, Jason was bitten on the leg by a young rival, obviously hungry for victory. Although Jason, at the end of the game, stormed off the field refusing to shake hands with the perpetrator, he was secretly glad it had happened. The bite mark was a badge of courage, and the incident the major topic of conversation as the bottles of Fanta were being handed around after the game.

There was of course a downside to the heroic opportunities team sport provided, as he discovered while playing for the South West region against the Darling Downs in Roma as a 10-year-old. His team was just a minute away from an unexpected win over the hotshot kids from Toowoomba, when Jason, running the ball out from his own line, was stripped of possession by a chunky blond-haired opponent. The kid had no trouble galloping over for the match-winning try.

Jason was inconsolable for an hour after the game. It was the first time in his life he could remember letting other people down, particularly in something as important as sport. It was a good lesson. He remembered that night never wanting to feel that way again.

As much as Jason enjoyed his football at the time, it was very much the poor relation of his sporting interests during those formative years. Cricket was definitely the number one priority, athletics the second, and football a distant third. 'I absolutely loved cricket,' he recalls. 'Everything about it—the sound of ball on the bat, the feeling of hitting a ball in the middle, the mind games that went on, even all the gear that you wore when you played—I just lived for it. Athletics I enjoyed because it was so clearly defined. Unlike cricket or football, there was never any doubt. Either you jumped over the bar, or you didn't . . . you ran faster than the next person, or you didn't . . . It was so cut and dried. But football—I could take it or leave it. It was something you were almost expected to play. I enjoyed it, but nowhere near as much as the other two.'

His preference manifested itself, not only in his constant requests for cricket-related presents, but also in the report cards he would bring home from Jimbour State at the end of each school year. GRADE THREE: What do you want to be when you grow up? Jason: A farm. GRADE FOUR: Farmer, Crikseter. GRADE FIVE: Pig Farmer, Criketer.

He could go a long way in the game . . . if only he could learn to how to spell it.


Meanwhile, back on the farm the Horan household was doing it tough.

Four years ago, rookie farmer Mike, unwilling to take the risk of being hit by drought, had deliberately bought a farm which backed onto a river. The way he'd structured the finance, a good cash flow was essential . . . for a good cash flow, you needed a good supply of water . . . for a good supply of water you needed a river. The logic was sound enough, but what he'd left out of the equation was the weather.

Perhaps he should have given long range forecaster Lennox Walker a call before he put down the deposit. The inimitable Mr Walker may have been able to warn him that in the next six years, Kandanga would be hit by two of the worst floods in living memory—the notorious Australia Day flood in 1974, and the winter flood of 1976. On both occasions, large parts of the property went asunder, pastures were ruined and cattle were lost. Compounding the Horans' problems was the beginning of the world cattle price slump. While Mike was still sloshing around the farm in his Wellington boots, inspecting damage and mending fences, the diminishing value of his herd was sending the family deeper into the mire. The Horans' life was like a game of snakes and ladders. Every time they started moving up the board, down they slid again.

'It was a hell of a battle,' Mike reflects, 'not just for us, but for everybody in the area. I think out of the 184 dairy farmers in the area, 180 of them supplemented their income in some way—we ran the Gympie Turf club, others worked in hotels, some grew pineapples, others branched out into tomatoes . . . they had to, just to make ends meet. We had one week's holiday in six years, and we weren't the worst off by any means. I remember walking into a neighbour's house at Christmas, and seeing four small presents, wrapped in newspaper under the tree. They couldn't even afford the wrapping paper. People were really hurting.'

With Helen's time divided between running the house, looking after her three-year-old daughter Emma, finding jockeys and printing race books for the weekly Gympie gallops, Matt and Tim, out of sheer necessity, were enlisted to help their father run the farm.

They worked like little men, fixing electric fences, pumping diesel, and shifting irrigation—duties far in advance of their years. They were tough, hardy little souls, from a very early age.

Helen remembers driving along Goomong Road one afternoon, and seeing Tim's blue bike—a freshly painted, second hand Malvern Star he'd been given for Christmas the previous year—lying next to a cluster of giant boulders on the edge of the road.

Just as she was about to panic, Helen was flagged down by her next door neighbour, June Sommerville, who half an hour before had scraped young Timothy, bleeding and bruised, off the gravel road.

'When I first saw him, I thought: "Oh my God". He was black and blue. Cuts and grazes all over him,' Helen says. 'He spent two nights in hospital while the doctors examined him and patched him up. It only occurred to me later that not once did he cry. He was a very tough little kid, and I'm sure that had a lot to do with being brought up on the farm, and having to perform the duties he did.'

To help keep the money coming in, Mike even dusted off his old Adidas football boots, last in service at Parramatta's Cumberland Oval in 1969. He signed a one-year contract with the Gympie club, Suburbs.

It was good money—$100 a game. Play six, and he'd have enough funds to meet the annual repayments on the farm loan.

The comeback also delighted Tim . . . he could go down and play ball boy, sit in the dressing shed with Dad before the game, take the sand out to Dad when he was having a shot for goal . . . and be paid 20c for doing it. He was in Heaven.

He loved the sound of the metal tags on the concrete floor, and the smell of liniment smeared over the bodies of players. He can even remember the 'crreeeeaakk' of the dressing room door, which meant kick-off was just seconds away.

There was also a one-armed winger—Arthur Potsbeam—who was a bit of a celebrity in the town. Tucking the ball under his only arm, Arthur would make a long weaving run then trot back into position, from where he'd flag Tim or one of the other ball boys over to give him a block of ice to suck on. Hardly the sort of stuff you'd see at Lang Park, or the Sydney Football Stadium, but this was Gympie. And Tim loved it.

He simply couldn't pack enough football into a weekend. He'd often play three games on Saturday morning, stay in his jersey and boots while he ate lunch, then play a couple more games by himself in the afternoon.

By this stage the less robust Matthew was almost playing out of sufferance. Helen tells the story of an Under 9 final, which finished in an 8–all draw. Both boys were delighted, Tim because he'd get to play 10 more minutes, Matt because he thought he might find some more money.

'He'd found 10c out on the field in the first half, and 20c in the second half,' she laughs. 'It goes to show how interested he was in the football!'

In early 1978, the big break came. Mike applied for, and was appointed to, the position of general manager of the Toowoomba Showgrounds. He was perfectly qualified for the position. Having survived six years on a farm, with two floods, a cattle slump, and three children under the age of eight, he and Helen were qualified for almost anything.

Helen saw Toowoomba as their passport to freedom. She had enjoyed the farm, all its trials and tribulations, but life had been an incredibly hard slog. It was clearly time to move on. You can only play so many games of snakes and ladders.

The family conducted the largest 'garage sale' Kandanga had ever known, selling off every piece of farm equipment they owned, from tractors right down to tool boxes. They packed what was left, and headed for the Downs.

Toowoomba. The big smoke. WOW! Tim could hardly believe his eyes . . . the gardens, the shopping centres, the hotels, the traffic lights, the cars . . . look at all those cars. And he thought Gympie and Noosa were the two biggest places in the world . . . how wrong can an eight-year-old be.

He was a tad sad to be leaving Kandanga, all that open space, the animals . . . the tractor. But he would be well compensated—his new home was located right inside the Toowoomba Showgrounds . . . a 20 hectare backyard, right in the middle of town. He would be the envy of every other kid at Toowoomba East State School.

There were exciting new opportunities, too, like cricket, and tennis, and swimming. He'd never been in a swimming pool before. He wondered why the water was so blue. *Shouldn't it be a murky brown colour?*

School was fantastic . . . if only he didn't have to go to those stupid classes in between sessions on the oval, before school, during school, after school.

As the report cards arrived home, a distinctive trend started to emerge . . .

Timothy Horan 5B . . .

Language Arts D C C
Maths C B B
Social Studies B C D
Music C C D
Art B B B
Phys Ed A A A.

Timothy Horan 6A . . .

Language Arts D D C
Maths E C D
Social Studies C C B
Music D C D
Art B C B
Phys Ed A A A

He survived on a bare minimum of schoolwork, spending the vast majority of his time out in his giant backyard, rolling his cricket pitch, or kicking the football, or hitting the cricket ball that dangled in the toe of an old stocking rigged up between the house and the laundry.

The idea was to stroke the ball 200 times, off the middle of the bat, without it hitting either wall . . . 121, 122, 123 . . . *Damn!* One, two, three . . .

By grade six, his obsession with all things athletic was starting to reap rewards. He was the school's fastest runner, he played lock for the Toowoomba Clydesdales rugby league team, and had just graduated into the ranks of Shell Shield cricket, as a batsman/wicket-keeper.

While the game of cricket was a little drawn out, a little slow moving to ever hold the fascination that football did, he was still captivated by the challenge, and enjoyed the weekend trips away with his mates . . . two hours in the car to Redcliffe, one and a half hours to Brisbane . . . two hours to the Gold Coast, and, once a year, an hour out to Dalby.

Dalby were a good side, they had two big mean fast bowlers. 'Both about seven feet tall,' Tim remembers. 'The only way you could score runs from them was by snicking them through the slips. It really annoyed them too.'

They also had this blond-haired kid—a really good batsman. Tim didn't know his name, although he'd swear he'd seen him somewhere before. This kid had the greatest array of cricketing apparel Tim had ever set eyes on—expensive Gray Nicolls bat, thigh pad, chest pad, forearm pad, batting helmet, spiked shoes . . . if it had been invented, this kid had it. And—he kept it all in this magnificent cricket bag—it was the envy of the entire Shell Shield competition.

'Here we were,' Tim says, 'in our white stubbies and T-shirts, a plastic bag, with a pair of gloves and a protector in it—This kid had the lot, proper cricket shirt—a spare bat—even his own scorebook! He probably would have been considered a bit of a poser, but he could really play, so he got away with it.'

That afternoon, driving back to Toowoomba in the car, slurping on the traditional post-game bottle of Fanta, the question started to eat away at Tim: *Who WAS that kid with all the gear . . . I'm sure I've seen him before . . .*

Then the penny dropped. It was the kid he'd stolen the ball from, to score the match-winning try in a footy game out at Roma last year. He was sure that was him.

Three months later, the seasonal sporting dial having swung around to athletics, Tim was in Townsville, where he was representing the Darling Downs in the State primary school championships.

Having bombed out in the first heat of the 200m, Tim was back sitting in the grandstand, making paper planes with a few of the other early relegation victims. He was just about to launch another one into orbit, when he heard this tumultuous applause . . . 'the winner of the high jump, with a leap of 1.6m, J. Little of South West Region.'

*There he was again! The kid with all the cricket gear. The kid I stole the ball from. He was everywhere. He must like sport as much as I do.*

'I remember somebody telling me it was the first medal of any kind the South West had ever won,' Horan says. 'That's why they were making such a fuss of him.'

Come late May, the pair would cross paths again, in a Probables v Possibles trial to determine the Darling Downs/South West team for the State Zone Rugby League Championships.

Ironically, the two zones—Darling Downs and South West—had been amalgamated for the first time just four weeks before, which meant Tim and Jason would be playing with, instead of against, one another.

Tim was considered a certain selection, until fracturing his wrist in a game three weeks prior. It was compulsory to play in the trial to be selected, so against the better judgment of his parents he strapped up the wrist—just 24 hours out of plaster—and ran on for 10 minutes.

An hour later, in the shadows of the large trees behind Toowoomba's Athletic Oval, the Bundaberg tour squad was read out . . . D. McGrath (Dalby), G. Willmett (Roma), T. Horan (Toowoomba), J. Little (Jimbour) . . .

Backslapping all around, with some parents even more excited than their children.

With approximately half the kids from the city—Toowoomba—and half from the outlying areas, billet arrangements had to be put in place for when the team assembled in Toowoomba in a fortnight's time.

Tour manager Terry McNelley asked the boys to pair off, Tim was standing beside Jason at the time. Neither can remember the exact specifics of what happened next, but it went something like this:

HORAN: 'You can stay at my place if you like.'
LITTLE: 'Yeah OK. Thanks.'
HORAN: 'I promise I won't steal the football off you again.'
LITTLE: 'Whaddya mean?'
HORAN: 'Out at Roma that time, when I stole the ball from you in the last minute, so we won the game.'
LITTLE: 'Was that you?'
HORAN: 'Yeah. That was me.'
LITTLE: 'Maybe I'll stay with somebody else.'

Two weeks later, Tim was proudly parading Jason around his giant playground. The wooden goal posts nailed to the fence, the cricket pitch complete with roller, the speedway track—exactly 400m around the inside—the swimming pool. Jason thought he'd set up his backyard pretty well . . . this was FAR superior.

He stayed with the Horan family for a week, going to school with Tim at East State, practising with the rest of the team in the afternoon, then mucking around in Tim's 'playground' until after dusk. At the end of the seven days, the seeds of a strong friendship had been planted. Identical interests, very similar abilities, very similiar personalities, both agreed they'd found the perfect playmate.

In Bundaberg two days later, team manager McNelley was allocating billets to local families. He had at his disposal just one family willing to take two billets. He'd seen Tim and Jason mucking around together, so instinctively sent them off to the home of Ron and Gloria Kelly on the outskirts of town.

A foreman at the Bundaberg Sugar Mill, Ron Kelly had three older daughters but no sons. He loved his sport—he could think of nothing more uplifting than having a couple of boisterous young footballers running around his house. To this day, a photograph of the pair of them sits on the mantelpiece in the loungeroom of the Kellys' modest weatherboard home.

'We've probably bragged about them to 2000 people over the last 10 years,' Ron Kelly admits. 'They were great kids. So happy all the time. Tim loved his Milo. He'd drink about five glasses a day. He had this fascination with Cocoa, our little dog who we'd taught to fetch Gloria's purse whenever we were about to go shopping. Jason was a bit quieter, but just as happy and well-mannered. We loved having them to stay.'

Of very little importance now is the fact that Darling Downs and South West won the State Regional Championships in Bundaberg that year.

Of far greater consequence was the dawning of one of Australian rugby's most celebrated partnerships. A partnership of world renown, and one to serve as the marketing focal point for the code's vibrant new image in the 1990s.

# Chapter Four

## Old School Ties

*'In sport, you'll learn things on the way. You'll learn about life and human frailty . . . if you're lucky you'll learn about honour and trust. Most of all, you'll learn about yourself.'*
AUSTRALIAN GOLFER PETER THOMSON

Toowoomba Grammar School is situated right in the heart of Toowoomba, at the top of the range which bears down across the Lockyer Valley to Brisbane and the Gold Coast.

Liberally spaced on 20 fertile hectares, the school's neo-Gothic architecture and lush green surrounds serve as a ready reminder of Grammar's rich heritage and tradition.

For more than 100 years, the school has been the learning ground for the children of many of the region's wealthiest and most prominent graziers, who enrol their offspring not just to formalise their education, but to prepare them in the ways of life.

In the eyes of middle-class, semi-rural Toowoomba, the school is seen as a bastion of conservatism, a sanctuary of propriety and discipline.

The Little family name is one well known to past principals of the school. Apart from Ray's fleeting visit in 1952, his younger brothers, Neville and Garry, were also prominent students during the 50s and early 60s. Neville in fact was dux of the school in 1958, and on the way to becoming a surgeon when he was struck down by Hodgkin's Disease. He died tragically the following year.

More recently, older brothers Ashley and Stephen had both been boarders, although that only served to confuse the impressionable 12-year-old Jason, as the fateful day drew near. Ashley spoke in glowing terms about Grammar—the facilities, the opportunities, the friends, the fun. But Ashley's endorsement had to be weighed up against earlier accounts from Stephen, who couldn't find a single complimentary word to say about 'the joint'. A strong-willed, at times belligerent youngster, Stephen left school at the end of grade 10, and went back to Jimbour to work on the farm.

Young Jason was confused. He didn't know what to expect, but he reasoned that any school with eight ovals, six cricket pitches, eight tennis courts, a swimming pool and a gymnasium, couldn't be all bad. At the very least, it would allow him to do what he liked doing best . . . playing sport. Only time would tell.

Some four kilometres away, on the north-western outskirts of town, his good mate was experiencing similiar trepidations, as he strolled into the quadrangle at Downlands College for the first time.

Of the 60 boys in grade seven at Toowoomba East State School, only one other was being sent to Downlands, and he was a 'muso'—the impolite term used to describe those kids who preferred playing the trombone or clarinet to kicking a football. Tim hardly knew who this kid was, let alone be seen in his company.

Closer to home, older brother Matt had now been at the school for two years, and he seemed comfortable enough, but Tim was no longer sure what sort of barometer that was. In recent years, their common interests had gradually dissipated—whereas Matt now enjoyed a staple diet of learning and knowledge, with an occasional side serving of sport, Tim, as always, gorged himself on football and practically anything else athletic.

He was particularly concerned by the football aspect. Ever since he'd lived in Toowoomba, he'd played rugby league for the All Whites, but his new school didn't play rugby league. Downlands played rugby union, whatever that was. Somehow, he would have to get out of playing union, and escape back to his mates at Glenholme Park. There was a lot to think about, so many problems to solve.

KELLY?
Sir!
LEE?
Here Sir!
LEO?
Here Sir!
LITTLE?
Sir.

The Senior's voice boomed out across the stark, sterile dormitory, as 120 sleepy 'grots' shuffled into line for the first of the day's three roll calls. It was 6.45am, the military style operation was moving into gear. There was no time to waste. Beds had to made, shoes cleaned, showers taken and uniforms donned, all before breakfast up in the main dining room. AND IT HAD TO BE DONE RIGHT! The slightest indiscretion, the smallest toe out of line and a punishment of some kind was a formality.

Life in the boarding house revolved around a pecking order. As grots—the less than flattering term for grade eight students—you couldn't get any lower. If a senior told you to get him a cup of tea, you'd get him a cup of tea. If he told you to take it back and put some sugar in it, you'd ask: 'How many sir, one or two?' No grot dared defy the pecking order. To do so would have been distinctly hazardous for his health.

Jason Little hated those early boarding school days with a passion, but no more than the rest of his peers. He could tolerate the disciplinary aspects: the endless roll calls, the rules and the regulations. But right from day one, he took exception to the infantile punishments inflicted by the seniors.

Late at night, it was not uncommon to see a grot, standing with his back against the wall, knees slightly bent, with a brick in either hand for an hour on end. Other nights, very late, the sound of muffled laughter would filter up from the oval, where a couple of the seniors were supervising what was commonly referred to as 'the fountain run'. They would force the grot to guzzle two litres of bore water, then make him run around the oval until he vomited.

Highly intelligent stuff, Jason thought, but like all good grots, he copped it sweet. At the very least, he reasoned the puerile punishments were helping bond together all the new kids at the school . . . the tiny tyros, in the trenches together, fighting the common enemy. It gave him a sense of belonging.

Every now and then though, the veneer of false bravado would crack, as the realities of being away from home for the first time sank in. With the dormitory's open floor plan, it was not uncommon at night to hear the sound of muffled whimpering from across the room. Crying was acceptable, just as long as nobody saw you doing it.

As homesick as Jason got in those early school months, it was outweighed by the enjoyment he derived from having people around him all the time. He simply loved having people around him and there were 120 grots crammed into two levels of Groom House.

Within eight weeks of arriving at the school, Jason had already gained a small piece of notoriety. That he was captain of the 13A cricket team counted for precious little, but in the fifth game of the season, against BBC, he had scored an unbeaten 134 out of a total of 174. Centuries in 32 over games were hardly common, particularly at a school like Toowoomba Grammar which had gone without a GPS 1st XI premiership for almost 50 years. The achievement warranted a special presentation in front of 850 students and 60 staff at the school assembly the following Monday. The masses now knew that somewhere down in the bowels of the school buildings, there was a 'Little grot' who could play cricket.

The onset of the football season usually arrives with a chilly blast in Toowoomba. There are some very cold pockets in Queensland during winter. Toowoomba is one of them. And the dramatic seasonal change trumpets the end of cricket for the year, and the dawning of another rugby season. Touchlines are drawn, football posts erected, and cricket pitches watered, and watered, and watered.

While all GPS sport is contested with intensity, pride and purpose, none is more competitive, more combative, than rugby union. There is hardly a GPS school on the eastern seaboard that doesn't pride itself on the strength of its 1st XV. Rugby is the ultimate symbol of strength, a game which transforms wide-eyed young boys into hardened, principled young men.

Cricket teams can lose outright, rowing boats are allowed to sink in the middle of dams, and debating teams can be humiliated, just as long as your 1st XV side performs with distinction throughout the winter months. Lesser schools are constantly exploring methods of improving their rugby standing, while those at the top work towards fortifying their positions.

Unfortunately Toowoomba Grammar, for most of its natural life, had fallen squarely into the former category—GPS premierships were a rarity. However, the saving grace was the existence of a competition within a competition. If the school beat Downlands, their arch rivals from across town,

LEFT: The Little children meet a furry friend. Stephen 11, Jason 10 months, Janelle 9 and Ashley 4.

BELOW: Little terrors – Jason 6, with Ashley 8 and Stephen 15.

LEFT: Ray Little applauds the boys' first footballing success together – Jason (bottom left) and Tim (top middle) after the State under 12 carnival in Bundaberg.

LEFT: Jason's first race, aged 3.

BELOW LEFT: Tim catching chooks at Kandanga.

BELOW: Life on the farm. Mike Horan with Tim (4), Emma (6 months) and Matt (6).

LEFT: The Horan children off to school at Toowoomba East State – from left, Matt (11), Emma (5) and Tim (9).

BELOW: Tim's first rugby league team, the Mary Valley Tigers. Tim is second from the left in the front row, brother Matt (far right, middle row) and father Mike, the coach, far right.

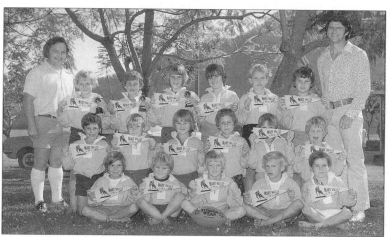

LEFT: Getting ready for Bundaberg, Tim and Jason, with Ashley Little between them.

RIGHT: A game of cards on the Littles' floor during their first year of high school.

BELOW: The Little kid with all the right gear.

ABOVE: Caught in perfect pose before the under 12 titles in Cairns.

RIGHT: Jason clearing one of life's early hurdles.

BELOW: The two always had one another covered, this time in the Downlands v Toowoomba Grammar under 15A match.

TOP LEFT: Side by side in the Queensland Schoolboys cricket team in 1987.

ABOVE: Little's loping stride was a trademark, even at high school.

LEFT: The proud Australian under 17s celebrate the victory over New Zealand in 1987. From left: Michael Brial, Little, Horan, Brett Johnstone, and David Furner, who later switched to rugby league.

Top left: Cadet Under Officer T.J. Horan, Downlands College 1987.

Top right: The happy couple, Horan resplendent in black chiffon, while being billeted together in Brisbane in 1987.

Right: The happy schoolboy pairing, 1987.

ABOVE: Teammates in
the Darling Downs
1st XI.

RIGHT: Which sport?
Little weighs up his
options in 1987.

ABOVE: Side by side in green and gold for the first time. The pair celebrate the historic victory over France in Strasbourg in 1989.

LEFT: Jason and that Wallaby in France 1989. He doesn't remember who the baby belonged to, but he swears it's not his!

RIGHT: Horan 'knows' that club games can be just as tough as Tests. Souths teammate Damon Emtage gives Horan 'a hand' halting the progress of Sunnybank's Simon Hooten.

SUN NEWSPAPERS

LEFT: The three wise
men of the Queensland
mid-field in perfect
sync – Horan, Little
and Michael Lynagh.

GARRY TAYLOR

ABOVE: The Horan wedding day (from left to right): David Francis, Matt Horan, Jason, Mike Horan, Helen Horan, Tim, Katrina, Cathy Ferris, Rob Ferris, Emma Horan, Emma Ferris, Anna Nason.

LEFT AND OPPOSITE: Meeting Princess Diana before the World Cup pool match against Wales in Cardiff. 'I'm sure it's why we got off to such a slow start,' Little says.

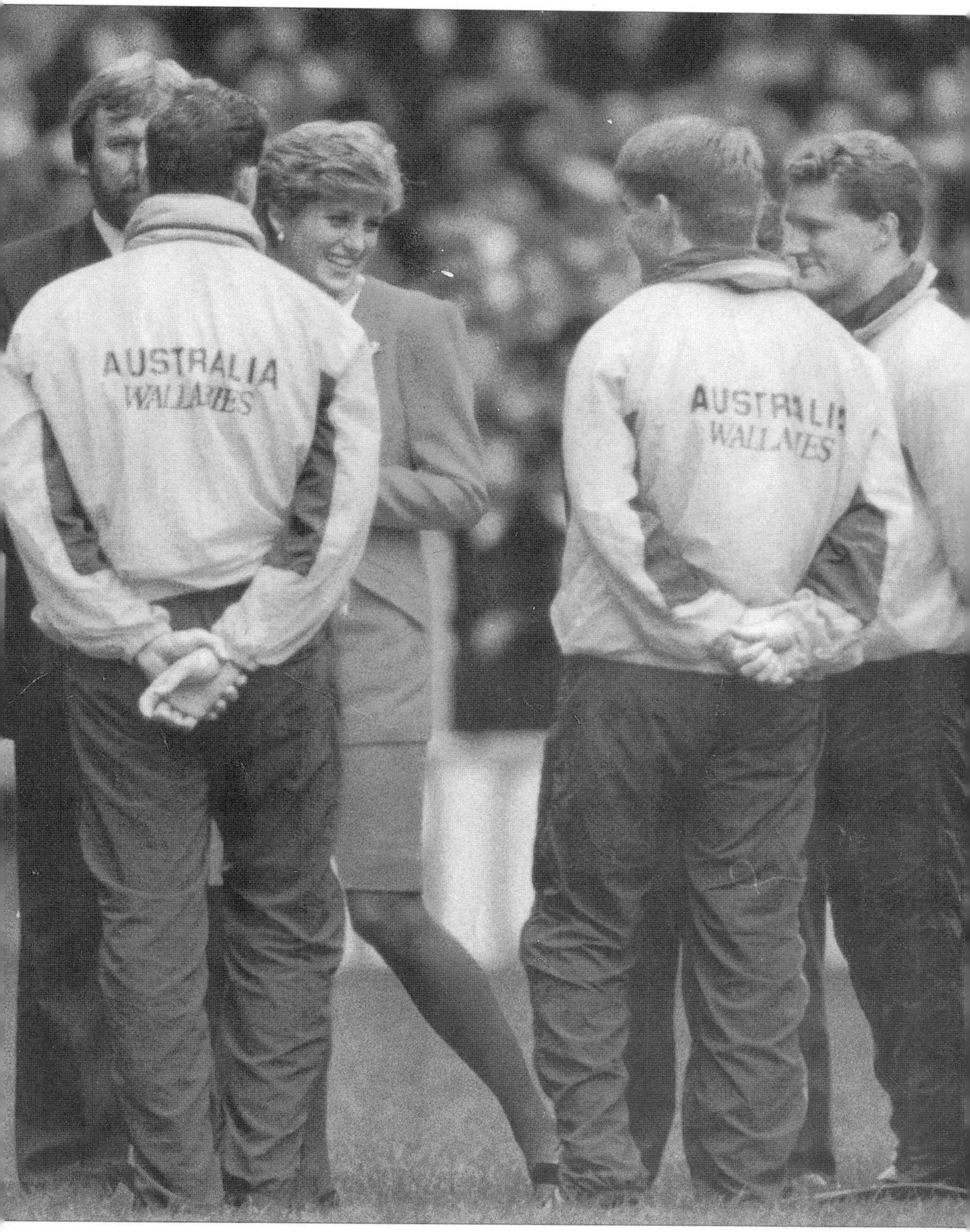
AUSTRALIA

ACTION PHOTOGRAPHICS

ABOVE: Skipper Nick Farr-Jones and deputy Michael Lynagh accept the World Cup spoils from the dignitaries.

RIGHT: The Webb Ellis Trophy is secure.

in the annual O'Callaghan Cup match, they were entitled to hold their heads high for another 12 months.

Jason at least knew what to expect from rugby. As a 10-year-old he had come to the school with his mother and father to watch older brother Ashley play on the wing for the 13As against Gregory Terrace. Like all good, loyal Toowoomba Grammar families, they had stayed to watch the 1st XV game.

He has vivid memories of the huge crowd, and the giant human tunnel which kids formed for the 1sts to run through when they took the field. He remembered how formidable they looked—in their deep blue jerseys, two gold bands around the waist, with numbers on the back.

Formidable they might have looked, but formidable they definitely were not. By halftime, the cheering had long petered out, with Gregory Terrace romping to a 40-something–nil lead. They were an awesome side, led by this blond-haired boy named Lynagh—number 10. Nobody could lay a hand on him. Gregory Terrace ran out 68–0 winners, which today is still the biggest defeat in the history of the school 1st XV.

Hardly the perfect introduction for an aspiring young sportsman, but Jason found a silver lining. He had been seduced by the sheer enormity of the occasion—the atmosphere, the fanatical support of the school, and all the families. He never dreamed for a moment that he'd be part of it—the older Brimblecombe boys were pretty handy players, and they were in school's 'Bs' and 'Cs'. But when he got to school, he would definitely give it his best shot.

A cold, blustery afternoon in the first week of May, 1983, signalled the start of Jason Little's rugby union career. He was just one of 150 'grots' who made their way up to the school's top oval—Kent Oval—to trial for the Under 13 grades. To this day, Jason can never remember being involved in a greater shambles. A sea of willing but aimless humanity, dressed in yellow jerseys and running around in a space fit for about 50. Half the kids, not knowing what they were doing, acted on instinct, and the other half followed. The end result was a giant yellow blob of bodies, arms and legs, contorting across the field, the ball buried somewhere beneath.

It reminded Jason of feeding time at the piggery—when his father dumped a bucket of grain into a pen, and the tiny piglets pushed, shoved and jostled for their share of the rations.

With his Jandowae rugby league background, Jason had some idea of what rugby was all about, but not much. Old habits died hard. The first time he touched the ball, there was no way he was going to let it go. He hung on for dear life, until the shrill sound of the referee's whistle: 'Penalty—not releasing'. *Those rucks and mauls. How do they work again.*

Despite being an automatic choice as flyhalf for the 13As, Jason didn't really enjoy his first year of rugby. His strongest memory of the long, cold, wet winter was the grating, nasal voice of his coach, Mr Curry, who spent the entire season on the sideline, screaming at them for this, screaming at them for that, not doing this, not doing that.

In Mr Curry's defence, there was ample cause for frustration. The team's best result was a draw, and flyhalf Little, with seven, was the leading (and only) point-scorer for the season. Rugby could only get better.

It did. By Under 15s, the team was in the hands of a convivial Science teacher by the name of Graham Samford, who was far more 'user friendly' than any other rugby coach Jason had been exposed to. Mr Samford got into the rucks and mauls, and would come out bleeding—he would put his body on the line for tackling practice. He told the players to take pride in what they were doing, and insisted they have a good time while they were doing it.

'It's something that I've always remembered,' Jason says. 'No matter what level you're playing, if you're not enjoying yourself out on the rugby field, you shouldn't be there. Obviously in some games it's harder than others, but I think it's a very sound philosophy.'

By the end of Grade 10, the sporting seasons were starting to meld into one. Cricket in first term, rugby in second, athletics in third, with gymnastics, cross country and a bit of swimming in between. It was all becoming a blur. He was on a treadmill.

An above average student, with the grades to match during his first three years, Jason's academic wheels were starting to wobble badly by the first semester of Grade 11. The amount of time he spent away from school—at athletics meets, at cricket carnivals, at rugby tournaments—was almost criminal. When he was at school, he was simply too tired to study. Midway through the afternoon, two or three times during a week, he'd sneak across to sick bay, and get a yellow slip from dear old Sister Kluck, so he could go back to the boarding house and have a sleep.

Clearly, something had to give—either sport or study.

Jason remembers addressing the problem with his parents, while driving back from the National Junior Athletics Championships in Perth in 1986.

Sprawled out in the back seat of the family's silver Ford Fairlane (the wheels of the old Ford station wagon had long since stopped spinning) he lobbed the question to Ray—which of his three sports—his three loves—should he sacrifice?

His father, always the deep thinker, ever analytical, bounced the issue around in his mind, before carefully selecting his words. If the problem was time-related, then perhaps that was a good place to start.

'Well,' said Ray, 'which sport takes up the greatest amount of time?'

'Probably cricket, but that's always been my main sport. I can't give up that.'

Fifteen–love, Jason. Ray was already on the backfoot.

'OK then, which one do you think you're best at?'

Modesty prevented Jason from saying so, but he was exceptionally good at all three. He had already represented his state in rugby and cricket, and just two days before, he'd broken the national Under 16 high jump record with a leap of 2.07m.

It was a poorly phrased question. The criteria laid out was obviously not going to shed any light on the problem. Ray had foot-faulted. Thirty–love, Jason.

'Well, which do you enjoy playing the most?' Ray asked in one last desperate bid to slide a serve past his agile young opponent.

'I love playing them all. I don't want to give up any of them.'

Ray remembers staring through the windscreen, at the straight flat road ahead, and smiling to himself. Forty–love, and on the ropes. Clearly it was not a game he and Pat were going to win. In a roundabout way, Jason was forewarning them that his grades mightn't be all that flattering for the next couple of years.

The kid could even play tennis.

No . . . no . . . please . . . please . . . *Damn!*

The big kid strutted away with his mates, laughing and guffawing. Another victim!

Young Horan looked down helplessly at the contorted red and blue strip that, seconds ago, was a necktie. Now it was a disgrace, twisted and askew, with a knot the size of his fingernail. But the tie would have to stay that way until the morning, when his mother could tie it for him again.

Oh what a difference a couple of months makes. Only last December, he was the king of the castle, ringing the school bell in the morning, running the cricket games at lunchtime, and pushing into the tuckshop line whenever he so desired.

It had taken seven years to earn those privileges. Now he'd lost the lot. The empire was gone. He was back to being a tiny fish in a giant pond . . . a 'greaser'. Greasers were exactly the same as grots, except they wore blue and red uniforms, instead of the blue and gold. That Downlands was a Catholic boys college, predominantly for day students, made very little difference. Greasers were treated just as contemptuously as their counterparts from across town.

Tim spent most of his first term at Downlands working out what he could—and couldn't—get away with. He had all sorts of new rules and regulations to obey—surely some of them could be bent or stretched a little. During the ensuing weeks, he would inadvertently put a few to the test. One lunchtime, in a high speed chase through the boarding house dormitory, he'd lost sight of his quarry. 'Shit' he said, at that very second swivelling around to see the large bulbous face of a teacher staring down at him. *Whooops!* Off he went, dragged by the ear to Brother Tattersall's office to have his mouth washed out with one of seven different flavoured shaving creams on the mantelpiece of the master's office. OK. Thou shalt not swear—he knew that rule was largely non-negotiable.

Despite the enjoyment he extracted from captaining the Downlands 13A cricket team, Tim still had reservations about playing rugby when winter arrived. He was determined to persevere with league. Somehow though, he feared he wasn't going to get a say in the matter. Right from the earliest of sporting days, his father had been very supportive, without ever intruding. But on this occasion, he recommended strongly that Tim give rugby a go. 'If you don't like it, you can go back and play league, but at least give it a try,' his father advised.

*Perfect!* That gave Tim the out clause he'd been hoping for. He had his plan carefully mapped out. He'd go along to the trials, get in a team, play a few games, say he didn't like it, and within a month, he'd be back with his mates playing league.

Everything was going beautifully, until one Thursday morning in early May, when the 13A team was posted up on the main sports noticeboard, outside the Sports Master's Office.

Out centre: D. McGrath
In centre: J. Carswell
Wing: J. Wright
5/8: T. Horan (Capt)

*Captain? They're kidding! What did they make me captain for?* His tidy little plan, suddenly, was looking a little messy. How was he going to quit after a few games if he was captain? He was trapped, until he could come up with Plan B. But while he thought, he may as well play.

Tim Horan's entry into the rugby union ranks was anything but smooth. Just as his snowy-haired chum across town had struggled to come to grips with the complicated new rules, so too did young Timothy, by now a stalwart of seven seasons of junior rugby league.

He wanted to play lock—or No 8—just as he did in league. But his father suggested he have a run at five-eighth—he'd probably see more of the ball in that position. This part was true. He did see more ball, but exactly what he should do with it, he didn't rightly know. So he tucked it under his arm, and charged ahead, time and again. To his astonishment, each time, a few of his teammates would then try to steal the ball from him. *Imagine that . . . guys on your OWN team!*

There was also confusion about the kicking rules. In an early game against Gregory Terrace, Horan booted the ball out on the full. Just as he was about to chastise himself, his teammates started slapping him on the back. *Oh, you can do that, can you?* He tried it again, this time there were groans of disapproval from the sidelines, as the referee brought play back to where he kicked it.

'I really didn't have a clue what I was doing,' Tim recalls. 'In one other game we were trailing by two points, and the kid next to me suggested we get down the other end and have a shot at field goal. I thought to myself: "What good would that do us?" I'd only ever heard of a one-point field goal. I knew my maths wasn't flash, but I thought this kid had lost the plot. As it turned out, he had a shot, it went over, and we won the game.'

Midway through his first winter at Downlands, Plan 'Get Back to All Whites' had long been abandoned, and replaced by the goal of playing for the 1st XV. If he was excited by his own rugby, Horan was simply entranced by the 1sts. He watched their games religiously—he'd decided there was no more important sporting event in the world than those games at 3.15 on a Saturday afternoon. From the first time he saw players run out through the long winding tunnel, in their special jerseys, white shorts, blue socks with red bands, he wanted to be part of it. And he would. No matter how hard he had to train, he would get one of those special jerseys, and run out through that tunnel.

Halfway through his third season of rugby, the dream was coming closer and closer to reality. The word around the school was that Downlands had this 'gun' Under 15A team, and the two most lethal attacking weapons were the halves, five-eighth Horan, and halfback Brett Johnstone, a slender lightning-fast kid who the year before had transferred from Goondiwindi High school—350 kilometres west.

Instead of arriving at 3pm to watch the 1st XV, parents and supporters were turning up at midday, watching the hot-shot Under 15s, going away to get some lunch, then returning for the 1sts game.

Under 14A coach, Sports Master John Coonan, took the unusual step of staying with the team the following year, so great was his desire to coach them for another season.

Coonan, now a teacher at Daramalan College in Canberra, ranks a try Horan scored against Brisbane Grammar as the finest individual effort he has ever seen from a schoolboy.

'He picked up the ball about 10m from his own line, cut across field to the sideline, straightened, then ran past or through or over about nine tacklers. At the time, it was the most extraordinary thing I'd ever seen a schoolboy do, and I haven't seen anything better since.'

While Horan was making a big impact on the sports field—he was also captain of the 15A cricket side, and the fastest 400m runner in the school—nothing of the sort could be said of his efforts in the classroom. Not that he was a bad student, he just wasn't interested.

'I could never understand as a 15-year-old, how doing an assignment on Beach Erosion or The Fall of the Roman Empire was going to help get me a job. At that age, I didn't think of education as a learning process—in my mind, school was something you did until you were old enough to get a job.'

His flippancy towards schoolwork was accepted by some teachers, but there were others who fired the old staple line at him: 'You have to study—you're never going to earn a living playing sport'. But every time Tim heard the words, his eyes narrowed, and jaw clenched. The translation of the body language: *By all means have your say. But you're wrong, and I'll prove you wrong.*

Much later in Horan's life, World Cup coach Bob Dwyer would notice that same steely glare, whenever he told his star midfielder something he didn't want to hear. *Yes Bob, sure Bob . . . we'll see Bob.*

As if there weren't already enough distractions to Tim Horan's scholastic pursuits, by grade 11 another had spawned—with the arrival at the school of the girls from St Ursula's.

Downlands was boys only for the first three years, but became co-ed in Grades 11 and 12. For 260 young males, smack bang in the middle of adolescence, the addition of 200 girls was a distraction, but a good one. They looked forward to having them around—it was going to be fun.

For the first few months, the new 'co-habitants' warily eyed each other off, like prize fighters prancing around the ring.

A pattern quickly emerged. Every morning, the girls would get off the bus, they'd walk across the lawns, up past the library, around the Dwyer Building and down the 'Emu' steps to their lockers. The 'Emu' steps were so named because of the width of each step. Upon descent, each abnormally large step required about one and a half paces, which meant you either had to take two smaller steps, or stretch out in a stooped fashion, like an Emu.

As the only short access route to the lockers, the Emu staircase was also the best place for the boys to stand in the morning. They would line up in predatory fashion, and rate the girls as they stooped their way down the stairs . . . 'Five, Four, Wow! Eight, Yuk—One.'

It was sexist, it was cruel, it was crass. They were 15. It was a lot of fun.

One girl that Tim and his obnoxious cronies never had a chance to rate was a slender but athletic brunette by the name of Katrina Ferris. Far too shy to be rated, Katrina and her friends would walk right around the back of the main oval—a further 500m—just to avoid the scrutiny, and the ogling eyes.

The Equal Rights Commission would be pleased to hear that the intimidatory behaviour didn't last long—the novelty of having girls around gradually wore off, and the young Downlands men discovered more polite, and ultimately more fruitful means of interaction. No longer was it 'uncool' to talk to girls. Good friendships, rather than relationships, became commonplace.

Tim and this girl Katrina Ferris enjoyed one such alliance. Katrina had also grown up in the country, on a grazing property at Surat, 400 kilometres west of Toowoomba, and as an excellent middle distance runner and netballer, shared Tim's love of sport. But it was just a friendship. No matter how many times his friends—and her friends—said they were just made for each other, Tim felt they would never be more than buddies, even though he hoped they could.

Tim can't remember exactly when it was—he suspects in the middle of Grade 11—but he was standing in a group, talking to Katrina and a few of her friends.

Katrina was perched on the pipe railing of Emu stairs, but as she laughed she toppled backward, cracking her head on the cement below.

The pain and the acute embarrassment were bad enough, but when she clutched the back of her head, and realised blood was gushing from the wound, she went into a state of shock.

It seemed a very natural thing for Tim to do . . . to put his arm around her, comfort her, then take her down to the infirmary to have her head stitched.

As the nurse rushed around, piecing together the parts of a pain-killing needle, Tim sat beside Katrina and held her hand tightly—*for the first time*. The crucial step had been taken. The pair started seeing each other more and more regularly—a new but very strong relationship had been born.

And along with it, according to his loyal school chums, came a second Tim Horan personality—a heavily modified, toned down version of the one he displayed when he was with them.

Brett Johnstone, who would later join Tim in the Queensland and Australian teams, explains: 'I guess, at school, everybody's a bit different around girls. But with Tim, it was like chalk and cheese. Around his mates, he was an absolute ratbag, always playing practical jokes, and pulling black acts on people. Around Katrina, he was the perfect gentleman.'

A big strong kid by the name of Garrick Morgan admits to being an early victim of the mischievous Horan humour. Morgan, formidable schoolboy second-rower, who like Johnstone would later rejoin Horan on the representative rugby scene, arrived at Downlands in Grade 11, transferring from Brisbane's Marist Brothers College. An imposing figure, even at that age, Morgan went straight into the 1st XV, which is where he got to know Horan.

'He was a real little shit—not unlike he is today,' Morgan says. 'He was always getting me in trouble. I'd go to sit down, and he'd pull my chair out. When I fell over, I'd be sent outside. No matter what he did, I'd get the blame.'

Morgan recounts frequent forays into town on Friday and Saturday nights, where Horan would simply toy with people in a distasteful, but nonetheless typical manner.

'We used to go into places like McDonalds,' Morgan says, 'and Tim would walk up to the counter in disabled fashion, and order in sign language, pretending he was deaf and dumb. The girl behind the counter would be really sorry—really embarrassed—and apologise for not being able to understand him. Then Tim would snap out of it: "OK then, just give us a couple of Big Macs and some fries." He did it all the time. Just having fun. One night, I can even remember him rap dancing in the middle of a circle of gospel singers. They were stunned. They just didn't know what to do.'

According to his teammates, and coaches, Horan never lost sight of that sense of fun when playing sport. He always managed to focus tightly on the task at hand, but could switch on and off, just like a light. When there was fun to be had, wisecracks to be made, Horan was right in the thick of it all.

Enjoyment was also one of the catchcries of his school mentor, Downlands 1st XV coach, John Elders. Elders is the man most frequently credited with elevating Downlands rugby to the lofty status it enjoys today. A mild mannered Englishman from Leicester, he coached England on an undefeated tour of South Africa in 1972, and to a joint Five Nations Championship the following season. He arrived at Downlands more by accident than design. As coach of the England Schools side, he was billeted at the school in 1979, at which time, the headmaster, Father Jim Littleton, had the foresight to ask him if was interested in a job as a fulltime Maths teacher.

Elders politely declined, but expressed interest in a four month posting. That was good enough for Downlands. He arrived in 1982, and stayed . . . and stayed . . . and stayed . . . appropriately, long enough for Horan and Little to bring the Webb Ellis Trophy back to the school to show him.

His effect on the school's rugby was immeasurable, not only in terms of the technical expertise he offered, but also the belief he instilled in pupils and coaches alike. He redirected attitude, and heightened enthusiasm. Almost overnight, under Elders' supervision, the school—from the 13Es up to the 1sts—went from easybeats to battle-hardened competitors, capable of mixing it with the best GPS schools. The red and blue jersey was a garment to be worn with pride.

Elders, now semi-retired and living back in England, remembers Horan as an extraordinarily gifted youngster, one whose sporting success centred on a formidably strong competitive spirit more than anything else. 'He had natural talent, certainly. But the quality that really stood out in my mind was his determination to improve, to learn, to win, to compete . . . in every sport he played, cricket, athletics, rugby . . . he was exactly the same.'

No matter how many rough edges Elders might have knocked off, or deft tactical ploys he might have added, Horan believes that Elders' primary, and most profound influence was philosophical.

'John had a very uncomplicated approach to rugby,' Horan recalls. 'He always used to say three things—prepare yourself properly, keep the game simple, but most of all, enjoy yourself. He said it was a laudable aim, wanting to play for your state, or your country, but you should never feel like you've failed if you don't. The rewards are merely a bonus, the icing on the cake. I think that was very good advice, not only to schoolboys, but to everybody who plays sport.'

Back at the Jason Little Sports Institute, known to some as Toowoomba Grammar School, time was not improving the Little lad's quest for academic excellence.

No matter what the season—cricket, football, or athletics—he seemed to be away. Two weeks in Los Angeles representing Australia at the World Junior Athletics Championships, another two weeks in New Zealand with the Australian Under 17 rugby team, six days in Sydney for the Australian Schoolboys rugby team, another 10 days for State cricket trials. As the study months rolled by, he simply got further and further in arrears.

Ray Little remembers one GPS athletics meet at QEII Stadium, where Jason had to catch a flight to Cairns for cricket the same afternoon. Ray had the Falcon engine running in the car park, waiting for Jason to finish his final event—the 4 x 400m relay. Crossing the line first, Jason dropped the baton, and continued running, and running . . . straight out of the stadium, not unlike Forrest Gump, the American cult hero of celluloid fame.

They made the flight by a matter of minutes.

One instance Jason recalls a little less fondly is the aftermath of a five-day cricket carnival in Gladstone. His bus arrived back in Toowoomba at 3am, six hours before a 40 percent Earth Science exam. He knew only too well, that at 9 o'clock, his academic garden bed wouldn't be flowering.

'Gentlemen, you may start your exam. You have two hours.' A single bead of sweat trickled down his forehead, as Jason fearfully ripped open the test paper, and scanned the page of questions. Not one could he answer with any authority, or genuine knowledge. He just sat there and stared blankly around the giant assembly hall, a nauseous feeling welling up in his stomach. Four seats away to his left, he remembers seeing his best mate, Tony 'Simple' McDonald, head down, pen ploughing furiously across the page. The nausea worsened. 'Even Simple knows some answers,' he thought. They were two of the longest and loneliest hours of his secondary school life.

While Jason didn't exactly surrender to study in his final two years, his outlook and attitude were definitely affected by the apparent hopelessness of the situation. To say he became a disruptive influence would be overstating the case, but he was no longer the 'goody-two-shoes' who first arrived at the school in 1983. He'd had a couple of close shaves, without ever having to front the school disciplinarian, deputy headmaster Mr Ron Bourne.

On one occasion in Grade 10, he'd conspired to be part of the midnight raid on nearby sister school, Fairholme College. The three raiders, one of whom tried desperately without success to wake Jason, were subsequently expelled.

A semester later, Jason managed to defuse a potentially damaging 'smoking in the toilet' allegation, by scoffing a mouthful of talcum powder. Not a great taste, but the desperate action was enough to convince a rampant boarding house master, Mr Goodman, that he and his mate, William Rackemann, hadn't been partaking of the evil weed.

Finally, however, the good fortune cookie crumbled. One night, after a 1st XV game against Brisbane Boys College, arrangements were made for a Grammar Old Boy to drop some beer into the boarding house. Rule No 1 of the 'Sneaky Schoolboy Handbook' already broken: If you're going to drink, don't do it in the boarding house. Rule No 2: Never leave a note saying: 'The beer for Ben Mason and Jason Little is in the fridge of the House Prefects Dorm', and Rule No 3: Definitely, under NO circumstances, let the boarding house master find the note!

Jason was oblivious to the fact that Rules 2 and 3 had been breached until 11am the following Monday, when he was hauled out of his Economics class by senior boarding house prefect, Hamish McIntyre, and escorted to Ron Bourne's office.

Mild concern turned to major panic when he saw Ben Mason, ghostly white, sitting on the seat outside the deputy headmaster's office. The penny dropped, the blood pressure rose. The penalty for anyone caught drinking in the school was automatic expulsion.

Ron Bourne, an imposing figure, with broad shoulders and a stern voice, proceeded to tear strips off the two wayward youths. It didn't matter—or seemed not to at the time-that Bourne had been Jason's 1st XI cricket coach for the past three seasons, or his Under 14 rugby coach.

Jason was then told to take the rest of the day off, go back to the boarding house and think about what he had done. *Beauty, another afternoon off.* That was virtually the last he heard of the incident. There was no expulsion, no suspension, just a promise to Ron Bourne that it wouldn't happen again. The same applied to Ben Mason.

There were subsequent phone calls to the office of headmaster Mr Bill Dent, from parents alleging preferential treatment for Little, the school's No 1 sports star, the captain of Cricket, Rugby and Athletics. But to this day, Ron Bourne denies the allegations. Now the headmaster of a school in North Queensland, Bourne says he 'made deals' with a lot of students. 'Young people are prone to making mistakes. But they should not be punished for the rest of their lives.'

Pat and Ray Little, however, acknowledge that Jason would have been expelled had it not been for Ron Bourne's intervention in the matter. So too does Ben Mason.

The O'Callaghan Cup showdown . . . the cabbies in Toowoomba insist there's no bigger day in the year than when the two private schools, Downlands and Toowoomba, clash to determine rugby pre-eminence for another 12 months.

You could call it a matter of life and death, but in the eyes of most Old Boys, it's a lot more serious than that. It's a rugby game, a game which invariably attracts a crowd of between 6000–8000.

Interested parties—families, friends, even friends' families —travel thousands of kilometres, from Mackay, Charleville, Julia Creek, to be in Toowoomba for the weekend of the local derby. And those who witness the O'Callaghan Cup games on a regular basis insist the atmosphere has to be ex-perienced before it can be believed. Old Boys arrive the night before, and park their utes in the prime vantage points, before heading off to the Spotted Cow Hotel to regale stories of past glories.

There are many grounds for the two schools' rivalry, not the least of which is religious, with Downlands proudly Catholic, and Toowoomba Grammar non-denominational. But perhaps of even greater significance is the fact that Toowoomba Grammar is part of the prestigious GPS com-petition, while Downlands is not. That's not to say the Downlands students cannot wear blazers, so large are the chips on their shoulders. But there is definitely a touch of the 'Haves' against the 'Have Nots'—or more accurately, the 'Ares' versus the 'Are Nots'. Downlands' annual game against Toowoomba is the bout they have to win to prove they are not the poor relations. And they will go to practically any measure to make sure they get the first punch in . . .

On the eve of an O'Callaghan Cup game not so many years ago, Downlands students conducted a midnight raid on the TGS swimming pool, dumping untold amounts of red dye into the water. The prank re-defined the battle lines for the game the following afternoon.

On another occasion, witches hats, signifying road work in neighbouring Margaret Street, were strategically re-arranged, so that morning traffic went through—instead of around—the Toowoomba Grammar grounds. The culprits were never caught, but there were no prizes for guessing the origins or motives of those responsible.

Remarkably enough, even members of the opposite sex have been embroiled in the issue of school rivalry. Any Grammar student successfully dating a girl from St Ursula's—Downlands' sister school—is immediately issued with a Superman cape. Likewise, any Downlands student romantically linked with a girl from either Fairholme College, or Glennie.

Jason Little and Tim Horan, in some respects, pioneered new levels of conviviality between the two schools during the years 1983–87. By Grade 12, they had both represented Australia at schoolboy rugby, and played together in the Queensland Under 17 cricket team. Their profile, coupled with the friendship they conducted across school boundaries, persuaded other students that it wasn't compulsory to hate somebody, just because he wore a blue and gold tie instead of a blue and red one.

The pair would regularly rendezvous down town on Friday afternoon at George's Cafe, for the mandatory gravy and chips, the cheapest—and best—item on George's menu. But it wasn't uncommon for them to walk in and see blue and gold ties on one side of the room, and blue and red on the other. Depending on who was there, intermingling often began soon after Horan and Little broke the protocol—and the ice—by sitting down together.

As unshakeable as the friendship was, it had to take a back seat come O'Callaghan Cup time. Particularly this year—1987—the *last* year. The result would stand forever—no 'we'll get them next year' available. The Grade 12 winner would be winner for life.

Horan and Little had enjoyed a remarkable rivalry through their secondary school lives, going head to head in cricket and rugby for five years, frequently as rival captains.

Cricket honours clearly rested with Jason, with Toowoomba Grammar the far superior cricketing school. But that didn't deter the ever-resourceful, doggedly determined Horan from trying every ruse he could think of to balance the ledger any time the two schools met.

In the Under 14 cricket match, played at Downlands, he even reverted to bending the rules—just a touch. One of the Downlands boarders had arrived back at school after the holidays with a two-headed coin, courtesy of some clever handiwork from one of his uncles. With the TGS game coming up on the weekend, Horan simply couldn't let the chance go by—he borrowed the coin, went home, and put it in the pocket of his cricket pants.

Come Saturday, the young captains strolled out onto the field.

'Here mate, you're the visitor, you toss, I'll call,' Horan said.

'Heads.'

*Surprise, Surprise! Heads it was.* 'We'll bat,' said Horan, quickly retrieving the bogus 20 cents and putting it back in his pocket. Cheats, as they say, never prosper. Despite first use of a perfect batting strip, the Horan XI was bundled out cheaply, and lost badly.

Jason remembers more clearly their head to head clash in Grade 12. As reigning GPS premiers, Toowoomba were clearly the better side. They'd dismissed Downlands for 120, a target TGS were never going to have any trouble reaching.

As opener Sandy Mettam hit the winning runs, the Downlands players motioned to walk off the field.

'Where the hell do you think you're going,' Horan, the captain, squawked from behind the stumps. 'We came here to get them out, and we're going to stay until we do.'

The act of defiance probably had something to do with the fact his arch rival, opposing captain and best buddy Little was down the non-striker's end, unbeaten on 38.

An over later, he was out, caught behind by Horan for 39. Hardly a time for cartwheels, but Horan allowed himself the luxury of a small, private airpunch. 'That's the sort of competitor Tim is,' Jason acknowledges. 'No matter what he's doing, he hates to lose. He doesn't even entertain the idea.'

For the first two years of their secondary school lives, their personal duel even extended as far as the swimming pool. Identically ranked in 1983 as the eighth fastest swimmers in their grades, they lined up alongside one another, on the blocks in the annual swimming meet between the two schools.

In one of the earliest Horan 'gotchas' on record, Tim baulked to start—Jason plunged in and swam 25m at full speed before race officials hauled him back by dropping a rope across the lane. A few moments later, the fresher Horan comfortably claimed the crown as the faster swimmer.

The following year, the same scenario, both on the blocks, kicking-off the 'B' relay. But no matter how hard Tim tried to induce a false start, the battle hardened Little refused to budge. Little comfortably hit the wall first, fuelling Tim's suspicions his foe had trained in the dams at Jimbour over the Christmas holiday, to prepare himself for the contest.

At one—all, both agreed to call it quits. Swimming in Toowoomba, after all, was a bit like sunbaking in the Sahara Desert. Only at very select times did it have any appeal at all.

So to rugby, and THE most important O'Callaghan Cup duel . . . the duel which reduces tough weather-beaten graziers' sons to whimpering marshmallows when they lose. In the four years to date, the Horan/Little Footy Ledger read two—all, with Downlands winning in 1983–84, and Toowoomba in 1985–86. This game would decide the issue.

O'Callaghan Cup veterans say they've never seen a bigger crowd at Toowoomba Grammar's Old Boys Oval; spectators snapping up every conceivable vantage point—trees, car roofs. They'd been there for hours before kick-off, priming themselves for a mammoth night of celebration—or sorrow drowning.

The game swayed from one end of the field to the other . . . No 10 for Downlands, Horan, a sharp break, pulled down from behind by Little, No 10 for Toowoomba. Little kicks and chases, cleaned up by Horan, and into touch . . .

The time ticked away. Neither side would budge an inch. 3–0 Downlands . . . tick tick . . . 3–all . . . tick tick . . . Toowoomba penalty goal 6–3 . . . tick . . . Downlands, a smart field goal from Johnstone 6–all . . . ticking . . . ticking . . . ticking . . . FULLTIME! A 6–all draw.

The issue had been resolved. There was no loser, just a couple of well-matched winners. They could now get on with the rest of their lives.

# Chapter Five

## Games Young Men Play

*'Before everything else, getting ready
is the secret of success.'*

HENRY FORD

When Pat Little telephoned her son in early August, 1988, to ask him what he would like for his 18th birthday, he didn't have to stop long to think.

'A piggery in Brisbane would be nice Mum, if you could arrange it . . .'

As flippant as the remark was, it mirrored the jumbled thoughts that were swirling through Jason's mind at the time. He had lived on a farm—or in a boarding house—for all of his 17 years 11 months, and loved it. But at the start of 1988 he'd moved to Brisbane in the pursuit of a sporting career. He was now betwixt and between . . . half farm boy living in the city, half city slicker, pining for the piggery, the cows, and the cotton fields.

However, where to live was only half the problem Jason was wrestling with in 1988. Of just as much concern was which sport he would pursue—cricket, rugby or athletics.

The dilemma had played on his mind for more than 12 months. Throughout his final year of schooling, he had canvassed practically everybody whose opinion he respected. He digested the lot, but there were three people in particular whose advice he valued—his ever-supportive parents, Pat and Ray, and Ron Bourne, the man with whom he'd made the 'deal' after breaching Rules 1, 2 and 3 of the 'Sneaky School-boy Handbook'.

Bourne had coached Little for three years in the First XI, and the pair had grown quite close. Jason saw him as a voice of reason, a person with a very balanced view of the world. During the many long afternoons, sitting in the cricket pavilion, while his teammates batted, it was not uncommon for Jason to send down the googly: 'Mr Bourne, seriously, which sport do you think I should play after school?'

Bourne had always played with a straight bat: 'Jason, I think you're the only one who can answer that. The decision is entirely yours.' It went on for months—Little hurling down the questions, the diplomatic deputy headmaster padding the ball back. Finally, one afternoon, while sitting underneath a giant Bunya pine after training, the persistent Little got the breakthrough he'd been looking for. Bourne swung lustily across the line: 'Well to be perfectly honest Jason, I think you're a better cricketer than you are rugby player. I believe you've got a brighter long-term future in cricket than any other sport.'

Bourne wouldn't have said it unless he'd really meant it. No doubt, the boy could play rugby, he was a very gifted all-round athlete. But in three years as 1st XI coach, he had seen Jason perform some unbelievable feats on the cricket field. 'I distinctly remember the first ball of the match against Anglican Church Grammar in Brisbane in Grade 12,' Bourne recalls. 'Their opener cracked the ball to cover where Jason was fielding. With his baggy hat pulled down over his face, you'd have sworn he was asleep. But in the one movement, he swooped on the ball, picked it up and threw down the stumps from side on. It was world class. In all my years of cricket, I've never seen a better schoolboy fieldsman. I really didn't want to nominate a sport—I didn't think it was my place, but he kept on asking, so I finally volunteered my opinion.'

Little had certainly had a profound effect on Toowoomba Grammar cricket. Before he arrived, the school had not won a GPS premiership since 1937, but while Jason was there, propping up the middle order, opening the bowling, and throwing down wickets from side on, TGS won two in succession. At 17, he was a cricketing colossus. A natural.

When he was picked in the Queensland Under 19 team to contest the national titles in Brisbane in January, a month after school, the cloud lifted. The picture had become a little clearer.

He had walked out of the school gates for the last time on December 2, firmly believing he was going to be a cricketer. Three months further down the track, he wasn't sure.

The Under 19 titles, featuring such celebrated Sheffield Shield names as Stuart Law, the current Queensland captain, Brendon Julian, Wayne Holdsworth, Darren Lehmann and Joe Scuderi, had come and gone without ever making him feel this is what he wanted to do for the rest of his life. Jason had won the award as the carnival's Best Fieldsman, and picked up a few runs, but precious little else. But the first seed of doubt had been planted. He went back to the farm at Jimbour, to play out the cricket season with the Mets, his club team in Toowoomba.

A couple of weeks later, with the Mets firing on all 11 cylinders, Little was selected to play for Eastern Downs, in an invitation match against Western Downs at Chinchilla. The appeal of another game of cricket was strong enough, but when he learned the Western Downs side would include one Ian Terrence Botham, his childhood idol, he was simply ecstatic. Botham was playing for the Queensland Sheffield

Shield side at the time, and his contract included the odd invitational match in the Country.

For a week before the game, Jason was delirious, each day sifting through all the possible scenarios. *I wonder if I'll get to meet him. Maybe I'll get to face him. What if he smashes one at me when he's batting. It'll probably take my hand off . . .*

He cast his mind back to Jimbour, and the Test matches he once played against brother Ashley in the backyard. He wondered what Botham would have thought, if he'd known he'd been a mandarin tree, fielding at backward square leg, in one of the many Australia v England Ashes series. *Gidday Ian, Jason Little, did you know, a few years ago, you were a mandarin tree in the . . .*

No. He didn't think he'd tell him.

The biggest crowd ever assembled at Chinchilla—about 4000—turned up to watch Botham, and the other star attractions—Test cricketers Carl Rackemann, Greg Ritchie, and John Maguire strut their stuff on a fine hot Tuesday in early February.

They weren't disappointed—Botham smashed 109—including a handful of mammoth sixes—in a total of 250. And the innings will not be remembered for the fact it was terminated by a skilful catch on the boundary by a fresh-faced blond-haired kid because it was also the only century Botham scored during his season in Queensland.

Set 252 to win, Eastern Downs were in early trouble until experienced local Lindsay Mason—Horan's cricket coach at Downlands—was joined at the wicket by an inexperienced and extremely nervous young Little.

Very few of the 4000 people in the crowd would have known who he was, or how many he scored that afternoon, but they may well remember him hoisting the world cricketing icon Botham over mid-wicket for six midway through an unbeaten innings of 43 which helped seal victory.

Almost four years later, Botham would be at Twickenham, watching the same kid who hit him for six in that game cut down his fellow Englishmen in the World Cup final.

As good as the Chinchilla experience was for nostalgic purposes, it didn't make Jason any less ambivalent about his sporting future.

He saw out the season with Mets, then headed down to Brisbane, for no reason in particular . . . just to play sport. Which sport, he still didn't know. The rugby season was about to get underway, but driving down to Brisbane, Ron Bourne's words came ringing back through his ears: *I think you're a better cricketer than you are rugby player. I believe you've got a brighter long term future in cricket than any other sport.*

Maybe he'd play a few games of rugby, and see how he went. He didn't know. He had plenty of time. He'd just play it by ear.

There were no such dilemmas, or demons of doubt, bombarding his buddy from across the other side of Tooowomba.

Well before he walked out the main gate at Downlands, and climbed aboard the No 4 West Bus for the final time, Horan knew exactly what he was going to do the following year. He was going to move to Brisbane, find a place to live, find a job, get some money behind him, buy a car, and play football. In that order. No fussing around. As his parents Mike and Helen realised at a very early age, Tim would grow up a very determined, very single-minded young man—a person who knew exactly where he wanted to go, and was in a hurry to get there.

Tim got out of the blocks even more quickly than he'd hoped, when he was offered a job with Castlemaine Perkins, Queensland's largest brewery, just three weeks after the completion of school. His father had arranged the interview a month earlier, but during the initial discussions the subject of TE—Tertiary Entrance—scores arose. Far from having a trump card to throw on the table, Tim had a ball and chain around his foot, and a noose around his neck. His school results were anything but flattering. He walked out of the interview, resigned to the fact that he'd be working in the markets, stacking boxes of fruit. But that didn't matter. *Get a job, find a house, get some money, buy a car, and play football.* He would be underway.

Then, out of the blue, a phone call to the family's holiday unit at the Sunshine Coast. 'You've got the job. When can you start?' Tim was on holiday, his first decent break for years now school sport was over. But it didn't matter. 'Immediately, of course.' He was in a hurry.

His first day at Castlemaine was a character building experience, to say the least. From the phone call three days earlier, he knew he had a job, and like every other Australian, he knew Castlemaine Perkins made beer, but in the heat of the moment he'd forgotten to ask exactly what he'd be doing. Would he be making beer? Would he be driving a beer truck? Would he be sticking beer labels on beer bottles? He had no idea. So, looking very much the young executive, wearing one of the four ties he had borrowed from his father, he turned up at the brewery, punctually at 8.30am, to learn just how he would be starting his working life.

Mr John Sheraton greeted him at the entrance, and took him into a large room, and sat him down in front of a computer: 'This is how you switch the computer on, this is how the computer works, this is what the computer does . . .'

Horan cursed himself. *Damn! Computers. If only I'd listened to what Mr Elders was saying in his school computer classes, instead of reading* Rugby League Week *under the desk.*

Much to his relief, a couple of days later, he'd established he wasn't in fact a computer operator, he was a beer order clerk. The computer was merely a tool of his trade. His task was to process beer orders from hotels around the state, and arrange delivery.

He impressed superiors with his conscientiousness, but every now and then, like all 17-year-olds, his mind would wander: How was Katrina coping out at Surat . . . won't it be good to start football training . . . I wonder what Jason's going to do . . . . .' During one such moment of absentia, a hotel in Townsville rang up requesting a pallet of beer—80 cartons. A few days later, three trucks carrying eight pallets—640 cartons (15,560 cans!)—arrived at the delivery dock. Fourex was on sale in town for the next two months. His immediate boss was frothing at the mouth for weeks, but Horan escaped with a caution on the run.

After three months, stages one, two, three and four of the master plan—get a job, find a house, save some money, and buy a car—had already been achieved. It was time to have a shot at his fifth, and far the most important goal for the year.

The Souths club at Yeronga, a pocket in Brisbane's inner south-east, was a logical launching pad. His coach in the Australian Under 17 side, Peter Francis, was looking after Colts, and several other of the club officials also had made contact, offering to assist with employment and career opportunities. He and the other Darling Downs-based Australian Schoolboys made a pact. They flocked, en bloc, to the Magpies' nest.

Horan's job at Castlemaine was perfect for football, in so much as it allowed him to arrive at training fresh, contrary to how he would have felt he had been lumbering boxes of pineapples and cumquats around the markets for eight hours a day.

After a couple of training sessions, and two early season trial matches, Tim was asked by the first grade coach, Gary Bird, what he thought about playing open grade rugby. 'Thanks but no thanks' was Horan's rapid-fire response. After the pressures of schoolboy rugby—playing in front of 3000 people each week for two years—he had earmarked 1988 as a season of fun and frivolity. Footy, mates, beers—he wanted nothing more than to have a good time.

And how! With total freedom, and money to spend for the first time in his life, Horan and his Colts mates were a party waiting to happen. Just add beer and stir.

Katrina had decided to go back to the family property, to repeat her final year of schooling, which meant there was no sign of Horan Personality No 2. Just No 1—24 hours a day, seven days a week.

Before the season was a couple of months old, a pattern had emerged. After training on Thursday nights, the entire team would head across to the 'Paddo Tavern', a boisterous watering hole in Brisbane's inner west, to celebrate anything they could think of celebrating. Sometimes, in the absence of anything better, they just celebrated the fact that it was Thursday night, but it was always good fun, particularly since the bouncer on the door refused point blank to believe fresh faced coach Francis had reached the required drinking age. Francis in fact was 33, and the only one in the party who was legal. They drank, they played pool, they played darts, they caused havoc. They had a great time.

But the festivities and frivolity certainly didn't conclude at closing time. Early in his bachelor days, Horan had made a pledge with his flatmate, Shane Kelly, that neither of them were allowed to return home late at night without plundering at least one pot plant from an unsuspecting neighbour. It became very competitive. Over a period of months, the pot plants got bigger and bigger, more and more expensive.

One night, Horan, so moved by the beauty and grandeur of one specimen, even borrowed a friend's utility to ferry the foliage back to their humble two-bedroom abode. The sight of a white Holden utility, careering through the streets of Toowong at 2am with a third of a jungle sticking out the back was always going to arouse suspicion but, somehow, he arrived at the unit undetected.

However 'Operation Date Palm' had one major flaw. After a 20-minute battle to get the leafy beast up the steps, he couldn't get the spoils through the front door. At times, even the best laid plans come unstuck. Under great sufferance, he took the plant back to where he found it.

In typical teenage fashion, personal hygiene and cleanliness also took a back seat in these formative years. The hours of the week were neatly divided up between work, training for football, playing football, and celebrating football. Any left over were devoted to stealing pot plants, well in advance of cleaning, washing, and tidying up.

Helen Horan remembers coming down to Brisbane one weekend and dropping into the unit unexpectedly. It was probably a good thing the occupants weren't at home. What she saw resembled a bomb testing station. The dairy shed at Kandanga had been cleaner. Under great sufferance, she put on eight loads of washing, and spent three hours cleaning, before leaving a two page foolscap 'you ought to be ashamed of yourselves' letter on the kitchen table.

There was *one* thing which did impress her though . . . all those beautiful pot plants on the verandah. She wasn't aware Tim was such a 'green thumb'.

Personality 1 v Personality 2. If only she knew.

While Tim was playing Colts, and stealing pot plants, Jason was playing grade and stealing the march on both him and the other young guns from the Downs.

He fully intended linking up with his mates—Horan, Johnstone and Co., but that's not the way things panned out. After missing the start of the season, he played a couple of games in Colts, but didn't really enjoy them. Tim was side-lined with an ankle injury at the time, so the attraction of playing with him wasn't available. Jason just sensed something was missing. There were so many kids, the training sessions were a rabble and the intensity was lacking. He might not have been sure which sport he wanted to play, but he was certain of one thing—he had come to Brisbane to learn, to improve. He wondered if that was possible playing Colts. It seemed a step down, not up, from his school days.

The very next night he went down to the club to do some extra kicking practice. While he was still gathering up the footballs, the first grade training session started to move into full swing. Thwack. Thud. Whack. Some 15m in front of him, Australian Test hooker, the mammoth Tom Lawton, was ploughing into people, tackles were hurting, muscles were straining . . . there was desperation, there was pain. Jason stood by the side of the field, entranced. *That* was what he wanted to do. If only Colts was like that . . .

Out of the blue, four days later came a phone call from Gary Bird, Souths first grade coach. Bird had seen him play the previous weekend, only for about 25 minutes, but had been suitably impressed by his speed, his long stride, his agility. Bird asked Jason what he thought about playing open grade. Jason didn't need to think. The steely in-built determination took over. In his quiet, shy, country manner, he accepted the invitation immediately, with the words of 'Yes please, Mr Bird.'

However, it was not going to be that simple. Not everybody in the club embraced so warmly the concept of a 17-year-old kid, however promising, matching football mind and muscle with fully grown men. The principal adversary was Colts coach Francis, who wrote a caustic letter to the club's committee, drawing attention to this act of irresponsibility from the first grade coach, which he claimed would do untold damage to Little's long term career prospects. The following week, Bird was summoned to appear before the committee, to explain his actions, and his thinking. He did just that, impressing upon the meeting that he had observed all propriety by approaching the player through his father. Ray Little, while not exactly wild about the idea, had agreed to let Jason make up his own mind. And Jason had. He wanted to play grades. The matter was resolved. The Francis challenge was thrown out of court, with the six man jury ruling in favour of Bird.

Bird recalls: 'It was a red hot issue at the time. There were quite a few people in the club who really had their noses out of joint. But I firmly believed in the adage that you're old enough if you're good enough.'

Not more than three days later, the theory would be put to the test. After just one training session, Jason ran out onto Chipsy Wood Oval against competition leaders University, playing inside centre, and 'absolutely shitting' himself.

'Well, I was and I wasn't,' Little says, correcting his own phraseology. 'I remember being really nervous, but in the same breath, I realised nobody had any expectation of me, or even knew who I was. So that made me feel good . . . but I was still petrified.'

Whatever his state of mind, it mattered not the slightest. The 17-year-old produced a slashing all-round performance, dynamic in attack and fearless in defence. A slightly embarrassed Francis stood watching on the sideline, shaking his head harder and faster as the game progressed. Six years on, Francis concedes he might have been thinking a little selfishly, but honestly believed at the time Jason was not physically ready for first grade rugby.

The match reviews in the local press the following day confirmed he was well and truly ready. *The Sunday Sun*'s Jim Tucker wrote: 'Relishing the treat of blue skies, Souths displayed their capacity for 15-man rugby at Yeronga yesterday, and unearthed a player who will keep the sun shining on Australian rugby for years to come . . . 17-year-old inside centre Jason Little, an Australian Schoolboy representative and Queensland Under 19 cricketer, shone out of the Magpies' emphatic 28–6 disposal of the competition pace setters University.'

Wayne Smith, in the *Sunday Mail*, was just as complimentary: '. . . as elated as (coach Gary) Bird was with his side's emphatic five-try to nil performance, it was the astonishing debut of 17–year-old centre Jason Little which really had him beaming'.

From such lofty heights, there was no looking down, or no turning back. Little, inside the space of a couple of weeks, would establish himself as a crucial member of Souths' first grade side. But there was a down side. As an open grade player, he was no longer eligible for the Queensland Under 19 side. Point One. Point Two—the State selectors believed that Little was too young to be included in the Under 21 side to play New South Wales and the ACT.

Without warning, he was stranded in no-man's land—too far advanced for one rep team, not far enough advanced for the next. Queensland Under 21 coach John Connolly argued Point Two by adopting the Bird view—'if you're good enough, you're old enough'—but the selectors wouldn't budge. They headed off south without him. Finally, on the sheer weight of his outstanding club form, Little was included in the Under 21 team to play New Zealand at Ballymore in mid-July. Lining up against rising Kiwi star, Craig Innes—the player he would later encounter in the World Cup—Little was outstanding, spearheading a victory widely acclaimed as good as any recorded by a Queensland team that season.

Three weeks later, the familiar moustachioed figure of national coach, Bob Dwyer, was sitting in Ballymore's McLean Stand, watching a Brisbane side go around against the touring London Irish club. With a Wallaby squad jetting off to England, Scotland and Italy in a month's time, Dwyer was on a final scouting mission to review the form of a few Queensland fringe candidates, among them prop Dan Crowley, No 8 Brendan Nasser, and winger Paul Carozza.

Not five minutes into the game, with Brisbane's blond-haired outside centre having already set up a try with his first touch of the ball, and scored himself with the second, the national coach began shuffling through his match program, trying to find details of the local line-up.

*Flick, flick, flick . . . No 13 Jason Little (Souths)*

'Where the hell did this Jason Little come from,' he asked assistant national coach, Bob Templeton, who was perched beside him. 'How come I didn't see him in the 21s?' Templeton started to explain that Little was only 17, and the selectors considered him too young to be playing at Under 21 level. 'Jesus, Tempo—Under 21s—it's an upper age limit—not a lower limit,' Dwyer argued. 'I reckon he's the best outside centre I've seen in the country this year. Not *potentially* the best—but the best—bar none.'

In the post-match reception, there were quite a few Irishmen, thrashed 46–7 in the game, who agreed. 'I'm wondering if your No 13 has any Irish blood in him?' London Irish manager Willie Lemon politely inquired during his speech. 'He looks a superb prospect. I'm sure we could accommodate him if he would like to play for a nice club in London.'

The Irish plaudits would probably only last a couple of hours, until the fourth pint of Guinness was slopped on the table. But Dwyer's impressions were far more permanent. He etched the Little name into his brain before dashing back to the airport to catch a flight to Sydney.

Ironically, had the national coach arrived at Ballymore a couple of hours earlier, he would have seen an equally startling display from Little's old sparring partner, the equally anonymous Tim Horan. Captaining the Queensland Under 19 side against Italy Under 19, five-eighth Horan was nothing short of devastating. Everyone in the grandstand would have seen him beat seven tackles in a 65m run to the line, but it took the much keener eye of a video camera operator to notice that Horan had changed the ball in his hands no fewer than six times, while fending off pursuers in his multi-directional rampage. His talent was instinctive, his speed and strength exceptional. The try-scoring effort alone may well have commanded another entry in the Bob Dwyer 'Players to Watch' book.

With the rugby season drawing to a close, and cricket gearing up for another long hot summer, Little's sporting life once again started to become complicated. On Saturday afternoons he was crunching opponents into the turf at Yeronga, and getting crunched himself. On Sunday mornings he was rolling up at the 'Gabba, for Queensland Under 19 cricket training, to face hostile fast bowlers off long runs. His shoulders were sore, his reflexes a little slow. Every now and then, while at the crease, a rearing delivery would sneak through his guard and cannon into his aching rib cage. *What the hell am I doing here?* It was time to make THAT decision. Something had to give. Either cricket or rugby.

There had been some speculation in the press of Little being included in the Queensland squad to tour Argentina the following March. This was his chance. He drew up the guidelines: 'If I'm picked to go to Argentina, I'll concentrate on rugby. If I'm not, I'll play cricket.' It was as simple as that.

On October 18, 1988, the Queensland selectors made one of the better decisions in the 106-year history of the Union. They included Little, aged 18 years and 40 days, in the 27-strong squad for South America.

Sorry Mr Bourne, Rugby it is. Cricket's gotta go.

Over at Yeronga, Horan was having a whale of a time. As much as he admired Jason for having a crack at the grades—and applauded his success—he knew he had made the right decision to stay in Colts. Moving to a new city, starting a new job, and living away from home for the first time was enough to digest for one year. Besides, the winter of '88 had been very good to him. He'd captained the Queensland Colts, exactly 25 years after his father Mike had done the same from exactly the same position. He'd also spear-headed Souths to a Colts premiership, and been bestowed with the QRU's prestigous 'Colt of the Year' award. There was quite a bit of celebrating to do . . .

THUMP THUMP THUMP THUMP, CRASH!

Even over the chatter, the laughter, and the loud music blurting from the juke box, the large gathering in the Souths clubhouse could hear the pounding of footsteps on the roof.

Peter 'Doubles' Daly, the Magpies' longest-serving and longest-suffering official—a player so bad that he was once sent from the field by his own teammates—had simply had enough of this loutish misbehaviour . . . premiers or cellar-dwellers, it didn't matter, it would simply not be tolerated.

He stormed outside and yelled at the top of his voice: 'WHOEVER IT IS ON THE ROOF, GET DOWN OR YOU'LL BE KICKED OUT OF THE CLUB AND BANNED FOR LIFE. YOU'LL NEVER PLAY FOR SOUTHS AGAIN . . .'

Seconds later, a bleary-eyed Horan poked his head over the guttering and peered down at Doubles, his thick glasses having fogged up with fury.

'Oh . . . um . . . Tim . . . I didn't realise it was you. Be careful up there. It's quite steep you know, probably pretty slippery as well.'

Doubles went back inside to get himself another Bundy rum and coke. No point in getting upset over a little roof party on grand final night, was there?

Even Doubles Daly knew that.

# Chapter Six

## The Big Time Beckons

*'There are 199 ways to get beat,*
*but only one way to win—get there first.'*
AMERICAN JOCKEY WILLIE SHOEMAKER

Queensland's trip to Argentina in 1989 is remembered by the 27 players, two coaches, manager and physiotherapist who left Australian shores on March 1, as one of the most memorable in the state's long and varied rugby history.

It was memorable for many reasons . . . the atrocious refereeing, the hair-raising bus ride across the Andes, the absurdly high inflation rate, the great leather goods shopping, the tough rugby, the huge steaks, and the post-match functions which invariably started between 1am and 2am.

But for the great majority, the most vivid memory of all was the wide-eyed innocence of the 18-year-old farm boy from Jimbour. In the four months between the time he was selected, and the time the plane took off, Jason Little had done everything possible to prepare himself for the tour. He had trained his butt off. In fact, he had trained so hard, and so often, that one afternoon shortly before departure, the team sprint coach elected to send him home from training, so run down was his body.

But no amount of physical toil was going to ready him for the mental and cultural challenge of four weeks away, in a foreign country, with 30 or so men, most considerably older than he. He was 18, he was from Jimbour, he was a little bit vague, he was making his first Queensland tour, and it was to Argentina, a country in which very little English was spoken. What chance did he have? Absolutely none. He was a bit like Crocodile Dundee in New York, but with football boots instead of a knife.

By the time the plane had touched down in Buenos Aires, the word had spread . . . there was a bunny on board. A very raw rookie. It was going to be a fun four weeks.

As the team bus weaved its way through the ramshackle outskirts of the Argentine capital, down towards the picturesque seaside resort of Mar Del Plata, the room list for the first game was read out . . . King/Korst, Lillicrap/Little, Lynagh/McCall . . .

Jason at the time couldn't decide what he was more nervous about—playing his first game for Queensland, or rooming with Cameron Lillicrap, a big bearish prop, who'd first played for Australia when Jason was just 13, and being yelled at by Mr Curry in the Toowoomba Grammar 13As.

'Crappa' didn't say too much, but when he did, Jason listened. And obeyed. The big prop's instructions were quite clear. 'Whatever you do Jason, late at night don't answer the door. Just don't open it, no matter who it is. I don't care.' Jason was petrified. He didn't know what 'Crappa' meant by his instruction, and was too afraid to ask.

At 2am, there was a rap on the door. QUICK HELP, SOMEBODY HELP, IT'S AN EMERGENCY.

Jason jumped out of bed, ran to the door, and opened it. A cardinal sin. Three early morning revellers, armed with a large bottle of Bundaberg Rum, barged through, sat down, and made themselves at home.

JASON, WHAT DID I TELL YOU? NEVER, EVER, EVER!

'But Crappa, they said it was an emergency, they said they were in trouble.'

Round one, and the kid from Jimbour had been knocked to the canvas.

Little wasn't listed to play the first tour game against Mar Del Plata. Instead, he made his mark as a waterboy, walking head first into a goal post after providing his teammates with a drink. The reserves bench was doubled over with laughter, as Jason picked up all the water bottles he'd dropped and hurriedly vacated the in-goal area. Round two—he'd just knocked himself down.

The second game, against Mendoza, at the foothills of the Andes Mountains, on the other side of the country, was Jason's Queensland debut. It was expected to be a searching test for the tourists, with the local side having finished runners-up in the national championship the previous year. Assistant coach, dual rugby international John Brass, had asked the players, prior to kick-off, to set personal goals. Lineout specialist Rod McCall planned to take eight two-handed catches, winger Antony Knox vowed to score two tries, and flyhalf Michael Lynagh, to find touch with every kick. If necessary, he would kick a field goal, to clinch the result. And so on.

The game went perfectly to plan. Queensland were in command, leading 49–24 with just minutes remaining. Knox had collected his two tries, McCall his eight clean catches, somebody else hadn't missed a tackle, and Lynagh boasted a perfect record with his touch-finders. As a scrum packed down, 10m into Queensland's half, Little, himself an outstanding contributor, sidled across to Lynagh. 'Noddy, time's running out. Don't forget you have to kick a field goal.'

Lynagh can remember just looking at him, to see if Jason's facial expression gave any clue as to whether he was serious or not. Nothing. Just that increasingly familiar half frown, half look of bemusement. 'I could only assume he was serious,' Lynagh recalls. 'I had trouble finishing the game, I was laughing so much.' Round three: Little was down and out.

Lynagh reported the incident at the team's 'Kangaroo Court' session that night and, right there and then, in Mendoza's Hotel Plaza, 'Jasonisms' were born. It was the generic term for any ridiculous comment, suggestion, or action, by any member of the touring party. Over the ensuing weeks, there would be Jasonisms aplenty.

At the same happy hour, team physiotherapist Col O'Brien piped up with a request that Jason had made, prior to the game, to have his wrist strapped. Minutes after the job had been completed, Little came back seeking further attention.

'Can you do this again, Col?' he asked.

'Why—is it too tight?'

'No. It's on the wrong hand.'

The court also heard how Jason had requested some ice, to put on his thumb, immediately after fulltime. O'Brien hauled some out of the Esky, and filled a plastic bag. 'Would you mind bringing it back when you've finished Jas—I'll need it for a few other injuries,' O'Brien said. Jason just stood there and looked at him inquisitively. 'I'll try, but I think it will melt,' he replied.

By the fourth game, the happy hours had become a circus. The entire gathering would be rolling around the floor of the team room, laughing at the 'Jasonisms' from the previous three days. So complete was Jason's dominance of the traditional 'Nigel Holt Award' (named in honour of the Wallaby second-rower who in 1984 had claimed not only to have a broken arm, but much worse still, a haematoa) that fullback Greg Martin moved a motion that the category be amended to read: 'The Jason Little Award'.

Martin recalls: 'It had become a one-horse race. Nobody else in the team stood a chance. Obviously Jason and Tim had one brain between them—that's why they hung around together so much at home. But the brain was apparently back in Brisbane with Tim—Jason had come away without one. So I figured we had to do one of two things—either we can the award altogether, or rename it in Jason's honour.'

The touring party unanimously agreed on the second option, on the proviso that Jason could be nominated for the award. Everybody was happy.

As cruel as the in-house ridicule might have seemed from a distance, it was merely a way of welcoming Jason into the team, and making him feel part of it.

Jason sensed that, but by the end of the tour he was hardly game to open his mouth. 'No matter what I said, it was twisted around. I learned to shut-up.'

Michael Lynagh was one who knew exactly how he felt. He too had gone away on tour with a Queensland team as an 18-year-old, with a few teammates old enough to be his father, and he remembered what a daunting prospect it was.

Lynagh says the most appealing thing about Jason on that tour was that he knew he was not a particularly worldly person. 'There was no false bravado. He just called things as he saw them. It was refreshing, and very entertaining at the same time,' Lynagh recounts. As much as the senior players enjoyed having Jason around, it didn't even come close to the satisfaction he extracted from being on tour. He thrived on the late night chat sessions—the stories, the experiences, the knowledge. He soaked up information like a sponge. The sessions reminded him of his latter years at boarding school—without the discipline. He loved the mateship, and the feeling of belonging.

Jason was particularly chuffed by a conversation he'd had with the 'grandfather' of the tour, winger Peter Grigg, while sitting around a beach bar in Santiago, Chile, one afternoon. Grigg, at that time a veteran of 28 Tests and 105 games for Queensland, revealed that he'd deliberately tested the youngster out in a game between Brothers and Souths at Ballymore late in the 1988 season. Twice the intensely competitive Grigg had ventured in off his wing, and absolutely hammered Little, a touch high, and a touch late. To Grigg's astonishment he got up both times, without so much as a whimper.

'I remember the first time, Jason looking at me, as if to say: "Why did you do that? I haven't hit you". I'd heard all these glowing reports about this kid—I just wanted to see what he was made of. After I hit him the second time, and he didn't flinch, I said to myself—"Yep, you'll do me son. You can play on my team anytime you like".'

While the off-field education had been a steep learning curve, Little had measured up to on-field expectations, at least until his fourth and final tour outing against Buenos Aires. He had a shocker—'probably the worst game of football I've played in my life'—and in the process Queensland tumbled to the first and only loss of its eight-game tour.

The 80 minutes reaffirmed what backs coach Brass had already identified—Little was an outstanding athlete—in fact the finest 'rugby athlete' he had ever laid eyes on, but his football at the time was not terribly mature. Brass suspected it was a legacy from school, where he could try practically anything he liked, and would normally get away with it. At the elite level this was not possible. Wrong options led to mistakes, and mistakes led to losses. There were a lot of rough edges to knock off the talented teenager's game. Brass took him aside and explained the areas he should concentrate on, and the areas which needed improvement.

There was a certain irony to all this. In October the previous year, when the selectors sat down to pick the squad for Argentina, Brass had tossed Tim Horan's name onto the discussion table. He'd been monitoring Horan's progress closely since early in the season, when he made a special trip out to Easts ground to watch him play in a seven-a-side competition. Brass remembers standing behind the goal posts by himself, absolutely stunned by the array of skills he was witnessing. There was the blinding speed, the acceleration, determination, the vision, the chip kicks, the tackling . . . the kid seemed to have the lot. He was so excited he had to tell somebody . . . anybody. He rang his wife Pam. 'Darling, I've just been watching this kid, he's unbelievable. I reckon he's the best young footballer I've ever seen . . .'

'That's nice dear, when will you be home . . . ?'

Brass' suggestion to take Horan to Argentina hadn't exactly been hit on the head in the selection meeting. The panel unanimously agreed he was a fine prospect, but they were locked into taking Anthony Herbert and Richard Tombs, two centres who had already worn the Wallaby colours. There was just the solitary 'rookie' spot available, and Little, after his sizzling effort against London Irish, had a mortgage on it. However, Brass had a sneaking suspicion that in terms of football maturity, Horan was a good 12 months ahead of his old school rival.

The early part of the 1989 domestic season was something of a black hole for Little. He had arrived home from Argentina, with little expectation of being named in the state side for the early representatives matches. He was well aware of his shortcomings, and just as determined to rectify them. He went back to Souths to work on his game.

While his confidence wasn't exactly sky high at the time, he was trying hard to remain positive, using the encouragement of the Queensland senior players to dilute the lingering self-doubt. But he was anything but heartened when he arrived back at Yeronga by Souths' decision to play him on the wing in first grade. He had been squeezed out there by the club's wealth of backline talent. He wasn't sure in which position he was best suited, but he knew it wasn't wing. He didn't like it out there, nor did he think he was particuarly good at it.

The only saving grace at the time was the fact that Tim had joined the open grade ranks. The pair hadn't seen much of each other in 1988, with Tim working during the week, and playing on Saturday, and Jason combining Sunday rugby with a tedious job as an insurance claims clerk from Monday to Friday. It was the first time in seven years they had drifted apart. Jason looked forward to being around the barrage of smart remarks, the practical jokes, the lively banter.

Horan's impact on the club scene was immediately felt. After just two first grade games, he was picked at five-eighth for Queensland B against Otago Sub Unions at Ballymore—a game scheduled on April Fool's Day, and just 48 hours after the Queensland squad's arrival home from Argentina.

Still 49 days before his 19th birthday, Horan looked anything but a fool, stepping up a class with the aplomb of a precocious young genius. In the *Sunday Sun* on April 2, Mark Oberhardt reported: 'Anyone who doubted the talent of former junior star Tim Horan needed only the first 10 minutes of yesterday's Queensland B v Otago Sub Unions match to become a believer. In that time, Horan displayed all his class to play a major role in the Reds' first two tries, setting the way for a 37–0 dunking of the hapless Kiwis.'

Back at Souths, an amazing game of musical chairs developed, with Horan and club captain John Mulvihill being switched, almost week to week, from inside centre to five-eighth, and vice-versa. But it didn't matter where he was stationed, the tune he played was always music to the ears of new club coach, Noel Mather.

Such was his impact at club level that Horan was being touted, with increasing regularity, as worthy of a chance in the Queensland side. But to some extent, the hands of Queensland coaches John Connolly and John Brass were tied. They were only too aware of Horan's talents, but where could they fit him? Michael Lynagh was at flyhalf, and centres Anthony Herbert and Dominic Maguire—a surprise inclusion in the side after being overlooked for Argentina—were doing a highly commendable job, both in attack and defence, during what was the wettest autumn in Queensland's history.

Horan was bound for the highest representative honours. There was no doubt. But he would simply have to bide his time. In the meantime, his career path followed the conventional channels, with his selection at flyhalf in the Queensland Under 21 team to play New South Wales at Sydney's Concord Oval.

The weather in Sydney that week was no better than it had been in Brisbane for the previous month. The game was played in appalling conditions, with ground staff on the morning of the game dumping a truckload of sand on the playing surface in an attempt to absorb some of the two inches of rain which had doused the city over the previous 48 hours.

With Queensland plundering both the Under 21 and the main game from their arch enemies, the visitors' mood in the post-match function was decidedly buoyant. Tim was standing with Jason, and a few other teammates when, out of the corner of his eye, Jason saw Bob Dwyer shuffling his way through the crowd, in their general direction.

He tugged on Tim's jumper: 'Hey look, Bob's coming across to say hello,' he quipped. No sooner had Tim turned around, than Bob was standing beside the two of them, extending his right hand.

'Tim, Bob Dwyer. Gidday, Jason.'

Jason had met Bob once before, at Ballymore the previous year, but to Tim he was merely a bespectacled, moustachioed figure he'd seen on television. Horan, for one of the very first times in his life, had been caught on the hop: 'Ah, er, Gidday . . . Mr Dwyer?'

'Please, call me Bob. Have you got a minute, Tim?'

With six beers on board, he already had a buzz. *Oh well, I suppose so, but can you make it quick! How ridiculous! Of course I've got a minute. I've got an hour. Two hours if you want.*

Exactly what about, Tim didn't know. He suspected at the time, it would have something to do with the way he'd been passing the ball, or his alignment, or his running lines. The pair sidled across to a less cluttered section of the room, where Bob explained: 'We've got a selection meeting tonight to pick the Australian B team to play the British Lions in Melbourne in 10 days time. Do you think you could get time off work?'

Tim was stunned. Stupefied. He just nodded obediently. The national coach had just asked him to play rugby. The beer orders in the office could wait. The drinkers weren't going to die of thirst.

He staggered back across the room like a punch drunk boxer to tell Jason, who was just as excited, but not that surprised, in light of Tim's consummate performance in the mud and slush that afternoon. He'd seen Tim do a lot of freakish things on the football field, but that afternoon, he'd clearly been in another league to the other 29 players on the field.

Some 15 minutes later, with the ramifications of Bob Dwyer's conversation having sunk in, Tim remembers quite literally 'floating' out of the function room and onto the team bus downstairs.

'Jason and I spoke about nothing else all the way home. On the way to the airport, on the plane to Brisbane, in the cab at the other end. I was just stunned. But I remember asking Jason not to say anything about it to anybody, just in case it didn't eventuate.'

The following morning, with the winter sun still to poke through murky grey skies, Tim was running barefoot down to the corner shop to pick up a copy of *The Courier-Mail*. He just wanted to make sure . . . *rustle rustle rustle* . . . Phew! He'd been named in the team at five-eighth, with Jason one of six reserves.

'I can't believe it, I'm playing against the British Lions,' he said to himself, walking back to the unit. *Hang on a second, who are the British Lions?*

As strange as it seems now, Horan had no idea at the time who the Lions were. He assumed it was another name for England, like the rugby league 'Lions'. That Scotland, Ireland and Wales also contributed to the side was a complete unknown to the rugby minnow who only two years before didn't know who the Wallabies were.

He did all the homework he could, before dropping around to Michael Lynagh's house to borrow an Australian blazer to wear to the match in Melbourne. When he got back to his unit, he checked his flatmate 'Slappy' wasn't home, closed his bedroom door, and tried the blazer on in front of the mirror.

It looked good, he thought. He badly wanted one of his own.

If there had ever been a worse night for a 19-year-old to make his international debut, Bob Dwyer couldn't remember it.

The Melbourne weather was at its least hospitable. It had been raining for three days straight, the ground was a bog, and an icy wind was whipping across Port Phillip Bay to the west. After two minutes, the ball was so heavy Horan felt like he was kicking a sandbag.

Despite Australia's last minute 23–18 loss, Dwyer was suitably delighted with the 19-year-old's performance, citing in particular, a tackle he made on rampaging Lions lock Wade Dooley, one of the biggest men in world rugby at the time. 'Tim drove in with the shoulder, picked Dooley up and dropped him in the mud. It was an awesome display of physical strength.'

Jason remembers just as clearly sitting on the reserves bench during the game, under four blankets, and listening to the superlatives being tendered by management and players alike.

He, perhaps better than anybody in Australia, knew what to expect from his best buddy, and he wasn't disappointed. 'From being with Tim before the game, I knew he'd make a good fist of it,' he said. 'He was so calm, so relaxed. He just brained them.'

In the press the following day, Dwyer was quoted as saying: 'I certainly don't think it's out of the question that he (Horan) could play in the Tests if Michael Lynagh was injured'. Right there and then, Horan probably could have guessed what was in store, but he hadn't allowed himself the luxury of thinking that far ahead. When his brother Matt, by now a journalist with the *Toowoomba Chronicle*, rang two days later to tell him he'd been selected on the Australian reserves bench for the first Test against the Lions in Sydney, he was stunned.

'People kept telling me I was a chance, but you tend not to believe it. I guess in a way it's a self-preservation mechanism. If you don't have expectations, you won't be disappointed. But I was genuinely surprised to be picked, given that I still hadn't played for Queensland.'

The Australian team assembled in the Rushcutters Bay Travelodge four days before the Test, the first rugby international to be played at the Sydney Football Stadium. Horan can remember being thankful for his experience in Melbourne. It had given him an insight into Australian team procedure, the punctual meetings, the dress requirements, the intense training sessions. But that didn't stop him feeling a little intimidated by the grandeur and importance of the occasion. As he climbed aboard the team bus for his first training with Nick Farr-Jones, David Campese and co., he felt as if a lepidopterist had let his entire butterfly collection loose in his stomach. He was still putting names to faces. And it concerned him greatly that even Tom Lawton, with whom he played at Souths, and for Queensland B against the Lions in Cairns, didn't know who he was.

He sought solace in the company of Scott Gourley, a veteran of two Tests but only slightly older than Horan, who at 19 years and two months was the baby of the squad. The two of them were almost inseparable, sitting at lunch and dinner for hours on end, chewing the fat, and remaining inconspicuous. There was very little sign of Horan 'Personality One'. He was locked in 'Personality Two' mode—quiet, unassuming, polite, obedient.

Two nights before the Test, the new 'chums' had to meet the tailor up on the sixth floor of the hotel to try on their new Australian blazers. Greg Martin, Dominic Maguire, Dan Crowley, there were quite a few of them, lined up to make sure their No 1s—coats, slacks, long sleeve shirts and shoes—were suitable.

Horan ripped off his jumper, and slipped into the blazer. It was too short in the sleeves and uncomfortably tight across the shoulders. But he didn't dare ask for it to be altered. The Australian blazer was his and nobody, not even a tailor, was going to take it back, even for a New York minute.

The 1989 Lions Test series will be remembered, by different people, for many different reasons. For some, it will be Australia's magnificent victory in the first Test, when the team exceeded all expectations to whip the Lions 30–12. The rugby public in Brisbane may remember more clearly the rough-house tactics the northern hemisphere side used to turn the tables in the second Test at Ballymore, tactics which left the face of skipper Farr-Jones a bloodied mess, and Welsh prop David Young with a badly tarnished reputation as a stomper. But everybody, from the fourth grade prop at Gungadoo, to the most junior janitor at the Sydney Football Stadium will remember the David Campese blooper which, history shows, lost Australia the Test series in Sydney.

The whimsical winger, spitting in the face of convention, had tried to run the ball from his in-goal area. When caught he threw a poorly directed pass which caught fullback Greg Martin unaware, and resulted in a try to Lions winger Ieuan Evans. Australia were leading 12–9 before the incident, but never recovered, finally going down by a solitary point.

It is perhaps the most written about, most spoken about mistake in Australia's rugby history, one which prompted an English production house to use the slogan 'Watch Campese fumble anytime you like' to promote a video they had made of the Lions tour of Australia.

Skipper Farr-Jones was even moved to write a letter to the Editor of *The Sydney Morning Herald*, so disturbed was he by the 'constant and at times vilifying attacks by rugby followers, and the press on one of Australia's greatest sportsmen'.

Horan had watched the whole episode unfold from the sanctity of the Australian reserves bench, where he stayed for the entire three Tests, without actually removing his tracksuit top. He remembers going back into the dressing shed after the game, and seeing Campese, sitting by himself in the corner, totally inconsolable.

'I wanted to go across, slap him on the shoulder and say, "mate, don't worry about it". But I didn't think it was my place. Besides, I couldn't be sure he'd know who the hell I was! I hadn't really had much to do with him at that stage. But I did feel very sorry for him.'

The other aspect which sticks in Horan's mind was just how much fuss was made over a pass going to ground. 'I just looked at it as one of those things that happen when you're playing football. Sometimes there are misunderstandings. Sometimes passes don't go where they should. But people went on and on about it. I even remember seeing Campo on television, explaining what had happened. I guess in a way, the whole episode made me realise just what a big deal sport is. In the eyes of a lot of people, Campo hadn't just let himself and his teammates down, he'd let his country down. It was a bit scary.'

As unlucky as the Wallabies might have been to lose the Test 19–18, and with it the series, coach Dwyer was not convinced he had the right personnel to take Australia through to the 1991 World Cup. He'd been alarmed by the Lions' capacity to unsettle Australia through the use of intimidatory tactics. He questioned whether the current crop had the physical presence to ever command top billing on the world rugby stage.

'From where I sat, we definitely weren't heading in the direction we needed to be to win a World Cup. A lot of guys had been around for a while. In the second Test, we'd been dished up badly in the forwards, we weren't particularly inventive in the backs. We needed to make some major decisions, sooner rather than later.'

With the one-off Bledisloe Cup Test against New Zealand the only remaining international in the domestic season, the time was right for some speculative selections.

Dwyer can't recall the exact context of the discussions at the selection meeting, but he remembers being staggered by the absence of opposition to what he was suggesting . . . tossing Phil Kearns, a Randwick reserve grader, in at hooker, putting Tony Daly in at loosehead prop, and slotting Tim Horan, Australia B's teenage flyhalf, into outside centre, alongside Lloyd Walker.

'There was hardly any discussion at all,' he says. 'Here I was, ready to field accusations of being far too radical, and the response was: "Well, OK, let's pick them".'

Nick Farr-Jones was one person who had grave reservations about what Dwyer and co. were doing.

He'd never met Daly or Kearns, and oddly enough, had no real impression of Horan, despite the fact he'd sat on the Wallaby reserves bench for the entire Lions series.

'I remember thinking: "Gee, what are we doing? Should we really be rushing these guys". I must admit, I was particularly sceptical about Tim—it worried me that he hadn't played for Queensland and he looked very small, particularly to be sending in to bat against the All Blacks first up. I guess at that stage I didn't have the confidence in Dwyer's judgement that I have now. Two years down the track I would have trusted him implicitly, but in 1989, I thought: "Gee Bob, do you *REALLY* know what you're doing?" '

Shortly after 9am, on August 11, Tim Horan was sitting at his desk, on the third floor of Castlemaine Perkins' Milton headquarters, in Brisbane's inner-west.

He'd just taken a phone order from the Boggabilla Hotel. Little did he know it would be the last order he'd take that day. As he was filling out the necessary paperwork for Boggabilla, extension 420 snapped him to attention.

'Tim, Wayne Smith from *The Courier-Mail*. Congratulations!'

'Congratulations? What for?'

'For being picked in the Australian Test team to play the All Blacks.'

GULP! 'You're kidding? When was this? Are you sure? Who else is in the team?' The questions wouldn't stop.

He tried to get back to work, but the phone calls just kept on coming as the news spread. Television stations, radio stations, family members, friends, fellow players . . . no hotel in Queensland was going to get through to extension 420 that day. It was probably a good thing. They may well have finished up with a delivery the size of the one Townsville's Railway Hotel received during Horan's early employment days at Castlemaine.

COME ON, RIP IT! THAT'S IT, NOW DROP. BACK ON YOUR FEET—QUICKLY! TIMMY HORAN YOUR TURN. LET'S GO . . .

Bob Dwyer barked out the instructions, as the Australian players wrestled around on the ground, trying to dispossess one another of the ball. Horan was with Simon Poidevin, the old warhorse, and prop Andy McIntyre, both of whom had been recalled to the team for the All Blacks Test. They were still in the warm-up of their first training in New Zealand, but Horan's arms and legs were already burning. As they paused momentarily for a quick drinks break, he hunched over and threw up, as furtively as he could, to conceal the pain from his teammates.

So THIS was the preparation for a Bledisloe Cup match? The intensity excited him.

Under normal circumstances, the four days before a Test are used to add the finishing touches, rehearse the moves and run through the match plan. But with so many changes from the 3rd Lions Test—six in all—Dwyer was virtually starting from square one.

First priority was for the players to get to know one another—as best they could in such an impossibly short period. It was important for instance, that Horan strike up some sort of rapport with Lloyd Walker, the scheming, sleight of hand New South Welshman who would be his centre partner at Eden Park. When Horan first laid eyes on him at the start of the Lions series, he thought Walker was either the team physio or the baggage man. 'He didn't look much like a footballer at all,' Horan admits. 'But Lloydie was a great guy. He made me feel very welcome.'

(Walker was the player Dwyer, earlier in the month, had bestowed with virtual immortality by referring to him as 'Rugby Union's answer to Wally Lewis'. Walker's critics north of the border suggested Lewis could take out a defamation action.)

But Horan was only worried about his own little patch. In three days time he would be running out at Eden Park in front of 40,000 people to make his Test debut against Joe Stanley who, along with France's Philippe Sella, was rated as the most formidable outside centre in world rugby. He had enough on his plate.

The day before the Test, Australia's newest, youngest Wallaby went down town to do two things—to get a haircut, and to meet Jason for a chat over a cup of coffee. Little, appropriately enough, was in Auckland with the Australian Under 21 side, who were scheduled to play New Zealand Under 21s in the curtain-raiser. It was as if somebody had turned the clock back to Toowoomba—the old rendezvous down town on a Friday afternoon, for chips and gravy at George's Cafe. Only now, there were no uniforms, no ties, no chips, just nerves. The chat served as a great settler for both of them.

Australian rugby players know only too well when they are getting close to Eden Park on match day. Out the window of the team bus, they will see the fans, most wearing the national dress of black tracksuit pants and 'All Blicks' jersey, marching with ever-increasing urgency, towards the main entrance. First three, then 15, then 60, then 200, ultimately congealing into one black mass, as they neared the turnstiles.

Inside the bus, deathly silence. 'All I could hear was the sound of breathing. That's how quiet it was,' Horan remembers. 'When we got caught in traffic, close to the ground, the fans started banging on the side of the bus. As much as you try to shut it out of your mind, the noise does disrupt your concentration. I just couldn't wait to get into the dressing shed to get organised.'

The black trackie pants, the bus, and the deafening 'boo' which went up when the Australian team walked out onto the ground, are the sum total of Horan's pre-match memories. Before he knew it, he was standing out in the middle of Eden Park, arm in arm with his new teammates, bellowing out the national anthem. Well, a few lines of it. Unfamiliar with the words to 'Advance Australia Fair', he'd spent most of the flight across the Tasman reading an 'anthem card' to prepare himself for this proud moment.

It hadn't worked: *Australians all let us rejoice, for we are young and free . . . Hmm Hmm-hmm hmmm, and hmmmm, hmm-hmmm*
*Hmm hmmm is hmmm hmmm . . . ADVANCE AUSTRA-LIA FAIR!*

Thwack! The game was underway. Kick, catch, pass, hoist, catch, return, catch, tackle, pass . . . the speed was electrifying. Horan felt like he was in a high speed tumble-dryer with black and gold jerseys whirling around him. 'Noddy (Lynagh) and Lloyd and Poido (Simon Poidevin) had told me I'd find the game really quick—they were dead right. Everything seemed to be happening at a million miles an hour.'

Rated 20-point underdogs going into the Test, the Wallabies performed with courage and distinction, holding the Kiwis to a converted try (18–12) right up until the time All Black prop Richard Loe burrowed over with seconds left on the clock. Fulltime: New Zealand 24 Australia 12.

The plaudits for the three new caps—Daly, Kearns and Horan—came thick and fast, from wide and varied sources. Dwyer was at the forefront, declaring the trio would form the basis of a very strong Australian team for many years to come.

Horan was happy enough with his own performance, but was very disappointed to have kicked off his Test career with a loss. 'It's obviously the one game you'll remember for the rest of your life. The memories would have been so much sweeter if we'd won.'

However, he didn't exactly leave Eden Park empty handed. Moments after the game, with the mentally and physically exhausted Horan only having just sat down, the burly figure of Joe Stanley darkened the doorway of the Wallaby dressing shed. The bare-chested All Black centre was carrying the No 13 jersey he'd been wearing just 10 minutes before. He headed straight for Horan.

'Well done Tim, I thought you played very well,' Stanley said, offering first his hand, then his jersey. Horan stood up—swapping jerseys—it was obviously a tradition. As much as he wanted to keep his first Test jumper, he thought he should do the right thing. He gestured to remove it but Stanley stopped him. 'No mate, you keep yours, it's your first Test. Congratulations.' With that, he was out the door, back to join the raucous singing in his own shed next door.

Stanley, now in the twilight of his career and playing for NEC in Japan, explains his motives: 'Philippe Sella did the same thing for me when I made my Test debut against France in 1986. I remember at the time, really appreciating the gesture. I thought I'd do the same for Tim.'

Stanley's thoughtfulness left a sweet taste in the mouth of an impressionable teenager. He believed it said a lot about the game. Horan felt he had just joined a very select club, an international fellowship of rugby players.

He thought how wonderful life-long membership would be.

# Chapter 7

# Side by Side in Green and Gold

*'The difference between one person and another, between the weak and the powerful, the great and the insignificant, is energy—invisible determination.'*

THOMAS BUXTON

'And now, I'd like to make a special presentation . . .' Nick Farr-Jones was up in front of the team, and in full flight.

'As is customary on all Wallaby tours, the youngest member of the squad is entrusted with the all-important responsibility of looking after the team mascot. Jason Little, could you come forward please.'

There were cheers and jeers, as Little, 19 years and 49 days young, reluctantly made his way to the front of the room, to accept the offering of his skipper.

'Jas, you should consider this a great honour,' Nick told him. 'I'm sure you'll look after Shithead as if your life depended on it.'

Little nodded in agreement, shook Nick's hand, accepted his 'trophy', and made his way back into the crowd.

He examined the stuffed animal more closely. It was the ugliest thing he had ever seen. No eyes. Coarse, scratchy hair. And it looked nothing like a Wallaby. It looked more like

. . . like . . . well, it didn't really look like anything. He'd been in possession of this toy animal no more than 30 seconds, and already he hated it. No wonder, Jason thought to himself, Noddy (Michael Lynagh) named it Shithead when he had to carry it around France in 1983. It was going to cause trouble, he knew that for certain.

The final team meeting before any major overseas tour is a special occasion, with the anticipation of opportunities ahead. But in this gathering, on the 3rd floor of the Centra Hotel in North Sydney, there was a rarefied air of expectation, with no fewer than 15 of the 30 players just one unsettled night's sleep away from their first full scale Wallaby excursion.

Minds were racing, and heads spinning, but none faster than Little's. Four years ago, he'd never heard of the Wallabies. Now he was one. For weeks, he had been mentioned in media dispatches as a strong candidate, but when he actually got the phone call from the Australian Rugby Union, to say he'd been selected in the team, he was flabbergasted. In his customary self-effacing manner, Jason had refused to believe the speculation. By his own reckoning he'd had a shocking season, losing all confidence after a bright start to his representative career for Queensland in Argentina. As desperately as he wanted to go away with the Australian team, he didn't think he deserved to.

Dwyer had other ideas. From the moment he first saw him play for Brisbane against London Irish in August 1988, he'd ear-marked him for France and Canada, even though the tour was still 15 months away. In fact, he and the other selectors had even toyed with the idea of taking him to the United Kingdom the year before, but decided against it on the grounds of his impossibly tender age.

As fate would have it, Dwyer knew nothing about Jason's loss of form or confidence in 1989. Although a harsh critic of his own form—Jason estimated he had played just three good matches all year—such was Bob's impeccable sense of timing, he was there to watch all three.

Back at the Centra, the formalities were drawing to a close. Jason bent down to pick up the mascot . . . 'Oh no . . . where's he gone . . . who took him?!'

The tour might still be 12 hours away, but the game had already begun.

If a book featuring 'The Top 10 Most Desirable Rugby touring destinations in the World' was ever written, you could read it back to front without ever finding a chapter on France.

Even the dizziest of globe-trotting rugby players in the world claim there is no tougher tour than an eight match excursion through France, particularly in the lead-up to the Five Nations Tournament.

If language barriers, dietary upheavals and other cultural hurdles aren't enough to trip up the visitors, the Federation de French Rugby will invariably formulate a match itinerary which will.

In France there is no respite. Every match tends to be against Provincial Selection XVs, which are thinly disguised national team experiments, designed to spotlight the weaknesses of the touring side prior to the first Test. In the first game, the French selectors might pit together a big strong forward pack, with a kicking flyhalf. For game two, a smaller, more mobile pack, with a lightning-fast set of backs. Then a blend of the two, big pack, running flyhalf, quick backs. By the time the Test comes around, they have a fair idea which configuration will function most effectively against the touring team.

But regardless of who plays in which position in the lead-up games, one thing is as certain as the smell of garlic on a Frenchman's breath. The players will be pumped up and prepared to spill blood for their country. Vive la France.

Given the passionate nature of the Frenchmen, it is not uncommon for that brimming emotion to boil over in the heat of battle. On the Wallabies' previous tour of France in 1983, there was one brawl which made its way into rugby folklore, a violent affair which travelled almost the length of the field before the referee could break it up.

Hooker Tom Lawton remembers it very clearly: 'It was like something out of the old gladiator days—a small army of crazed men just belting anyone they could. The French were horrendous at the time—absolutely lethal. You could guarantee that if a Frenchman looked ugly and tough, he was ugly and tough. The uglier they were, the tougher they were, and the further you stayed away.'

Lawton in fact played the first of his 41 Tests a few weeks later, marking a notorious French strongman by the name of Phillipe Dintrans: 'He was the sort of guy who would belt you over the head with an iron bar, then hand it to you and say: "Your turn". Very tough fellow.'

Nick Farr-Jones was not on the 1983 tour, but he'd heard all the stories, not just about the on-field thuggery, but the uncomfortable touring conditions—the hotels right next to railway lines, the terrible food, the 10 hour bus trips, the liaison officers who didn't speak English . . . he wasn't particularly looking forward to the trip, but as captain it was his job to instil confidence and enthusiasm in the young, largely inexperienced Australian side. He sensed it was going to be a long, hard haul.

The Wallabies' two game stop-over in Vancouver was more for the benefit of Canadian rugby than Australian, but the two comfortable victories lifted sprits, and steeled the players for the fierce battle which awaited on the other side of the world. The first Canadian game, a lowbrow clash against the North American Wolverines in front of a mere 700 people, also carried a special significance for Little, in so much as it was the first time he pulled on the Wallaby jersey.

At the team happy hour that night, he had to 'skoll' twice, once to commemorate his first game for Australia, and a second time for leaving the Wallaby mascot in the departure lounge and having to go back through US customs to retrieve him. *Damn that stupid toy.*

The Wallabies flew straight into Toulouse, a thriving industrial city in the south of France, and checked into a stylish old hotel, beside a lake on the outskirts of town. As much as Argentina had been a culture shock for Jason eight months before, France impacted on Tim in an identical fashion. Two trips to New Zealand had been the extent of his previous overseas experience and the most discernible difference over there was the age of the cars. In France it took a little longer to acclimatise. 'I found it very strange not being able to talk to people, and even more importantly, make them understand what you wanted.'

Language was one problem, but it wasn't half as crucial as the second: Food. Two of the three French words Tim learned while he was in the country were 'bien cuit'—well done. The original 'steak, sausages, eggs and chips' man (or Truck Driver's breakfast as his teammates dubbed it), Horan liked his meat 'bien cuit'. The French didn't—they liked it raw. As much as he stressed to the waiter, 'bien cuit, bien cuit, merci' (his other word!), the steak would arrive back at the table as if the chef had forgotten to turn on the gas. Before the tour was a week old, he'd snapped. 'Bugger this,' he said, and stormed off into the kitchen. When he hadn't returned five minutes later, Queensland halfback Peter Slattery went off in search of him, just to make sure he hadn't been carved up by an indignant chef.

Slattery poked his head into the kitchen to see the cheeky Horan, complete with chef's hat, behind a stove merrily cooking his own steak. Before the head chef knew it there were half a dozen or more new apprentices, waiting in line to convert their 'blue' steaks to 'bien cuit'.

By the time the rugby was in full swing, the term 'bien cuit' was being used in a totally different context, quite often by Bob Dwyer and in appreciation of Little's tackling. Jason had been included in the tour party as the third winger—behind the established pairing of David Campese and Ian Williams—and that was where he played his first game on French soil, against Beziers. He had precious few opportunities in attack, with the team tumbling to a 19–10 loss, but his defence was impeccable. He tackled and tackled and tackled, on occasions bringing down two Frenchmen in the one movement. Up in the grandstand, Bob Dwyer can remember nudging assistant coach Bob Templeton: 'I don't know what you think, Tempo, but I reckon we might have made a blue here, playing Jason on the wing. Maybe we should have a look at him in the centres.'

Up until that moment, it was commonly accepted that Tim Horan and New South Wales youngster Darren Junee would be the centre pairing for the first Test in Strasbourg on November 4. In an article in the *Sunday Telegraph* headlined 'Centre Superkids', Terry Smith from France wrote on October 22: 'Two years ago the Australian Schoolboys rugby team boasted a five-eighth called Tim Horan and an outside centre named Darren Junee. Now, in just a fortnight's time, Horan, only 19, and Junee, just 20, are poised to become Australia's youngest ever centre pairing.'

Horan—no problem. He had secured his spot with a spectacular two-try performance while marking French Test star Denis Charvet in the tour opener against Toulouse. But Junee's claims were less authoritative. He'd merely marked time against Toulouse, neither climbing up the ladder nor falling off it.

The tour moved across to the coast, and up to Toulon, to prepare for the game against Cote d'Azur, yet another provincial team stacked with Test aspirants and uncompromising types whose eyes roll back in their head like oranges and apples on a poker machine the moment they take the field.

Approaching Test matches, the selectors' thinking becomes increasingly hard to conceal. For combination purposes, it is essential the 'A' team—the shadow Test side—has a couple of games together, so players don't have to have Mensa membership to work out who's in front, and who has fallen behind. Likewise, in the midweek games, no news is good news. If you're overlooked, you're overjoyed.

As the squad assembled in the team room—a large basement underneath the hotel—Jason saw Bob talking to Junee. *Hmmm, the selectors must have decided to give Herbie (Anthony Herbert) or Brad Girvan a run at outside centre.*

Team manager Andy Conway began: 'Right, the team for the match against Cote d'Azur: Marto (Greg Martin) fullback, Peabody (Ian Williams) and Campo on the wings, Jason and Timmy in the centres, Noddy and Nick the halves, backrow Tim Gavin, David Wilson and Dave Carter . . .'

Jason's ears pricked up. *Hang on a sec, I think he called my name.*

'I reckon they'd got to the second row by the time I realised I'd been named in the team,' Little admits. 'I was shocked. I had no idea I was going to be given a run in the centres. As much as I'd hoped of having a run with Noddy (Lynagh) and Nick, I thought it would be on the wing.'

While Jason didn't exactly have a Test jersey on his back, he definitely had one arm in the sleeve. A strong performance against Cote d'Azur, and the Test No 13 would be his.

Greg Growden, covering the tour for *The Sydney Morning Herald*, didn't even think Little needed that, writing on October 25: 'Tomorrow, Toulon will witness the first major appearance of a player combination which could easily become an invigorating international link in the Hawker-O'Connor, Burke-Papworth vein . . . Both are only 19, yet they have already shown extraordinary maturity and confidence in each other on this tour to indicate they will be together for some years yet.'

Growden's self-assurance proved to be well-founded. After another rousing defensive display against Cote d'Azur, Little was retained in the 'A' team to play Alpes in Grenoble four days later. The second arm was in . . . then finally, the announcement of the team he didn't want to be part of—the 'B' side for the game against Auvergne in Clermont Ferrand. It was to be the Wallabies' last pre-Test hitout. No J. Little . . . it was the sweetest announcement he had never heard. The No 13 jersey HAD to be his.

Guarantees or no guarantees, Little was shaking as he made his way down to the 'dungeon', the Wallabies' team room in the basement of the hotel in Strasbourg, four days before the Test. Staring blankly at the orange seat in front of him, Little remembers the house-keeping and general 'administrivia' dragging on and on . . . 'duty boys for tomorrow David Wilson and Dan Crowley, videos tonight in Craigy's room, trip to the Adidas factory tomorrow after training, washing to the foyer by 9am . . .' WHO CARES? CAN YOU JUST GET ON WITH IT?

This time he didn't miss his name—he digested every syllable as it reverberated around the room. Centres: Tim Horan and Jason Little. A nervous nod of the head as the squad applauded the announcement of the Test team. He was there. On Saturday, he would run out onto Du Stade De La Meinau, behind his best mate, in his first Test, aged 19 years and 70 days.

That Tim was 19 years and 71 days old when he played the All Blacks at Eden Park added yet another parallel in their curiously parallel lives.

It was just another lazy afternoon in Strasbourg. The cool October breeze wafted up the tree-lined avenue, and rustled large brown leaves which littered the pavement. Winter was clearly just around the corner.

The Wallabies' morning training session had been a searching one, hard, sharp, and very thorough, but the afternoon as usual was free. Jason, Tim and Darren Junee were sitting in one of the untold number of sidewalk cafes which lined the streets of Strasbourg and, they assumed, practically every other French city.

Just in front of them, a lady walked by, pausing momentarily while her small dog deposited a giant 'do-do' on the pavement. When the canine had completed its business, she opened up her handbag, and pulled out a tissue. Jason thought to himself: 'Isn't that nice, she's going to clean it up, and put it in the bin.'

Wrong. The lady, immaculately dressed in a tailored suit, wiped her dog's bottom, dropped the tissue on the pavement, and walked off. 'I just couldn't believe it,' Jason says. 'Where I came from, dogs were for rounding up cattle, not for having their bottoms wiped.'

The episode was significant, not because of the insight it offered into the toiletry habits of the country's one million canines, but because Horan, Little and Junee were once again knocking around together.

Teammates in the Australian Schoolboys side in 1987—Horan at five-eighth, Junee at outside centre and Little on the wing—the trio were inseparable in France and Canada. Junee might have already turned 20 but he was as big a 'babe in the woods' as the other two. And in the same way Jason had been caught out in Argentina at the start of the year, the naivety of the trio was being exposed on this even tougher testing ground of France.

Flanker Dave Carter, the laconic sheep farmer with the tinder dry wit from Quirindi, in the New South Wales central west, aired the thoughts of the entire squad by dubbing the trio Proton, Neutron and Electron. Carter reasoned that all three were required to make up an atom, which he believed was the collective size of their brain. Before too long, Proton Neutron and Electron had been abbreviated to 'Third-of-a', the suggestion being they had a third of a brain each. It was merely an extension of the 'brain time-share' theory that Greg Martin had devised in Argentina, but this time, there were three bodies instead of two on the roster.

The appropriate modifications were also made to the Wallaby team happy hours. At the beckoning of the Queensland contingent, 'The Julius Sumner Miller Award', as it had been for as long as the mad fuzzy-haired professor had been conducting his experiments on TV, was changed to the 'Jason Little Award'. But unlike in South America, the award was anything but a one-horse race. Little had champion gallopers either side of him.

'They were hilarious,' second-rower and resident French linguist Peter FitzSimons remembers. 'They had this very fraternal relationship. You sensed that Tim was the street-smart one who almost took it upon himself to look after the other two. But that didn't prevent him from regularly putting his foot in it.'

On one occasion, FitzSimons remembers sitting beside Horan at dinner. 'I don't want to eat any of this crap,' Horan bleated, totally fed up with looking at menus he couldn't understand. 'I can recommend the Soup du Jour,' FitzSimons offered in assistance. 'Nah, I had that yesterday, it was awful,' Horan replied, oblivious to the fact that the dish translated to Soup of the Day.

Earlier on in the tour, while the Wallabies were based in Toulouse, David Campese had announced plans of a day trip down to Nice, the ritzy French resort on the Mediterranean Coast. It was a popular idea and in no time at all, Campo had four or five willing travel companions. Horan, for the life of him, couldn't understand the attraction. 'What's everybody going down to see Campo's niece for?'

But the coup de grace came one night when team trivia buff Brendan Nasser triggered a general knowledge quiz around the dinner table. 'I've got one for you,' Nasser beamed. 'Name three countries in Europe that start and end with the letter A.' Almost instinctively, Jason was quick-witted enough to pipe up with Australia, Argentina and America, but Tim left himself badly exposed when he quietly inquired: 'Where's Europe?'

Mister Horan, how do you plead?

'Not guilty . . . well maybe a little bit guilty. Geography was never really my strong suit at school. I'm sure Mr Mason (at Downlands) would attest to that. I didn't really have a clue which country was where until I started going away on rugby tours. I think I learnt more from maps in the inflight magazines on aeroplanes than I did in five years of high school geography.'

In the meantime, the barbs would continue, and he would happily cop them. Life after all, was not to be taken too seriously.

Test players are not generally allowed out of the team hotel on the eve of a Test, but this was an emergency.

'Hotel Altea Pont De Europe, merci' Horan instructed the cab driver in his most fluent French, as he and Junee climbed in the back. Some 20 minutes later, after a hair-raising 10km trek across town, the pair alighted. Junee paid the fare, as Horan bounded urgently into the hotel. In the ground floor restaurant he located his mother Helen, who had arrived in the country just a couple of days earlier after a snap decision to join the supporters tour.

'Hi Mum, sorry to interrupt, but would you mind giving me a haircut?' Helen was in the middle of eating dinner, but she'd been expecting him. She dutifully dropped eating implements, excused herself from the table, and went upstairs to her room to get the scissors.

The haircut ritual was a carry-over from Auckland—Tim decided in New Zealand he simply must have a 'crop' before the start of any major Test series. 'I guess it's a psychological thing. I just feel a little sharper, a little lighter.'

Darren was there to see his mother and father, who were also on the tour, but decided that he too should make use of Tim's personal globe-trotting beautician. A quick chat, a kiss goodbye, and they were gone. They arrived back at the team hotel in time for their own dinner.

November 4, the first Test and Australian rugby's day of reckoning had finally arrived. The rain which had hovered for the past three days above the bustling city, near the German border, was starting to clear. Fine weather was forecast but the conditions were certain to be greasy.

A task of monumental proportions confronted the Wallabies. Not only had the French never lost a series to Australia on home soil, but the Wallaby line-up included no fewer than four new caps in the run-on XV—Little, Nasser, FitzSimons and lock Rod McCall were playing their first Test—and a further three, Kearns, Daly, and Horan, the All Black debutants, their second. Only Farr-Jones, Lynagh and Campese had played more than 10 Tests. Number eight Tim Gavin, with seven Test caps, remarkably had more than the sum total of the other seven forwards.

On top of that, the Wallabies' tour record up to that point had been, at best, modest, with just two wins in their five games in France. Bob Dwyer, since resuming his reign as national coach, had a record which read: 11 Tests, four wins, six losses, one draw. Clearly, the odds were stacked heavily in France's favour.

A mere three hours before kick-off, and the squad was huddled in their musty team room, strapped, dressed, and primed for battle. Before them was Dwyer, tears of emotion seeping out of the bottom of his glasses as he spoke about the virtues of pride—pride in your country, pride in the gold jersey, pride in your own performance. No-one in the room had seen the Australian coach so worked up—clearly this was a Test match he not only wanted to win, but needed to win. The knives at home were being sharpened.

As deeply as Jason was moved by Dwyer's overt display of emotion, he couldn't ignore the lighter side of the coach's sermon. Walking up the stairs to the bus, he muttered to Tim: 'I don't know what he's got to cry about. I'm about to mark Philippe Sella in my Test debut in front of 40,000 people. If anybody should be crying it's me!'

The bus trip over to Stade De La Meinau was a good hour. As the team's police escort worked its way across town, parting the heavy Saturday traffic, Horan and Little sat silently beside one another, halfway up the bus on the left hand side. Jason thought about home, how much he would have liked his mother and father to be here in Strasbourg. He'd spoken to them in Jimbour just four hours before. His mum said there had been dozens and dozens of phone calls to the house wishing him well. His father, as usual, didn't say much at all, just a casual 'You'll be right'. Deep down, Jason honestly believed it. He had the benefit of experienced players all around him, Farr-Jones, Lynagh, Campese, and his best mate Horan beside him. He couldn't have wished for better circumstances, a better combination, a better backline. But in between time . . . he wondered about the value of these bloody police escorts . . . *Jeeeezus, another near miss* . . . he couldn't wait to get to the ground and onto the field where it had to be safer.

The team climbed off the bus and headed straight into the dressing shed, a rather small claustrophobic setting in the bowels of the main grandstand. Little and Horan's blazers were hung up side by side, just as they had been in the Queensland Country dressing shed in Canberra in 1986, in the Australian Under 17 shed in New Zealand in June, 1987, and the Australian Schoolboys shed in Sydney later the same year.

Strolling around on the field, as the players habitually do prior to a game, Horan pointed to the north-western corner. 'There, I'm going to score there . . . in front of that Chat . . . Chaute . . . Chataset . . . that blue and white sign.' The long, peculiar French name on the advertising billboard had tripped him up, but Jason, Wallaby mascot tucked safely under an arm, got the drift of what Tim was saying.

Assistant coach Bob Templeton, something of a father figure for the two youngsters abroad, recalls following them out onto the field, for one final assuring chat. 'I wanted to stress to them that Mesnel and Sella were just two players, with the same number of arms and legs as them. But they didn't seem fazed at all. I don't think they understood what a big reputation the French pairing had. They were incredibly composed.'

'Mesdames et messieurs je vous present l'equipe Australienne.'

'Ladies and gentlemen, would you please welcome the Australian team.'

Moments later, amid a deafening crescendo of horns and trumpets, the game was underway.

They say there's a moment in every international rugby player's career when he 'arrives' as a Test player. If that is the case, Horan and Little 'arrived' together on November 4, in the 39th minute of the 1st Test at the Stade De La Meinau in Strasbourg. It was at that point they combined to finish off a movement which will be remembered by all who saw it, a moment which so excited ABC TV commentator Gordon Bray he told a national television audience he'd split his pants.

For all but fleeting moments in the first half, the Australians had been forced to defend grimly, denying the French time and time again through sheer desperation on their own goal line. First Lynagh, a magnificent front-on tackle on Eric Champ, the villainous French enforcer, then seconds later,

Horan burying his right shoulder into opposite number Franck Mesnel, lifting him up and dumping him into the moist Strasbourg turf. With Horan's fireman's lift, the French fire was all but extinguished—the Australians had the blaze under control. A dazed Mesnel spilt the ball, Australia was awarded the scrum feed, and fullback Greg Martin booted the side down field and out of trouble. In no longer than it took the ball boy to fetch the ball, the mood of the game had changed. France had played their aces, and been trumped on every occasion.

Almost from the ensuing scrum, Lynagh hoisted a kick long and high, high enough to enable Martin to hare after it, soar above the French players and catch the ball on the full. With Martin still airborne but descending, he lobbed a basketball pass to Little on his left. Even today, Little can picture the ball in front of his hands. *Just catch it, just catch it.* He did, and set sail for the line. Only a player as lightning fast as French winger Patrice Lagisquet, the man they called the 'Bayonne Express', could have nailed Little in so few steps, but with the aplomb of a 30-Test veteran, Little wrestled his arms free and popped the ball up for Horan, who had loomed up outside him. Neither of them can remember a call, it just seemed logical to Jason that Tim would be there. He was. He took the ball, sprinted, and slid across in the corner, almost collecting the blue and white 'Chaussettes' advertising sign he'd singled out before the game.

The try, Horan's first in Test rugby, meant far more than a reduction of Australia's deficit to a mere two points—12–10 at halftime. It provided an almost illegal injection of self-belief. The Wallabies sensed they had the Frenchmen's measure. Skipper Farr-Jones said just that at halftime. 'Just stick at it, just stick at it, we've got these guys. They're gone.'

They were. Five minutes into the second half, the perfect execution of a backline move, appropriately code-named 'Froggy', saw winger Ian Williams crash over beside the posts.

Lynagh, the player who unloaded the final deft pass, converted to give the Wallabies the lead for the first time in the game. The longer the match went on, the stronger the Australians became. Hearts were pounding, adrenalin was pumping, today they would simply not be denied. The French had arrived at the ground contemplating a date with destiny. The Australians had handed them an appointment with disappointment.

Further tries to Campese and Horan, with Little once again involved in Horan's second crossing, gave Australia an historic 32–15 victory. Jason can remember precious little of the second half, just Bob Templeton running up and down the sideline yelling and screaming, like the ugliest of ugly fathers, spurring on his child in an Under 8 district match.

'I do remember I got a bit carried away,' Templeton admits. 'But of all the rugby matches I have been involved with over a 30 year period, that Test goes down as one of my all-time favourites. It was such a courageous performance.'

The feeling in the Australian dressing shed after the game was one Little would have liked to bottle up and keep for the rest of his life. So many new faces, but all now with smiles a foot long. 'We all stood in a circle and belted out the most emotional version of the national anthem I can ever remember being part of,' Jason recalled. 'It was just magic.'

Ten minutes later, the players were arm in arm again, this time in the giant spa baths just across the corridor, re-living each and every one of the 80 minutes. The mood was intoxicating. They hadn't just beaten the French on French soil. They had flogged them. Four tries to nil, inflicting on France their worst loss at home since the Springboks' 25–3 demolition in 1952.

FitzSimons posed for the cameras, holding a bottle of champagne above his head. 'This is a preview of the 1991 World Cup final at Twickenham. If you see any rugby league scouts near our two centres, shoot them.'

Some 19,000 kilometres away, in North Queensland, Ron Bourne, the diplomatic deputy headmaster, sat alone in the loungeroom of his Mackay home. He looked wearily at his watch and yawned. It was 1.40am. As he turned off the television, and walked to his bedroom, the words came ringing through his ears: *Well to be perfectly honest Jason, I think you're a better cricketer than you are a rugby player. I believe you've got a brighter long term future in cricket than any other sport.* 'Yeah, good one Ron,' he muttered to himself. 'You're a genius.' He turned off the light and went to sleep.

*Repeat after me.*

Tim Horan stood in a crowded restaurant with his right hand on his mother's head as Peter FitzSimons, playing the part of the high priest, delivered the sacred French oath. Beside the big bearded lock was skipper Farr-Jones, the witness.

'*Je te jure sur—I swear to you* . . .'

Horan obediently repeated in French and English: 'Je te jure sur—I swear to you . . .'

'*La tete de ma mere—on the head of my mother* . . .'

'La tete de ma mere—on the head of my mother . . .'

'*Que je nirai pas a jeu a XIII—I will not consider rugby league* . . .'

'Que je nirai pas a jeu a XIII—I will not consider rugby league . . .'

'*Avant le coupe du monde—until after the World Cup* . . .'

'Avant le coupe du monde—until after the World Cup . . .'

Then the same for Jason. In the absence of his mother Pat, Helen was nominated as the surrogate, and the ritual was repeated.

'*Je te jure sur—I swear to you* . . .'

It might have started out as a bit of impromptu fun as the players revelled in the euphoria of their landmark victory.

But there was an underlying seriousness which FitzSimons did nothing to disguise.

*'Je te jure sur la tete de ma mere—I swear on the head of my mother* . . . it had always appealed to me,' FitzSimons explains. 'It's just such a wonderful oath. Not like "I promise" which is so often devalued. That's something a used car salesman might say. But swearing on your mother's head . . . think of the consequences—you just can't get any more serious than that.'

The serious underpinnings were not lost on Tim and Jason either. They knew exactly what they were getting themselves into. Some 12 months down the track, their commitment, their oath, would be put to the test.

The following morning, the enormity of Australia's achievement was rammed home as the Wallaby players, most bleary eyed and tragically short on sleep, scanned the local papers.

'La revolution de 1989' trumpeted the French rugby newspaper, *Midi Olympique*, featuring a full page 37cm wide photograph of Horan about to dump Mesnel into the ground.

On the other side of the world, the Australian press had a field day. In *The Australian* the following Monday, Ian Telford wrote: 'An immediate check is needed to see if Le Coq—the once proud rooster symbol of French rugby—suffered an embarrassing change of gender in Australia's stunning 32–15 triumph here on Saturday. So thoroughly was he plucked in the Wallabies four tries-to-nil rampage that the possibility of grievous fundamental damage cannot be ruled out . . . Many hands made light work of the plucking, but none worked more expertly than the two Queensland Country boys who know their way around a farm yard, Tim Horan and Jason Little. The debut of the Toowoomba born 19-year-olds, the youngest centre combination in world rugby, was nothing short of sensational.'

Brisbane's *Courier Mail* claimed Horan and Little had 'ushered in a new golden age for Australian rugby union', while on his segment on Channel 9's 'Wide World of Sport', Grand Slam coach Alan Jones said the Wallabies owed their victory to 'the naked enthusiasm of the two young Australian centres'.

The President of the French Rugby Federation, Albert Ferrase, however was appalled by the locals' effort, calling for the entire team to be axed. 'We made a complete mess of the match,' he said in an article carried by French news agency, Agence France-Presse. 'We haven't been given a thrashing like that in years. I'm not a selector, but if it were in my hands, I'd change all 15 players for the second Test.'

Monsieur Ferrase wasn't exactly granted his wish in its entirety, but he was granted half of it. The French selectors chopped eight players, including legendary fullback Serge Blanco and skipper Pierre Berbizier, for the Test in Lille, in the north of France the following Saturday.

The Lille Test match, played before another fervid capacity crowd of 40,000, once again proved just how much difference a week can make in sport. Farr-Jones and Dwyer had stressed to the Australian players: Beware the wounded Frenchman, beware the wounded Frenchman. But not until Horan ran out onto Stadium Nord and saw the anger in the eyes of the French players did he really appreciate what his skipper had been saying.

'I remember thinking, as soon as they came screaming out through the tunnel: we're in a bit of trouble here. The French players had this glazed look in their eyes. I'd never seen anything like it before. They were men on a serious mission.'

Serious indeed. Trailing 13–6 at halftime after an opportunist Australian try by hooker Kearns in the first term, the Frenchmen absolutely blitzed the Wallabies who gave the impression they had invested every centime they owned in Strasbourg a week before. They were bereft of ideas and answers. France rattled home to win 25–19, squaring the series and restoring immeasurable pride to a French rugby pysche which only seven days earlier was bordering on suicidal.

At the end of a dinner with the French team that night, Farr-Jones distributed song sheets with the phonetic spelling of the words to 'La Marseillaise', the French national anthem. On cue, the Wallabies stood and belted out the first few verses. The singing, the pronunciation and the tune were all horrifically out of whack, and probably not helped by the acoustics of the 300-year-old building, but the gesture was well appreciated by the host team. They responded moments later with an equally poor but just as sincere version of 'Waltzing Matilda'. Jason loved it: 'There seemed to be genuine respect between the players. You could go out onto the field and belt one another, but as soon as the rugby was over, you were the best of mates. It was a great thing to be part of.'

The following morning, as Tim was packing his bags in preparation for the flight back across to London, the phone in his room rang. 'Ello! Tim? It is Franck Mesnel speaking.' Mesnel, the player Horan had dumped on his back more than once in the two Tests, was ringing to congratulate him on his first series in France. 'I thought you showed remarkable skills and courage for a player your age,' he said. Mesnel told Tim he'd be seeing Michael Lynagh before he returned to Australia, and would give him some clothes from his fashion boutique, Eden Park to pass on. 'Merci beaucoup, Franck!'

Two Test series, and two gentlemanly gestures, one from Joe Stanley and the other from Mesnel. Horan was starting to cherish more than ever his membership of the international rugby fellowship.

# Chapter 8

## Injuries, Ill Feeling and Iced Water

*'The man who can drive himself further once the effort gets painful is the man who will win.'*
BRITISH ATHLETE SIR ROGER BANNISTER

On November 17, 1989, just two days after he had arrived back from France, Tim Horan marched through the door of Castlemaine Perkins' Brisbane headquarters.

It was a very different Horan to the nervous, confused 17-year-old who had first arrived at Finchley St some 20 months before, not knowing if he was going to be a brewery truck driver or storeman and packer. He was now an international rugby player, returning from abroad, from the heat of battle. His chest was puffed out, there was a spring in his step.

'Gidday Julie.'

'Gidday Tim.' His supervisor didn't even break stride. She just kept on going.

*Hmmmm, Gidday Tim. What? No Gidday Tim, how was the trip? How was France, how was the Rugby?* That's OK, he reasoned, she must have been busy.

'Gidday John.'

'Yeah, hi Tim, how are you going? Listen, can you track those Mackay accounts down for me? I'm fairly sure they're behind with their payments.'

*Oh sure I can, no problem. If I can remember how—I HAVE been away overseas for seven weeks, in case none of you have noticed. What is wrong with these people.*

He decided to ring his mate, Graham Hart, up in accounts. Surely he'd at least acknowledge the fact he'd been away, played a couple of Tests, scored a couple of tries, beaten France etc.

'Gidday Graham, Tim Horan.'

'Oh, hi Tim.'

'Yeah, I've just got back from France,' Horan said, trying to lure him into conversation.

'That's good. Hey, I don't know whether Jenny's spoken to you, I need a copy of those forms from North Queensland. When you get a chance, can you sort them out and drop them up to us? Thanks. I better fly. I've got a fair bit on.' *Click.*

Horan was shattered. The ballooned chest had returned to normal. The spring had deserted him. Two hours had passed and not a word. Not one question about France.

Finally, morning tea arrived . . . and the room was suddenly awash with streamers, balloons, cakes, and Eskys full of iced beer. People from all over the brewery converged on the accounts department to congratulate him, to slap him on the back.

Horan had been nabbed. 'I was just about to jump off a bridge. I'd spent hours preparing my answers for all the questions I thought I'd be asked and, after two hours, I didn't ever think I'd get to use them.'

The belated but nonetheless hearty acknowledgment of his colleagues at Fourex was not the first, nor would it be the last fuss made of Horan—and Little—when they arrived home from France.

From two relative unknowns prior to the tour, they had returned home the talk of Brisbane's rugby community. They were on television, on radio—they'd even been nominated for The *Courier-Mail*'s Sports Star of the Year award, and were the newspaper's first choice for any promotional photographs relating to rugby. Even cab drivers, normally a good barometer of public opinion, were mentioning them in dispatches, even if the commentary was heavily slanted towards the professional code. Bob Templeton remembers being told on a brief trip from the city one night, not long after the tour: 'Yeah, those two blond haired kids, Horan and Little, I reckon they'd go OK in league.'

Little had missed the initial wave of fanfare and fuss by accepting an invitation to fly from London straight down to Bahrain with Rod McCall, to play for the Bahrain Warblers in a Sevens Tournament. The glitzy moneyed carnival event is an eye opener for the most feted of international rugby players, let alone a wide-eyed 19-year-old farm boy from Jimbour. There were yachts twice the size of his parents' house, parties that went all night, and to ferry him and McCall around, a white chauffeur driven Jaguar, which they had at their beck and call 24 hours a day. It might well have been the most sleepless week in Felix's 40-odd years. They would phone him up at all hours of the night . . . at 2am, 3am, 5am.

'Hey Felix, can you come and get us?'

'Certainly Sir. Where are you?'

'We don't know.'

'Well describe what you can see.'

'Well just in front of me, there's a big white building with a blue awning, next to that . . .'

'OK, I think I know where you are . . . Stay put, I won't be long.'

If these were the trappings of playing international rugby, Little planned to play until he was 60. It was just sensational.

Injuries, Ill Feeling and Iced Water

Horan was determined to keep his feet firmly on the ground. Never a 'big head', he wasn't about to change. Whenever he went to club training at Souths, he chose what he wore very carefully. He'd rummage through his dirty laundry basket and pull out an old pair of Downlands socks, in preference to wearing a clean Australian pair. There was not a Wallaby logo anywhere to be found whenever he was among his mates at the club.

But like Jason, Tim did notice a few subtle changes in his life—the strange manner in which some people were treating him. On Sunday nights, for instance, he'd drive down to the nearby Cat and Fiddle, to pick up some takeaways for dinner. Whereas he once stood in line, with the rest of the great unwashed and waited to be served, the little bearded man would now spring to attention the moment he walked through the door. 'Tim, nice to see you. What can I get you tonight?' 'It was embarrassing,' Horan recalls. 'I'd never been treated like that before and it made me feel very uncomfortable. I'd point out there were other people who'd been waiting longer, and suggest he should serve them.'

On another occasion, when strolling through the streets of Surfers Paradise with Katrina, he stopped to get some icecreams. The young man behind the counter picked him out immediately. When Horan went to pay for the first cone, the young fellow waved his money away: 'No—it's on the house for that try you scored in France'. Now, there was a time and a place for modesty, and there was a time and a place to be smart. Clearly this occasion fell into the latter category. Horan couldn't resist. 'Hang-on a second, I scored two tries.' It worked a treat.

There was a certain irony to all this mollycoddling. The ice-cream boy probably didn't realise—nor would he have cared—that three-Test hero Horan, precocious young talent that he was, had still not played a game for his state. When he headed off on a pre-season tour to Western Samoa and

Fiji with the Queensland team the following March, he arrived at the airport wearing a red Queensland Rugby Union official's tie, as opposed to the blue player's version. An enormous amount of fuss is made over those blue polyester strips, which would retail for not a cent more than $15, were they available through retail outlets. But they were not. They had to be earned. And Horan as yet had not earned his. It was an anomaly he wanted to quickly rectify.

It was reasonable to assume, given Little and Horan's heroic deeds in France the previous November, the pair would have been a walk-up start for the state team at the beginning of the 1990 season. That was not the case. Coach John Connolly was an ardent believer in players earning their spurs. Since taking over the coaching reins from Bob Templeton 12 months earlier, Connolly had focussed on restoring the pride in the Red jersey. He sensed it had become, in the latter stages of the Templeton era, no more than a means to an end—a stepping stone to bigger and better things. In Connolly's mind, playing for Queensland was the biggest and best thing the game could offer. He encouraged his players to think the same way.

In part, that is why Horan and Little were not seriously considered for selection during Queensland's domestic program the previous year. The incumbents, Dominic Maguire and Anthony Herbert, were doing the job very capably, therefore his loyalty rested with them. And his loyalty would stay there, until somebody else gave him a very good reason to sway.

The remote Southern Pacific isle of Western Samoa, in some respects, is like France. Not physically or culturally, but in as much as it too would struggle for inclusion in that imaginary player's bible, 'The Top 10 Most Desirable Touring Destinations in World Rugby'. A dusty port city protecting a sweeping harbour, Apia offers limited recreational opportunities for visiting players, other than a challenging hike up nearby Mount Vyae to visit Robert Louis Stevenson's grave site. If players are not into grave sites, they're more or less confined to the comfortable poolside surroundings of Aggie Grey's hotel, the premier accommodation in the bustling city of 160,000.

The first of Queensland's three tour matches was against a Western Samoa Invitation XV at Apia National Stadium on March 8. In the 56th minute, Connolly was presented with his *'very good reason to sway'*. Darting around the blindside, debutant Horan burst through three Samoan defenders, chipped ahead, regathered, chipped ahead again, and won the race to the ball for his first try in Queensland colours. Connolly just looked at assistant coach John Brass. Both of them shook their head in amazement. Two seats further along, sitting on the reserves bench was Dominic Maguire, the Test centre in the series against the British Lions the previous year. Maguire looked across at Connolly, Connolly looked at Maguire, but not a word was exchanged.

'Dominic knew from that moment, it was all over red rover,' Connolly says. 'Dead right,' agrees Maguire. 'I could play my best 15 games in a row and not come up with an effort like that one Tim produced against Samoa. The guy was in a class of his own, even at that age. I was well aware the next selection meeting wouldn't take long.'

By the end of the game, Horan had scored a further two tries, with Queensland running out convincing 37–9 winners. He'd earned his blue tie, and a permanent spot in the Queensland side for as long as he desired to play the game.

Little on the other hand was struggling. Connolly was more reluctant to dispose of Anthony Herbert, a strongly-built outside centre who had first worn the Wallaby colours just prior to the 1987 World Cup. A big, strong fellow, Herbert might have lacked the finesse of other players, but he was incredibly competitive, and an integral part of the social fabric of the team. Little was selected in the centres, alongside Tim in the opening game against Samoa, but was squeezed out onto the wing for the first consequential outing of the season, the South Pacific Championship game against Fiji in Suva 10 days later. Little in fact was lucky to be in the starting XV at all. He was reserves bench bound until Queensland's Fijian winger, Isei Siganiyavi—so excited to be home—was dropped for missing three successive team obligations.

Little found the whole scenario very frustrating. While he didn't necessarily expect to be in the team, he knew his game had been vastly improved by the experience and knowledge he'd banked in France. He feared being stationed out on the wing would drain his confidence, just like the previous year. 'I was a useless winger. I might as well have been playing in the second row. I didn't have the confidence to go looking for work, because I was so preoccupied with getting the basics right. So it was not uncommon to play a game, and only touch the ball once or twice. I needed to be much more involved than that.'

He arrived back in Brisbane as frustrated as he ever had been in his sporting career. Still, he was quite prepared to accept that he hadn't had the worst run in the world. He would try to be patient, and use the experience to toughen up mentally.

THE RUSSIANS ARE COMING! THE RUSSIANS ARE COMING! In a tour which once again exemplified just how far and wide rugby's tentacles stretched, the Soviet Union team arrived in Queensland to kick off the 1990 Ballymore representative program.

Their game against the Reds in late March would hardly be remembered as Horan and Little's first outing in a Queensland jersey at Ballymore. Of much greater significance was the incredible bravery the Soviet team showed in actually *playing* the game. Arriving in North Queensland in March,

straight out of a Soviet Union winter, the visitors were mesmerised by both the warmth of the Queensland welcome,
and the climate. But despite repeated warnings from North
Queensland rugby officials, who even went to the trouble of
buying bottles and bottles of sunscreen, the Soviet players
declined to apply the lotion. They were determined to go
home bronzed gods, parading around in the midday sun with
their shirts tied around their waists. Some were even bare-
chested for seven straight hours during a charter boat trip out
to the reef off Cairns.

The end result was predictable. By the time the team arrived in Brisbane, many of the players had sun blisters on
their sun blisters. The Soviet team doctor naturally enough
had never had to treat severe sunburn before, and, rather than
seek advice from local medicos, he simply recommended the
players cover the sunburnt areas with as much strapping as
possible—sticking plaster, slapped straight onto sensitive skin.

The tackling of forwards like Sam Scott-Young and Brendan Nasser was ferocious enough without the excruciating
pain of third degree sunburn to compound it. One Soviet
player left the field in tears, followed not long after by both
first choice props who could no longer bear the pain of packing scrums on their red raw shoulders.

The piercing screams of the Soviet players as medical staff
removed their dressings—and further layers of raw sensitive
skin—could be heard in the neighbouring Queensland dressing
shed, even above the whirr of giant air-conditioning machines.

Jason felt he had a raw deal of a different kind, being picked
on the wing for the game against the Soviets, despite an
increasingly strong push from forces outside the team to have
him moved into the centres. Grand Slam winning skipper,
Andrew Slack, in his weekly column in *The Sunday Mail*
newspaper, claimed the continued choice of Herbert ahead
of Little was 'a classic case of picking a team to combat the

opposition's strength, rather than maximising Queensland's assets'.

The article, on April 2 continued: 'Horan and Little are obviously going to be the Test centres—playing Little on the wing is only going to create uncertainty in his mind.'

Even the Queensland Rugby Union administrators bought into the argument, with Executive Director Terry Doyle ringing Connolly at home to try to persuade him to play Little in the centres against Auckland—the side's next game. It was the only time in 15 years service that Doyle had meddled in team selections.

'I just felt so strongly about it. After France, Tim and Jason were the talk of the town, the absolute flavour of the month. Rugby fans were hankering to see them play together, and yet we couldn't seem to fit both of them into the state team. I rang John, and suggested that from a promotional standpoint it was important that we have Tim and Jason paired in the centres. There was no disrespect to Anthony—but the other two were who the public wanted to see.'

Finally Connolly relented, relegating Herbert to the reserves bench, and promoting Little to the No 13 jersey for the game against Auckland. The match proved to be anything but an auspicious occasion, with Queensland getting pummelled by the Kiwi heavyweights.

In many ways Connolly's act of defiance, in retaining Herbert ahead of the Test incumbent Little, was typical of the mood in Queensland at the time. While Queensland officials didn't exactly go out of their way to antagonise their New South Wales counterparts, Connolly in particular would always do what he felt was right for Queensland. If that fitted in with Australian plans, all well and good, but if didn't, tough luck. It was Queensland first, daylight second, the rest third.

The feeling between the two states came to a head in May, after Queensland had beaten New South Wales 12–3 in a boring, wet, midweek game at the Sydney Football Stadium.

As Queensland backs coach John Brass was just about to enter the post-match function room, he was savaged by a very disgruntled national coach.

'Did you get your job on false pretences?' Bob Dwyer asked Brass, his former Randwick clubmate, in an opening gambit which left no doubt as to his impression of the Queensland game plan. Dwyer was very critical of the manner in which Queensland had played the match, claiming the style of the Reds' victory had set Australian rugby back 10 years. He queried what Brass had been teaching, and reminded him it was a coach's job to improve his players' ability, rather than restrict them. He couldn't comprehend how Queensland could have these dynamic centres out on the field, and starve them of possession.

Brass found the whole episode bizarre. 'I thought Bob showed a serious lack of understanding of my role, given that I wasn't the one who decided how the game would be played—John Connolly was. But even more startling was his comment about the style of the game being more important than the result. Coming from the national coach, I found that comment unbelievable. It showed a complete lack of appreciation of the importance of results at that level. I think in retrospect, Bob had probably pre-ordained his Test team—he wanted New South Wales to dominate in the forwards, and Queensland to outplay them in the backs, but instead, we had taken them on in the forwards and beaten them. I suspect he became very frustrated watching it.'

Irrespective of the accuracy or relevance of Dwyer's comments, there was an appropriate time and place to address such an issue. An emotional outburst at the door of the post-match function room, within earshot of the players, didn't fulfil either criterion. Queensland team manager John Breen, who would later become the manager of Dwyer's World Cup side, lodged an official complaint with the Australian Rugby Union, via the QRU. Far from re-directing the ideology of Australian rugby, in particular backline play, Dwyer's outburst merely provoked the Queensland camp, and deepened their resolve to play the game exactly as they saw fit.

Horan and Little, in many ways the focal point of the debate, were caught between a rock and a hard place. There were distinct differences between the manner in which Bob Dwyer wanted them to play the game, and the instructions they were receiving at Queensland level. The national coach insisted they stand flat in attack, and commit their opposite number to the tackle, while Brass wanted them to be more flexible—flat in some instances, but on other occasions deep, hitting the advantage line with momentum. For Horan and Little—both still 19—it was all a bit confusing. They obviously didn't want to ruffle the feathers of the national coach, but by the same token, they were both extremely close to Brass. They respected him enormously, not only in terms of the technical knowledge he imparted but also his profound philosophical offerings, some of which had been relayed by legendary rugby league coach Jack Gibson, during Brass' playing days with Easts in Sydney.

*'If you must make a mistake, make it with speed.'*

*'If you shrug off a loss, you can't be a winner.'*

*'Never worry about signing autographs, worry when people stop asking.'*

*'If it ain't broke, don't fix it.'*

Or, in the case of the odd whinge or complaint: *'Who owns the problem?!'*

Brass was very much the mentor—he moulded their values, opinions and attitudes. But Dwyer moulded careers. They would have to learn to tread carefully.

When the national selectors announced the team to tackle France in the first of three upcoming Tests, it came as no surprise that Horan and Little were named alongside one another in the centres. What did create headline news was the unheralded axing of David Campese. Rugby's ultimate journeyman had just returned from club football commitments in Italy, but not in time to convince the national selection panel he deserved to be picked for the first international appointment of the winter. Campese lost his place to another Italian, Queenslander Paul Carozza. If Campese was the Italian Lamborghini—fast, flashy and full of class—Carozza was the Fiat Bambino—compact, economical, and very useful in heavy traffic. While the exchange of the Italian speedsters was probably never intended to be permanent, the Australian panel had for the first time served notice about the new hard-line approach to selections.

The much awaited appearance of Horan and Little, together in Wallaby colours for the first time on Australian soil, lasted just 65 minutes. In a dull, static first Test in Sydney, Horan, on one of the rare occasions he touched the ball, charged upfield only to be caught on an awkward angle by French scrumhalf Henri Sanz. *Craaaack*. The players in the ruck dispersed to reveal the sight of Horan lying on the Sydney Football Stadium turf, clutching his left knee. As he was being armchaired to the sideline by the team's medical staff, Bob Dwyer was hurrying down to the sideline to meet him. *Why this guy?*

The prognosis from team physio Greg Craig was not all that serious—four to five weeks at the most—but as long as he worked hard on the rehabilitation, Horan would be back in time for the Wallabies' full scale tour of New Zealand, starting in late July.

The French came and went, the three Test series wrapped up by the Wallabies in a memorable second Test at Ballymore, which yielded almost a point a minute. The viewing was not unlike a tennis match, as play swayed from one end of the field to the other. And while the final scoreline of 48–31 probably suggested there had been an abrogation of defensive responsibilities, it was more the creativity of the players, and the leniency of Welsh referee Clive Norling, which facilitated the 10-try spectacle.

Little's first try in Wallaby colours, on his home turf, brought a special cheer from the capacity crowd of 22,000, but nowhere near the applause of Serge Blanco's remarkable 100m effort from behind his own goal line.

It will be remembered by those who witnessed it as one of the greatest individual tries in Test rugby. The Ballymore beer garden was abuzz after the game. *Whaddabout Blanco . . . wasn't that just sensational.*

By 8 o'clock that night, the French fullback had run 150m, from out in the car park, over XXXX hill, beaten the entire Australian team twice—all while whistling the 'La Marseillaise'. There were still 5000 people in the ground five hours after fulltime. The atmosphere was just intoxicating.

A one-off Test match between Australia and the American Eagles, the day before a six-week Bledisloe Cup tour of New Zealand . . . it was a little like young Johnny asking his mother if he could take her prize piece of pottery to school for Show and Tell, just two days before the opening of her first major exhibition. It was asking for trouble.

The Wallabies would win the Test, there was no doubt. The primary objective was to have all players walk from the field safely, all limbs intact, and ready to tackle the All Blacks.

Surely little Johnny could be trusted . . .

CRASH! There goes the prize piece of pottery! Jason Little went tumbling to the ground, clutching his right ankle. As hard as he tried to get up and walk, he couldn't put an ounce of weight on the leg. The immediate suspicion was that Little had just badly bruised the joint in a tackle, but so severe was his pain, Greg Craig had no hesitation in sending him off for precautionary x-rays the following morning. The x-rays revealed what Little, if nobody else, suspected. A small fracture

at the the base of the ankle. The implications were horrific—
total rest for two weeks, no rugby for six. No tour. The first
major exhibition had been cancelled.

Little was absolutely shattered. He arrived back at the Parkroyal Hotel, x-rays in hand, just as the touring party was
having a group photograph taken. He had tears in his eyes.
He couldn't bring himself to face the rest of the players.

He went upstairs to his room, where his bags were already
packed and ready for New Zealand. Beside them was the
new Wallaby mascot, presented to him by Nick Farr-Jones
at dinner two nights prior. As much as he hated the little
nuisance marsupial, he wished he was carting it off to the
airport that afternoon. But he wasn't carting anything off
anywhere for two months. A freak tackle—a hard American
head—had denied him his first shot at the Kiwis.

Nick remembers walking past the open room, and seeing
Jason sitting on the end of the bed, tears in his eyes, clutching
the x-rays. 'I remember feeling so sorry for Jas that morning.
Looking back on it now, it doesn't seem that big a deal, but
at the time, rugby was his life. He just exuded this incredible
passion for the game. He obviously had a great desire to be
with Timmy. It was unbelievably hard for him. He was an
established part of the team, then all of a sudden, he was
watching it all from afar.

'It was disappointing for the team too. Jason was really
starting to come of age as a Test rugby player. In fact it gave
me a warm feeling, just watching those two young guys play
the game, and play it extremely well. They obviously enjoyed
every minute, training wasn't a chore, they just couldn't get
enough rugby. It took me back to 1984, when I first arrived
on the scene.'

As disappointed as the Australians were to have lost Little, it
was matched by the relief in the All Blacks camp. The previous
November, while on a six-week tour of England and Wales,
the Kiwis had huddled together in a room of their hotel in

Swansea to watch the Wallabies play France. Grant Fox recalls the occasion: 'By halftime, a lot of the guys were asking where the hell did this kid Little come from. We'd obviously seen Horan once before, but Little we hadn't really heard of.' There were a few things which struck the All Black players immediately—one was the obvious ingredient of speed, the second was the two centres' distribution skills. But what really stood out was the understanding they seemed to have. As Fox points out: 'There was obviously a very good rapport between the two of them, which of course is crucial in any good midfield combination. I can honestly say we were pretty happy when we heard Jason wasn't coming.'

One out, one in. Only an hour before the disconsolate Little arrived back at the Parkroyal, Horan was duck waddling across the floor of the first floor team room, trying to convince Bob Dwyer, Bob Templeton and Dr Fergus Wilson that his left knee was once again ready for rugby. The Australian medico had his doubts, but the other two—whose opinions seemed to weigh more heavily—were satisfied. By Horan's own estimation he was 95 percent—he'd be 100 in a few days, in time for the first match. The green light was given—Horan was on the plane.

'Three—nil, three—nil, three—nil . . .'

The chanting of the Kiwi fans outside the bus was just as obnoxious as Tim Horan remembered it to be. Dressed in their black trackie pants, thumping loudly on the side of the Australian bus . . . but this time they did have a point. What if the Wallabies lost this Test too? What would it feel like to be part of the first Wallaby team since 1972 to leave New Zealand without a single Test win? Just how would they front their fans back home? Horan's body shuddered. The consequences were almost too horrible to contemplate.

But there appeared to be a better than even money chance it would happen. The All Blacks had already secured the

Bledisloe Cup, comfortably accounting for the Wallabies in the first two Tests—21–6 in Christchurch and 27–17 in Auckland. In the process, they had extended their unbeaten record to 22 Tests, and more than 50 international matches. The smart money was on New Zealand.

August 18—it was one of those Wellington days when you were far better off inside. Gloomy, bitterly cold, with strong winds tilting rain to impossible angles. And up there in the grey, cloudy heavens, Athletic Park, arguably the most exposed Test rugby ground in the world, a stadium where 60m field goals are not out of the question, nor line kicks which finish 10m behind the kicker.

Michael Lynagh wasn't having anywhere near that amount of trouble, but there was a familiar banana shape to each of his kicks in the first half, when Australia were tacking into the fierce southerly wind. The halftime deficit of just three points was almost cause for celebration, especially when straight after the break, Australia's increasingly confident, increasingly assertive hooker Phil Kearns pounced on a loose ball at the front of a lineout to score the Wallabies' second try in four All Black Tests. Picking himself up off the ground, Kearns gave opposite number Sean Fitzpatrick one of the more famous verbal showers in trans-Tasman rugby history. The exact text may never be known, but the convivial Kearns, whenever asked publicly, maintains he was merely responding to Fitzpatrick's BBQ invitation, and specifying he would like 'two sausages' when he arrived.

There were few other snags the Australians had to contend with that afternoon. Kearns' feisty gesture epitomised the fire in the belly of every Wallaby player on the field. A couple were playing for their Test futures, most just for the pride in the gold jersey, but not one of the 15 who ran on were prepared to accept anything less than a win. They outpointed the All Blacks in every department, showing desperation and determination not seen since Strasbourg 10 months before.

With two minutes left on the clock, the result had already been decided with the Wallabies leading 18–9. As Lynagh was placing the ball on the mound for his fifth attempt at penalty goal, French referee Rene Hourquet turned to outside centre Anthony Herbert and said: 'You boys will drink a lot of beer tonight.' 'Too right Rene, too right,' came Herbert's smiling response.

The fulltime siren—21–9. The Australian players embraced—an outpouring of emotion based more on relief than elation. Before the game they were confronted with the prospect of being one of the worst performed Wallaby sides ever to leave Australian shores. But in just 90 minutes, the Woeful Wallabies had become the Wonderful Wallabies, inflicting on the All Blacks their first loss in 1373 days, since France defeated them in Nantes back in 1986.

The Bledisloe Cup may have long gone, but at least the black monkey was off the Wallabies' back.

The concierge at the Holiday Inn Hotel looked at Horan strangely, but didn't say a word. Why anybody would be walking out of the hotel with two towels draped over his shoulder at 10 o'clock at night, he had no idea. But he obviously didn't think it was his place to ask.

Two hours and 10 beers later, Horan was scouring Grapes nightclub, looking for his accomplice. One lap, two laps, three laps. Finally he located Nick Farr-Jones in a corner, quietly chatting with a small group of people, including his wife Angie. 'Come on mate, it's almost midnight. Let's go.'

The others looked at one another as Horan and Farr-Jones, without explanation, marched out the door of the nightclub, with Angie following. Farr-Jones flagged down the first passing car, if jumping out in front of its path qualifies as flagging down.

''Scuse me mate, this is an emergency. Can you take the three of us down to the harbour.'

The driver recognised the faces immediately. Despite the fact they'd just beaten his beloved All Blacks seven and a half hours before, it would still be a pleasure to have them in the car. 'Yeah Nuck, Tum, no worries, hop in eh?'

During the brief trip, the driver's curiosity got the better of him. He had less restraint than the concierge: 'If you don't mind me asking, why do you want to go to the beach at this time of night?'

'For a swim of course,' Horan replied. The car pulled up, the trio got out. 'Can you hang on a sec? We won't be long.' The driver and his two passengers sat on the warm bonnet and watched in amazement as Farr-Jones and Horan gingerly tip-toed across the small, pebble beach, stripped off, and plunged into the freezing waters of Wellington Harbour. They emerged almost blue, shivering uncontrollably. After taking a few very unflattering photographs, Angie handed them the towels . . . 'Good call those towels, Timmy'. They put their clothes back on and climbed back up the embankment to the car.

'Ahhhh, that feels better. I needed that,' Horan quipped. 'Eh, you jokers are crazy . . . absolutely crazy' was all their Kiwi chauffeur could mumble.

Farr-Jones explains the lunacy: 'We made the pledge after the first Test—when we played so badly in Christchurch—that we would go for a swim in Auckland Harbour if we won the second Test. When we lost that, we decided to carry it over to Wellington. There was no way Tim was going to let me forget it. I think the concept honestly appealed to him. He probably would have wanted to go swimming, even if we lost.'

Nick was only half aware of it at the time, but the icy feeling running through his veins that night was matched only by the cold feeling a number of Queensland-based players had for national coach Bob Dwyer.

The numbest of all was second-rower Bill Campbell, the Queensland skipper, who had surprisingly been recalled to the Test line-up after spending the entire tour as captain of 'Billy's Boys', the also-rans in the midweek team.

As the fulltime siren sounded at Athletic Park, Campbell, head down, trudged from the field in his jumbo size 15 boots, looking like a gambler who'd just blown his life savings. He sat down next to second-row partner Rod McCall in the corner of the dressing room. From McCall's memory, as Campbell was picking the mud out of his boots, all he could say was: 'What have we done, what have we done?'

He realised that by helping to end the All Blacks' winning streak, he had also helped to retain Bob Dwyer as the Wallaby coach for the World Cup. Years later, he suspects Dwyer would have been retained even if the Australians had lost the series 3–0, but the victory had removed any doubt.

Campbell's feelings were not based on a personal feud—he was simply not a great believer in Dwyer's ability as a coach. 'Whether he was doing something magnificent with the backs, only they could determine, but from a forward's point of view, he had very little understanding,' Campbell says. 'That's why he had (assistant coaches) Jake Howard and Bob Templeton in there. If Bob (Dwyer) said anything contrary to what they thought, it would be ignored. I know some people regard Bob as the guru, but in my opinion, it was Jake Howard who created the forward play which took Australia to the World Cup and won it. People don't realise how central he was. When I was there, Bob's input was minimal, Tempo had a reasonable say, but Jake was the policy maker, the ring leader, the guiding force.'

While Campbell never mounted a campaign to get rid of Dwyer, he did have a number of strong allies in fellow Queenslanders Sam Scott-Young and reserve hooker, Mark McBain. There were also three or four senior New South Welshmen who believed it was time to change the national coach, but elected to keep their views and thoughts private, through fear of retribution.

Scott-Young, who earned man of the match honours in Wellington after being called in as an eleventh hour replacement for Brendan Nasser, has always been forthright in his comments about the national coach, probably to the detriment of his international career. He claims skipper Nick Farr-Jones was central to the push to get rid of Dwyer.

'Nick will deny it now, but in New Zealand, he was doing most of the rebel rousing,' Scott-Young says. 'Like just about everybody else in the team, he'd had enough of Bob's erratic behaviour. I'll never forget his team talk prior to the (second) Test in Auckland. He wanted Michael Lynagh to try to hit the posts with his up and unders in New Zealand's 25. He asked Noddy: "Do you reckon you can do it, do you think you can hit the posts—we've got a 50–50 chance of scoring if you can". Noddy (Lynagh) was as stunned as the rest of us. He didn't know what to say, finally muttering something like: "I don't know Bob, it's a big ask". The players just couldn't believe it. I was sitting beside Bill Campbell and we just looked at each other: Bill said: "Shit—What are we in for here?" Bob had totally lost it. Anytime he was really feeling the pressure, he was totally erratic.'

Even Horan, who at age 20 was not willing to question too much of what the national coach suggested, remembers being bamboozled by the 'goal-post tactic'. 'I did wonder what page of the coaching manual that had come from, but Bob does tend to get very emotional prior to Tests.' Towards the latter stages of the tour, Horan was also aware of 'quite a bit of discontent' among the players, but made a point of not getting involved.

'You'd hear comments—anti-Dwyer statements—up in rooms, and around the hotel foyers every now and then, but I'd never really buy into it. I'm there to play football and enjoy myself. Having said that, I can appreciate how hard it must be for the guys who are not in the Test team to remain positive and supportive, especially if they don't think they're getting a fair go as far as selection is concerned.

'That's probably an area where Bob let himself down in the early days—by not talking to players—explaining to them why they'd been dropped, or what they had to improve on to force their way into the team. Otherwise, I enjoyed playing under him. I thought he had some really good ideas, and on the tour of New Zealand, he seemed a bit more flexible in his approach. Like when Noddy or Nick came up with an idea, he was prepared to discuss it and bounce it around, whereas in France in 1989, he had very firm ideas on the way things should be done. I thought he was improving all the time.'

The rumblings of discontent continued in small isolated pockets upon the team's return from across the Tasman, but gradually, the dissidents ran out of ears willing to listen. In December, 1989, Dwyer had been appointed national coach for the following two years, after warding off the challenges of New South Welshmen Dick Laffan and Paul Dalton, and Queenslander Alex Evans. The democratic process alone dictated that Dwyer deserved to take the Wallabies through until after the 1991 World Cup. The start of the tournament was a mere 14 months away. It was in the best interests of Australian rugby that everybody get behind him. And that's what the players in particular decided to do.

For his part in the drama, Farr-Jones concedes that Dwyer was definitely 'gone' had the Wallabies not beaten the All Blacks in the third Test.

'But then again,' he says. 'So was I.'

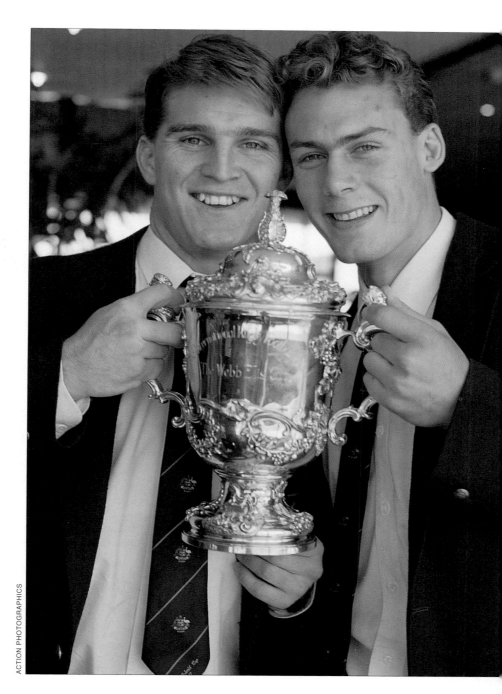

ACTION PHOTOGRAPHICS

Arriving home from the World Cup with 'Bill'.

ABOVE: Little evading the clutches of Will Carling (no. 13) and Stuart Barnes in the Barbarians match at Twickenham in 1993.

LEFT: Jason, back on the farm with Mum and Dad.

RIGHT: Celebrating the 1993 victory over France in Paris with winger Damian Smith, Little's long-suffering flatmate.

MIKE LARDER/SPORT. THE LIBRARY

ACTION PHOTOGRAPHICS

ACTION PHOTOGRAPHICS

Saluting the crowd after clinching the series against the South African
Springboks in 1993.

ACTION PHOTOGRAPHICS

ABOVE: England's World Cup captain Will Carling puts an end to Horan's audacious run during the final at Twickenham.

RIGHT: Little looks for a way around Irish winger Simon Geoghan during the World Cup quarter-final in Dublin.

SPORT. THE LIBRARY

SPORT. THE LIBRARY

ACTION PHOTOGRAPHICS

NEILS SCHIPPER/SPORT. THE LIBRARY

Opposite: Horan in possession: strength, vision, concentration.

Above: Horan, wearing 'Rest of the World' colours looks for a hole in the All Black defence during the New Zealand Centenary Test series in 1992.

Left: An autograph signing session in Goondiwindi.

MIKE LARDER/SPORT. THE LIBRARY

MIKE LARDER/SPORT. THE LIBRARY

Little begins the run which resulted in the first of his two tries against the Springboks at Ballymore in 1993. Forwards Garrick Morgan and Phil Kearns loom in support.

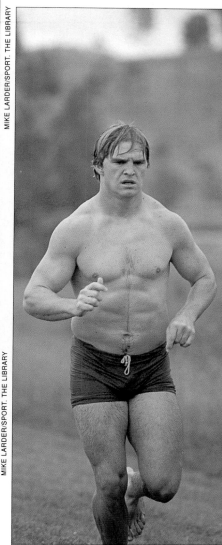

MIKE LARDER/SPORT. THE LIBRARY

MIKE LARDER/SPORT. THE LIBRARY

Sweating it out on the infamous pre-season Queensland training camps. (1992)

Horan on the burst for Queensland.

MIKE LARDER

MIKE LARDER

RIGHT: Taking the plunge together in a river out west.

SPORT. THE LIBRA

ABOVE: Little finds space against Wales in the World Cup pool match in Cardiff.

LEFT: Little runs into traffic against the Springboks at Ballymore.

MIKE LARDER

ALLSPORT/RUSSELL CHEYNE

ABOVE: Horan fields a crucial kick above England's Rory Underwood and teammate David Campese, before heading off on his crucial touchline run in the World Cup final.

RIGHT: Horan doing the dirty work during one of Queensland's torturous pre-season training camps.

MIKE LARDER

MIKE LARDER

ABOVE: The World Cup trophy hits the road.

LEFT: Little soaking up the sun in Fiji with Queensland coach John Connolly.

# Chapter 9

## In a League of Their Own

*'What are some of the most beautiful statements in the English language? I suggest these: I love you. You are wonderful. It's benign—not malignant. Your car is ready. I'm ready to sign.'*

WILLIAM A. WARD

'CONTRACT ON HORAN' 'Broncos, Eels, queue up to bid' screamed the banner headline in the Sydney *Daily Mirror*.

The mud on Tim Horan's No 12 jersey had not yet been washed off, nor was the immigration stamp on his passport dry, when talk of a defection to rugby league mushroomed out of control.

With Horan's three spectacular Test performances against the All Blacks giving the league talent scouts ample to drool over, sports journalists at last had the perfect excuse to give the story a whirl. The newspapers all had a crack.

'Dynamic Wallaby centre Tim Horan is destined to face a flood of rugby league offers in the wake of his superb display in Australia's third Test triumph against the All Blacks,' wrote Peter Jenkins in the Sydney *Telegraph*.

'Twenty year-old Toowoomba schoolboy Tim Horan who figured in the Wallabies' historic win is tipped to sign with the Brisbane Broncos next year,' Paul Malone speculated on the front page of *The Courier-Mail* on the Monday morning after the victory.

'Australia's exit from the Rugby World Cup next year will signal a rush by the Winfield Cup (rugby league) clubs to snare Tim Horan, the Wallaby dasher. More than any other Wallaby, the 20-year-old Queenslander carries a 'can't miss' tag as far as the professional game is concerned', Terry Smith claimed in the *Daily Mirror*.

Even at that early stage, it appeared not a matter of if Horan would switch to rugby league, but when. There was just one problem. Horan knew nothing about it.

'It was pure speculation,' he says. 'When I came back from New Zealand, I'd had two phone calls from coaches, but I still hadn't received one single offer. In fact the only rugby league official I had spoken to in the previous six months was (former Wallaby coach) Alan Jones. I can't imagine where the Broncos rumour started. Admittedly, I'd met with them once but it was more than two years prior. Besides, it was nothing more than a casual conversation with (coach) Wayne Bennett and (director) Paul Morgan over a cup of coffee at Paddington. They were just sounding me out, to ask me what my long term plans were. There was no offer—no pressure—just an invitation to give Wayne Bennett a call if I was ever thinking of switching. All of a sudden, I'm tipped to be playing for them. I guess it was flattering to be considered good enough to play in a competition like the Winfield Cup, but at the same time I found it a bit frustrating. Sometimes when you read the papers, you wondered whether rugby existed at all.'

The brazen approach from Jones came early in the 1990 season. Horan can't remember exactly when—he suspects March or early April. He recalls coming home from club training, and being stunned when his flatmate Shane Kelly told him Alan Jones had phoned, and wanted him to return the call urgently.

Horan had never spoken to Jones before, and had seen him just once in the flesh—in 1987—when he'd come down to the Australian schoolboys training at T.G. Millner Field. He had two lasting impressions. First, what a good talker the Grand Slam coach was, and secondly, what expensive shoes he wore. He remembers whispering to Jason at the time: 'Check out those shoes.' 'Yeah I know—the crocodile numbers.' The pair were only half listening to Jones' words of wisdom while they debated how much the shoes would have cost.

Casting aside footwear bias, the next morning Horan did call Sydney. The conversation began with a brief interrogation. Who answered the phone? Who was Shane Kelly? Was he OK? Did he have anything to do with rugby? Could he be trusted? *Yes, No, Yes, of course.* Satisfied that confidentiality would be observed, Jones told Horan he was coming to Brisbane on a speaking engagement, and would like to meet him for breakfast. *Fine.* While Jones didn't exactly specify what the meeting was about, Horan knew the radio talk show host wasn't coming to Brisbane to ask for his long range Melbourne Cup tips. Jones had not long taken over the reins of the Balmain Rugby League club. It could only be about one thing.

Horan recalls being very nervous as he parked his car in a city car park and made his way across to the Heritage Hotel. The man had an aura about him—Tim had never heard of the Australian rugby team until Jones took over the reins in 1984 and was therefore well aware of how he'd changed the face of the game. But from what several of his Wallaby teammates had told him, Jones was quite difficult to talk to. They said there were times when you just couldn't get a word in. The chat would be interesting, if nothing else. He arrived as scheduled at 7am, and was sent straight to Jones' suite, in the upper floors of Brisbane's most prestige hotel.

Jones greeted Tim warmly. Despite the early hour, he was immaculately dressed and looking as if he'd already done half a day's work. Tim couldn't help peeking down at the floor, just to check out his shoes. Nothing fancy. Moments after they'd sat down, there was a knock on the door. 'Mr Jones. Here's your breakfast. Mr Horan would you like an orange juice?' *Yikes, he knew my name.* Tim wondered whether he'd been recognised, or whether Jones had briefed the staff. Either way it concerned him. He feared news of the tryst would be all over town and in the headlines. WALLABY HORAN HOPS INTO TIGER DEN.

After very little chit-chat, Jones began. The time was right to play rugby league, rugby union wouldn't take him where he was capable of going, the national team was being very badly coached, the game was being run by a group of people who didn't have the interests of the players at heart. He went on and on . . . rarely pausing to hear what Horan had to say. The 20-year-old found it very disconcerting.

'I can understand he was there to convince me to play rugby league, but I was very disappointed in the way he was bagging rugby union. It gave me the impression he'd forgotten just how much profile and notoriety he'd got out of the game himself—it was rugby union which really put him on the map. I'd always seen him as an achiever, this great Australian, but here he was downgrading the national team and Bob—although he never used his name. I was obviously proud of what we'd achieved over the past couple of years so I found it hard to swallow.'

Finally having run out of trump cards to toss on the table, Jones offered to make Horan up a T-shirt with the figures '$150,000–$200,000' emblazoned on the front. Underneath he would print the words 'THAT'S HOW MUCH I AM COSTING MYSELF EVERY YEAR I PLAY RUGBY UNION'. A clever ruse, but Horan had heard it all before.

Not until Tim was halfway out the door did he feel as if he'd presented his case at all. Talking as fast as he could, he explained that he was pretty happy with union at the moment, the direction the game was heading, the number of things he still wanted to achieve . . . *yes, yes* . . . Jones accepted all that . . . 'but have a think about what I've said, have a chat with your father, and I'll give you a ring back in a week.'

Exactly seven days later, Jones did ring. Horan politely delivered the verdict the Balmain coach had already anticipated. 'I knew from the way you were talking, that your mind was already made up. Naturally I'm disappointed but I wish you well.' With that Jones hung up. He has not spoken to him since.

Horan remembers thinking at the time he was glad Bob Dwyer was coach of the Australian team, and not Alan Jones.

For the man they left behind, it had been a long and frustrating six weeks. Jason had watched the first Test from a beach bar on Fraser Island, a fisherman's haven some 200km north of Brisbane. Just Jason, his father, and two other grubby-looking types—their hands still ripe with the pungent odour of pilchards—clustered around a small television set high on the cliff at Indian Head. It was about as far removed as he could have been—both geographically and mentally—from Lancaster Park in Christchurch.

The Wallaby management had flown him over to Auckland for the second Test, but as hard as the other players tried to make him feel part of it, Little felt like a spare tyre—and a flat one at that. It's a feeling all injured Test players experience. They want to be part of the action, or well away.

The six weeks hadn't, however, been a total waste of time. While Tim and all the other Wallabies were negotiating the might of the All Blacks in Wellington, Jason was doing a little negotiating of his own—with the North Sydney Bears.

The phone call had come from Steve Martin, the North Sydney coach, even before the Australians had said 'au revoir' to the French. It was tentatively agreed Little would meet with them after the Wallabies returned from New Zealand but when Jason was ruled out of the trip through injury, the negotiations were brought forward.

Little had no genuine intention of switching codes at that stage, but like Horan was naturally curious as to what value would be placed on his head. There was one problem. Who was going to protect him from the predatory rugby league club negotiators? Though Jason was still only 19, he knew how intimidating talks with a league club could be, having partaken of one such meeting in August, 1988.

At the time he was just 17, going on 15, straight out of school, with no more than 10 first grade games for Souths under his belt. As hard as he had tried to erase the memory, he simply could not. The approach came from the Gold Coast Giants, the club which became the Seagulls in 1990. Little was to meet Gold Coast coach Bob McCarthy and a couple of other club officials for lunch at Brisbane's Crest Hotel. He was working in the mail room at Morgan's stock-broking firm at the time, and only had an hour off for lunch. He'd sprinted from one side of the CBD to the other, arriving for his secret luncheon appointment in a lather of sweat.

By the time entree was served, Little was glad he only had an hour. 'I felt like I was under siege. These guys were telling me I was wasting my time playing rugby, come and play rugby league, you'll be an absolute sensation, you'll earn heaps of money. They wouldn't let up. When I told them I was hoping to be picked in the Queensland team tour to Argentina in March, one of the guys said (Little unfastens two buttons on his shirt for extra effect): "Maaaaaate—if you play rugby league, you can buy as many trips to Argentina as you like". It was absolute drivel. I'd never been exposed to the hard sell of a rugby league club before, but that one hour session made me really wary of league club officials.'

The Giants' meeting had ended on a bizarre note, with the same henchman handing Little a napkin: 'Maaaate, this is the deal,' he snarled. 'Take it or leave it.' Jason unfolded the napkin to see the figure $30,000 written in blue pen. 'I couldn't help thinking on the way back to the office how the napkin would stand up in court if there was a breach of contract. I even thought about wiping a bit of gravy on it, to try to make the 30 look like 80.'

Whatever else the experience had taught him, he knew one thing for certain: he didn't ever want to go into a negotiation battle alone. The worldliness he had acquired in the past 18 months might have been sufficient for him to tip-toe unscathed through the minefields of Argentina and France, but Jason still knew he would not last 15 minutes under siege from hostile league scouts, loaded with ammunition. There were two things in life he hated: one was saying 'no', and the other was asking for money, particularly in relation to his own services. Hardly a position of strength in negotiations with any rugby league club, let alone a professional, hard-nosed organisation like North Sydney. He knew in the interests of self-preservation he had to seek assistance. He enlisted the services of John Brass, a highly-decorated dual international who had marched down the same track when he switched to the professional code in 1969.

Little didn't quite appreciate it at the time, but the invitation he'd extended to Brass to escort him to Sydney had placed Brass in an invidious position, given that he was the assistant coach of the Queensland team. How a rugby league scouting mission would be viewed by senior Queensland rugby officials, should they ever find out, he shuddered to think. But Brass knew from his own experiences how the league clubs operated—waving fists full of money before the eyes of impressionable young footballers. His gut instinct told him his first loyalty was to Little. Besides, he was not there to sway him one way or the other, he was there to protect him—and decipher fact from fiction.

On the flight to Sydney, the battle plan was drawn. Brass would do all the talking, Little the listening. If Little got stuck for an answer, look to Brass, and Brass would answer. No problems.

The pair sat down with Martin, and North Sydney Chairman David Hill in the loungeroom of Hill's exclusive home in central Randwick. As a loosener, Martin asked Jason how his injured ankle was progressing. Without so much as uttering a syllable, Little looked straight at his senior commander.

'At that moment, I was very glad I was at the meeting,' Brass recalls. 'Jason even wanted me to tell them how his injured ankle was coming along!' The convivial discussions lasted close to two hours, with Brass, as planned, doing most of the asking and answering, Little the listening.

'I was definitely very lucky Brassy was there,' Jason says. 'Goodness knows what would have happened if he wasn't. I might well have been talked into doing something that I later regretted.'

The exact financial details of Norths' offer went whizzing by Little in the meeting. Not until the pair were sitting down in the departure lounge at Mascot Airport did Brass relay the figure of $100,000 minimum for a season. It was a lot of money—an impressive amount in fact—but upon reflection, Little was never tempted to accept the offer. Besides, France, 1989—*Je te jure sur la tete de ma mere*—he had sworn on the head of his mother (well actually Tim's mother) that he wouldn't go to league until after the World Cup.

With rugby league commanding the spotlight it does in the media, such negotiations are always hard to keep quiet, even under the most clandestine of circumstances. But the secrecy of this particular rendezvous lasted only 45 minutes, until Brass and Little boarded the plane for Brisbane. Sitting two seats up in business class was the unmistakable form of Arthur Beetson, Brass' old teammate at Easts. Beetson, a rugby league commentator with the ABC at the time, was flying back from commentary duties in Sydney that afternoon, and was quick to put two and two together when he saw Brass sitting at the front of the plane with one of rugby union's hottest properties. After getting off the plane, the trio took a taxi to Artie's Queen's Arms Hotel in inner-city New Farm, where Brass and Little plied the big fellow with beers, attempting to make him forget he had seen them together on a plane out of Sydney.

Five hours later, Beetson could still remember the duo's seat numbers on the plane. Brass and Little could hardly remember their names.

In the first exhibition of his remarkable recuperative powers, Little's fractured ankle healed in time for him to take his place alongside Tim in the Brisbane club final series. A month later, with the national selectors believing the extra rugby would benefit him, Little was included in the inaugural Emerging Wallabies tour—an eight match excursion to Europe designed to expose the second tier of Australia's rugby talent to the rigours of international competition. It loomed as the ultimate rugby junket, with exotic destinations like Spain, Holland, and Italy, blended with the more searching on-field tests of England and France. But as the trip unfolded, Little, and indeed most of the other players, felt they were caught up in a B-grade movie, the cast of a low budget production being slapped together by a penny-pinching director. The players endured 32 hour train trips from Barcelona to Rome, 14 hour travel days covering no more than 480 kilometres, and hotels unfit for boy scout conventions.

If there was an up side, the trip did bond the players, as well as make Little fully appreciate the red carpet treatment he received anytime he was in camp with the Wallabies. On the down side, despite the fact he'd already played six Tests—more than any other player on the trip—he was still the youngest in the tour party. Consequently, he was once again lumbered with carrying the fluffy toy—the 'Emerging Shithead'—throughout the team's torturous travel itinerary . . . onto buses, off buses, onto trains, off trains. Over to a different platform. Onto more trains . . .

How he wished another new boy would arrive on the scene. Just as long as it wasn't another outside centre.

Little stayed on in England after the tour, to meet up with the remainder of the Queensland squad who were flying across to France to play in a world provincial championship in Toulouse. The tournament was significant for two reasons. One it heralded the real emergence of a gangly young second-rower by the name of John Eales. Remarkably agile and athletic for somebody more than two metres tall, Eales had played schoolboy cricket against Tim and Jason in Cairns as a 12-year-old. He had featured sporadically in the Queensland side during the 1990 domestic season, but had been the undisputed star of the 'B-grade movie' in Europe. Of all the Emerging Wallabies, Eales had emerged further and faster than anybody. When his 50 metre field goal attempt shaved the post in the dying moments of the Emerging Wallabies match against England B a couple of weeks earlier, Little knew he was mixed up with a pretty special talent. (Wallaby lock Rod McCall was to find out a little later . . . the week before the World Cup final, in fact, when he bet his second-row partner he couldn't walk from the tryline to halfway on his hands. Eales travelled 70m before flipping back on to his feet to collect a well-earned 10 pounds.)

The second significance of the French tournament was far less encouraging. In the semi-final against Fiji, Horan had suffered a re-occurrence of the left knee injury he first damaged against the French. While not as serious as the first, wire photographs of Horan being carried from the field sounded the alarm bells ringing when they appeared in newspapers back home the following day.

He had ample time to get the joint right before rugby resumed in 1991, but the mere fact that Horan had suffered two medial ligament tears on the same knee, six months before his 21st birthday, could only be a source of concern.

The Queensland players had walked away from the tournament empty handed after losing the final to hosts Toulouse, but the mood on the plane home was buoyant. It was December 23. The team would be back in Brisbane on Christmas morning—but no need to wait until then to kick off the festive season. The usual game of musical chairs was in full swing as the players broke up the boredom of a 40 hour journey with card games, board games, trivia quizzes and small private parties.

With dinner about to be served for the third or fourth time, Queensland manager John Brass returned to his original seat, next to an attractive New Zealand girl whom he'd already established had been living in England, and was on her way back to Auckland for Christmas. As Brass was unwrapping his knife and fork, the blonde-haired Kiwi lass spoke, a slight tremor in her voice: 'John, is it alright if I give Tim some of these presents.'

'What do you mean . . . what presents?'

'These presents,' she said pointing to the inviting bundle at her feet. 'I bought them for my friends at home, but it's just so sad about Tim and his brother.'

The picture was starting to crystallise. Brass knew exactly how fanciful the Horan fabrications could be. He had to find out more.

'I wasn't aware of it. Tim and which brother?' he asked the girl, who by this stage was swirling the red wine around in the bottom of her glass, trying to choke back tears.

'Tim and his brother, Matt,' she muttered. 'I asked Tim what he was doing for Christmas, and he said: "Oh nothing much, just swapping a couple of small presents". He and his brother never do much at Christmas any more, since their mum and dad were killed in that car accident on Christmas eve a few years ago. It's so sad, isn't it . . .'

'HORAN GET OVER HERE! You tell this lovely girl the TRUTH!'

Horan Personality No. 2 was alive and well, and living on Qantas Flight 463.

It was in a lecture theatre on the Queensland University campus in Brisbane in mid-January that the Wallabies' 1991 World Cup campaign began in earnest.

A hot steamy summer's morning, the Cup final at Twickenham some 20,000 kilometres and 280 days away, but the Wallabies were underway.

Bob Dwyer stood on the podium, in front of the 45 players, and a small army of support staff, and set out in no uncertain terms what was required between then and November.

'For the next 10 months rugby has got to take priority, ahead of careers, jobs, families, relationships, everything. If you're not prepared to make that commitment, to make rugby the absolute No 1 priority, you might as well leave the room now.'

Jason felt like putting up his hand, like an eager schoolboy who had finished his week's homework two days in advance. *Sir, Sir, I've already done that.* He did have that aspect well under control, but more by accident than design. With no obvious career path, only part-time study commitments, and no family or children relying upon him, Little was very well positioned to adhere to the national coach's demands. There were others less inclined. How, for instance, did Dr Bill Campbell tell his employers at the Royal Brisbane Hospital, his wife and his four children he would be devoting every second of his time to rugby until after November 2? He couldn't. Rugby, vintage 1991, he realised, was sadly beyond his 6ft 9in (205 cm) reach. Besides, with his paucity of faith in Dwyer, he feared he may—sub-consciously or otherwise—prove a disruptive influence on the team, and that was not going to help Australia win the World Cup. After two more pre-season training sessions, Campbell hooked the big size 15s over a peg in the Ballymore dressing shed, and wrote a letter to ARU President Joe French, regretfully announcing he had retired from all rugby—and the reasons why.

While total commitment was undoubtedly what was required if Australia were to win the Cup, there were some other senior players who thought Dwyer was putting the horse before the cart, or at least attacking the issue on the wrong philosophical front. Rather than exclude wives, families, girlfriends and employers from the year, they believed it would have been more productive for the players to *involve* all the people around them—ask them to get behind the team, and make them feel part of a worthwhile 10 month project.

Regardless, they respected Dwyer's singlemindedness. However erratic he might have been on occasions, the man clearly had a vision, and master plan to make it happen. The World Cup final, Dwyer reasoned, was not going to be won over 90 minutes at Twickenham on November 2, nor by playing well in the quarter and semi-finals. It was going to be won by the team which arrived at the tournament with the most meticulously prepared squad, the country which had left nothing to chance.

In a mechanical sense, Dwyer was building the ultimate piece of rugby machinery, assembling a flawless engine bit by bit over the two seasons leading up to the World Cup. When one bit didn't work to his satisfaction, he would take it out and try something else. If that still didn't work, he might go back to the original part, and modify it slightly. Still no improvement, a new part altogether. The experimental process had started way back in 1989, when Dwyer introduced three brand new parts—Daly, Kearns and Horan—for the one-off Bledisloe Cup Test against New Zealand. All three worked like a charm—Daly and Kearns up in the powerhouse, Horan as part of the steering mechanism at the back. All three were there to stay.

By the time the Wallabies had returned from New Zealand, the nucleus of a great side was already in place. In scrumhalf Farr-Jones, and flyhalf Michael Lynagh, the Wallabies had a halves combination without peer in world rugby. There were the mercurial talents of winger David Campese, the strength, drive and ball skills of No 8 Tim Gavin, the ball-winning capacities of lock Rod McCall, and the explosive powers of Willie Ofahengaue, a monstrous Tongan who'd burst onto the Test scene in Christchurch six months earlier.

All the major engine parts were already in place, there were just the vital cogs to find and install, then the fine tuning process would start.

To assist him in his search, Dwyer had a veritable army of helpers, monitoring, testing and evaluating the performances of all 45 players in the World Cup squad. Each player had their own evaluation panel member—mostly former Test players—who would sit up in the grandstand and scribble down every imaginable statistic . . . how many tackles a player made, how many he missed, how many times he stepped off his right leg, how many off his left, the number of times he entered a ruck, composure under pressure . . . there was not a minuscule detail which went unnoticed.

There was a supporting team of specialists—strength trainers, physios, psychologists, even a dietitian—whose task it was to collectively squeeze that extra one percent of performance from the players. For the more senior members in the squad, the 'old school', technical terms like lactic acid, rehydration, muscle fatigue, and arousal level sounded foreign at first. They toed the party line, initially under sufferance, but before too long even the major sceptics were starting to come around. They did recover more quickly when they drank water immediately after the game, they could train for longer if they ate properly the night before—a few small adjustments made a significant difference.

Well before the 1991 season began in earnest, Dwyer was preaching to the converted.

## TEN RUNGS—WE'VE GOT TEN RUNGS OF THE LADDER TO CLIMB THIS SEASON—ON SUNDAY WE'RE GOING TO CLIMB THE FIRST.

It was July 18, three days before the Wallabies met Wales at Ballymore in the first Test of the 1991 season. Dwyer was in the first floor team room of Brisbane's Parkroyal Hotel revving up his engine. This is it, he said. This is where it all begins. Dwyer was instructing the players to look at the Welsh match as the first small step in the direction of World Cup glory. They'd take it step by step, one at a time. Building and climbing all the time, up the ladder towards that ultimate pot of rugby gold. Each step was just as important as the next.

The Wallaby team, featuring a few new trial parts in John Eales, New South Wales fullback Marty Roebuck and unlikely looking winger Rob Egerton, just couldn't wait to get started. But there was nobody more eager than Horan.

Having spent the off-season working tirelessly on strengthening his left knee, Horan was jumping out of his skin to road test his sprouting confidence amid his Wallaby peers. Whatever face he might have worn publicly, when he first came into the team in 1989 he felt very much intimidated by the senior players. Farr-Jones, Lynagh and Campese in particular had an aura about them. They had, after all, been playing for the Wallabies at a time he was still captaining the Downlands 14As. Farr-Jones and Lynagh were always very supportive, but Campese was a little prone to giving the new boys a hard time. He and Jason used to dread when Lynagh called a backline move involving Campese. If a pass was a little high, a little low, or even a little behind him—like the first one Jason delivered in his Test career—Campese would bark out a few sharp instructions as to what he expected.

Neither Tim nor Jason ever questioned his right to do so—Campese was the world try-scoring record holder. He did have a few clues about playing the game. But at the same time, the beratings hardly engendered confidence or under-standing—two crucial components of backline play. Horan resolved to grind out a bit of respect. As No 8 Tim Gavin says: 'It's one thing to earn the admiration of the national selectors, it's another thing altogether to earn the admiration of your teammates.' So the young midfielder, for his first five or six Tests, adopted a stock standard policy—do the simple things well, don't make mistakes, play your part to perfection and the rest will look after itself.

Finally against New Zealand in Auckland in 1990, the real Timothy James Horan stood up to be counted. From a maul on halfway, he loomed up outside Gavin, took the pass and accelerated. With the defence closing in, he chipped ahead, threaded his way through a wall of All Blacks, and beat a further three defenders to the line. *Down around the lemon tree, chip over the clothes line, dodge the chooks and dive over beside the outdoor dunny.* Much the same as it was at Kandanga. Just 15 years on.

It was a display of individual skill which not only stunned and delighted Australian rugby supporters, but also grabbed the attention of the rugby league talent scouts. With his 30m, five second exhibition of speed, strength and vision, Horan had effectively added another '0' to his price tag, should he ever want to put his services on the market.

From that point on, there was no looking back. Horan the conservative, rock solid centre, became Horan the adventur-ous, lethal attacking weapon, willing to back his judgement and skill whenever the occasion arose. Little, sidelined with ankle trouble at the time, remembers sitting in the grandstand at Eden Park and watching the transformation unfold. 'It was strange, but up until that time, nobody had really seen the full array of Tim's talents at the top level. I guess only the people who'd watched him create havoc at schoolboy and Colts level really knew what an instinctive player he was. After he scored that try in Auckland, I thought to myself: "Hello. Here we go." He'd been like a bomb, just waiting to go off. Finally it happened.' Horan doesn't know if it was that immediate, but certainly remembers being buoyed by the try in Auckland. 'I suppose for the first few Tests, all you are aiming to do is secure your place in the team. In the back of your mind, there's a concern that if you try something out of the ordinary and it backfires, you'll pay the price. Obviously by the second Test, I must have felt assured about my place in the team.'

It came a little more gradually, but there was also a change in his on-field relationships with the senior players. Though never a shrinking violet, Horan had always been careful not to say too much on the field, particularly while surrounded by the Holy Trinity—Farr-Jones, Lynagh, and Campese. When Tim arrived on the scene, they already had more than 150 Test caps between them. But in his third season of international rugby, the time was right. He became more willing to make suggestions, to bounce ideas around, and offer solutions to any small tactical problems. The bad passes to Campese had also ceased. In 1991, there was no such thing as wayward service from Horan. If the ball was delivered a little behind Campo, he'd obviously been standing too flat. If he had to stretch for it, he must have been standing too deep. Too low—meant he was too wide. And so on. It made for some lively on-field banter between the two.

Little had ridden the same emotional roller coaster, scaling the peaks of the French series in Australia in 1990, but tumbling down the other side just as quickly when he missed the

Bledisloe Cup series through injury. Looking back, Little realises the broken ankle couldn't have come at a worse time in his career. 'As Tim says, for the first five or six Tests, you're really just looking to consolidate your position. I felt I'd done that, but when I was ruled out of the All Black series, I was back to square one. In 1991, I really felt like I was starting my Test career again.'

There was no better place for him to resume than alongside Tim for the first time in a Test at Ballymore. But that wasn't the sole reason Horan was waiting anxiously for July 21 to arrive.

His earliest recollection of international rugby had been the Wallabies Grand Slam in 1984. From watching the videos, he had three vivid memories implanted in his mind—one of a goose-stepping David Campese making a goose out of some unfortunate fullback, a second of Mark Ella scoring his fourth try in as many Tests, but the most vivid of all was giant hooker Tommy Lawton standing, arms aloft, saluting the reserves bench after the Wallabies' pushover try against Wales at Cardiff Arms Park.

'It was obviously unheard of at the time—the Welsh conceding a pushover try in front of their home crowd. From that moment on, I'd always thought of Wales as an awesome rugby team, a proud rugby playing nation. I was very keen to play them.'

Awesome they might have once been, but at Ballymore, awesome they were not. They were awful, the worst Five Nations team ever to set boots on Ballymore. The Australian engine hummed, as the side ran in 12 tries before the fulltime hooter saved the Welsh—and the crowd—from any further torment.

As happy as Horan was to win, and win so well, he honestly felt cheated. Late in the game, he'd watched Welsh halfback Robert Jones actually step out of the way of a rampaging Willie Ofahengaue, rather than attempting to tackle him.

Certainly it was a zillion to zilch at the time—what difference was one more try going to make? But Horan still found Jones' evasive action deplorable. It sparked memories of a game he'd played in his final year of school—a social match against the Downlands Past Students. At halftime his father, totally out of character, had stepped under the rope, hauled young Timothy out of the team huddle, and delivered a none too polite dressing down: 'If you don't want to play, give your jersey to someone who does, and get off the field. There's a hundred other kids who'd love to be out there.' Horan thought he'd got away with his little charade, but his father could read him like a book. He was dead right. Tim hadn't been trying, he'd just been going through the motions, shovelling the pass across field, not really running hard, not chasing, not tackling. He felt so humiliated he'd been caught out, and vowed never to give anything but 100 per cent anytime he played sport.

'That's probably why I was so disgusted when I saw Jones step out of the way. I'd seen him play for the British Lions in 1989, and he was such a feisty competitor. Two years later, he's playing for his country and not even trying. I suppose he thought one more try wouldn't make any difference, but I'm sure if the boot had been on the other foot, none of the Wallabies would have tossed in the towel like that.'

Having been beaten 63–6, it was doubtful Welsh rugby could sink any lower, but they did—just five hours later at the post-Test dinner in Ballymore's Murrayfield room. The players, having kept their pre-match pledge of not 'going the biff' on the Australians, went the biff on themselves during an ugly scuffle in full view of the Australian players and some 50 other guests.

The dissension, which centred on a rift between the Neath players and more urbane city types from the south, had been simmering for almost half an hour. The travelling Welsh press corps tried to warn team manager Clive Rowlands that tempers down the other end of the room were getting a little frayed, but Rowlands elected to leave them to their own devices. Finally, it erupted, and in the ensuing melee, British Lions centre Mike Hall was cut on the hand with a broken glass.

Little at the time was standing no more than 5m from the centre of the volcano. He wondered how things could have gone so bad. 'The Welsh were like a badly disciplined club team. Even on the field you could sense the disharmony. I suppose getting flogged like that was the straw which broke the camel's back. I almost felt sorry for them. The brawl was huge news back in Wales. My brother Ashley was living in the UK at the time, and he saw a re-enactment of the fight on television. Apparently even one of the church groups in Wales got involved, blaming alcohol for the team's shocking performances in Australia. Everybody bought into it.'

As the Welsh skulked out of the country, their tails between their legs, the attention turned to England, who had been touring Australia simultaneously, albeit with significantly more diplomacy and finesse. With Will Carling's men having marched undefeated through the Five Nations championship three months prior, the one-off Test was a good opportunity for the Wallabies to gauge their relative strength against the best the northern hemisphere had to offer.

If the engine had hummed against the woeful Welsh, it simply purred against the Poms in Sydney. The English Rose had been plucked petal by petal. Had Michael Lynagh's final attempt at penalty goal not rebounded from the right hand upright, England would have been subjected to the heftiest loss of their long proud rugby existence. Dwyer remained outwardly phlegmatic—with so few of the rungs of the ladder climbed he could not afford to be anything more. But much later, in his book 'The Winning Way', the national coach would describe the 40–15 triumph as one half of the best 80 minutes of rugby he had ever seen an Australian team play.

Eales, Roebuck and Egerton, the new parts installed for Wales, had once again performed admirably. More and more parts were in place, less and less tinkering was required. In their last three outings, the Wallabies had amassed 124 points and conceded only one try. Things were running smoothly.

As impressed as skipper Nick Farr-Jones was with the Wallabies' hard-nosed efficiency and clinical execution, what delighted him more was the consistency the team was finally showing. Ever since Farr-Jones had taken over the captaincy reins of the national side in 1988, their performance chart had been littered with peaks and troughs—brilliant one week, awful the next. The British Lions series in 1989—flogged them in the first Test 30–12 and tumbled 19–12 in the next. The tour of France—a stirring victory in Strasbourg, followed a week later by a limp-wristed loss in Lille. Even in New Zealand in 1990—awful in Christchurch, much better in Auckland, positively impregnable in Wellington.

Any good team could win well on their day, but a good team wasn't going to walk away from Twickenham with the William Webb Ellis Trophy. A great team was. By Farr-Jones' definition, greatness was only achieved by a team playing to its potential every time they took the field. That's what the Wallabies were aiming for.

Two Tests against the All Blacks—one at home, the other away—were the final rungs the Wallabies had to climb before boarding the plane for England in October. It would be the most searching road test yet for Dwyer's reconditioned engine. Six new parts had been added to the model which had finally run over the top of the All Blacks in Wellington 12 months earlier. A couple more successful hit and run missions in 1991, and the Wallabies would head off to the UK not just thinking, but knowing they were capable of winning the Cup.

When All Black skipper Gary Whetton and his men arrived in Sydney for the first Test in the second week of August, they did so carrying the most unfamiliar tag of underdogs. Exactly when the All Blacks last wore that label into a Bledisloe Cup Test, it is hard to say, but Little and Horan probably weren't born—Bob Dwyer might not have been either. Underdogs or red hot favourites—it didn't really matter—the Wallabies still had to win. But the new balance of power served as a ready reminder of just how much ground the Australians had made up since the 1987 World Cup, when the All Blacks were far and away the best team in world rugby.

When the Wallabies went into camp at Peppers Resort, their hideaway on the Central Coast at Terrigal, 90km north of Sydney, Little immediately noticed something different. Even four days before the Test, there was a tension, an urgency that he had never experienced before in a pre-Test assembly. 'It was my first Test against the All Blacks—I'd never witnessed it before. You could just feel the extra anxiety that comes with playing against New Zealand. The training drills were sharper, there wasn't quite as much laughing or mucking around. The team was totally focussed on the job ahead.'

Focussed indeed. New Zealand flyhalf Grant Fox remembers August 10 as the one time in his illustrious Test career he feared the All Blacks were going to be ripped apart. 'We knew full well the Aussies were a very good team, but they were absolutely on fire that afternoon. Somehow we managed to stay in touch, but at one stage I really thought we were going to be beaten by 20 points.'

The fulltime score showed Australia as 21–12 winners but the match will best be remembered for the freakish second-half try scored by Wallaby winger Rob Egerton. It was one of those wonderfully paradoxical moments which international sport serves up every now and then. Egerton, socks down around his ankles—looking decidedly like the kid on the front of the Mad Magazine with his marine style haircut—galloped after a kick and snatched the ball out of the grasp of All Black demigod John Kirwan—tall, blond, strong, apparently invincible. Kirwan didn't have time to turn and chase. Egerton was on his way—to the tryline and the World Cup. The tortoise had just beaten the hare. The skinny kid with the concave chest had kicked sand in the face of the bronzed Adonis, and walked off into the sunset with his gorgeous girlfriend. And the sell-out Sydney crowd loved it.

Three weeks later, the Kiwis would exact revenge by beating the Wallabies 6–3 in the slush at Eden Park. It might have been the first small slip on the ladder, but there was little cause for alarm. There were positives to be found everywhere. For a start, the team had played atrociously, Michael Lynagh, in a rare off day, had landed just one of seven penalty goal attempts, and yet the Wallabies had still finished within three points of the reigning world champions. And although nobody interrupted the team happy hour to say so, there were quite a few players who believed that a solitary loss in the lead-up to the Cup was not necessarily a bad thing.

Horan was one who subscribed to the theory: 'I remember back in 1990 when we ended the All Blacks' unbeaten run, going into the New Zealand dressing shed to have a quick drink and a chat with Walter Little. I got the distinct impression the All Blacks were more relieved to have been beaten than we were to have won. The pressure of winning all the time had just built up to an intolerable level for the Kiwi players. I reckon we were heading in the same direction. Losing the Test in Auckland released the pressure valve, and knocked out any complacency which might have been creeping in.'

So, it was one Test-all. If there had been a psychological upper hand gained, it probably belonged to Australia, but only marginally. One thing was certain though. The inferiority complex Australia had for so long carried into trans-Tasman rugby confrontations had been well and truly put to rest.

The post-1990 vintage Wallaby was a positive, self-assured type, almost convinced that Australia were bound for World Cup glory. They had prepared to win. They deserved to win. They could look forward to the UK with the utmost confidence.

It was one of those perfect spring days—cloudless skies, very little wind, the warmth of the sun irrefutable proof that summer was just around the corner. The Souths Magpies were about to take on Brothers in their march to yet another grand final of the Brisbane club competition. In the No 4 dressing shed underneath the Ballymore grandstand, Jason Little was attending to some last minute ablutions. There was a thumping on the cubicle door.

'Let me in.' It was Horan.

'Mate can't you tell I'm busy.'

'No mate, let me in, let me in. I've got something to tell you.'

Reluctantly, Little unbolted the door. Horan squeezed into the tiny space and closed the door. He seemed a little edgy. 'I've got something to tell you.'

'Yeah I know you told me. But couldn't it wait, like two minutes?'

'No. It can't. I'm going to ask Katrina to marry me.'

It sounded all too much like another Timmy Horan nab. Little wasn't having a bar of it: 'Yeah good mate. Now can you leave me in peace?'

'No seriously, I'm going to be a husband. But that's only half of it. I'm also going to be a father.'

Little's jaw dropped. He wanted to ask 100 questions, but there wasn't time—with the flurry of activity in the shed kick-off must have been mere minutes away. Besides, a cubicle at the rear of Dressing Shed No 4 was hardly the perfect place for consequential, life-altering discussions. It would have to wait. Jason took the field for the semi-final, still not knowing whether he was dangling on the end of a line, a giant hook through the side of his mouth.

Horan made a hasty retreat after the game, but promised he'd talk to Jason that night.

Soon after Little arrived home, the phone rang. Tim and Katrina were having a bite to eat at a Malaysian restaurant at Toowong, and would like him to come over. They had something to ask him.

Little put down the phone. If it was still a nab, it was a bloody good one. But he suspected for one rare moment in his life, Tim was telling the truth. He arrived at the restaurant to find Tim and Katrina tucked away in a quiet corner. Tim came straight to the point. 'Trine and I are getting married, and we'd like you to be our best man.'

During the brief drive across town, Jason had convinced himself it was true, but the announcement still came as a shock. Naturally he was delighted, but he couldn't help thinking just how far away he was from marriage, and settling down.

Over the ensuing two hours, all the blank spaces were filled in. Tim and Katrina had been officially engaged for 24 hours, they were getting married after the World Cup, and yes, they were expecting a baby.

Inside the boundaries of tradition, their sense of order might have been a touch astray, but in the modern context, it mattered little. Tim and Katrina had been inseparable for more than four years, since that fateful lunchtime mishap on the Emu steps in Grade 12 at Downlands. They planned to get married sooner or later—the latest developments dictated it would be sooner. While both initially had reservations about telling their parents about the pregnancy, they were heartened by the wholesale support they received.

The couple set a wedding date for December, just three weeks after the World Cup final.

Wouldn't it be fantastic, Tim thought, to have a dual celebration when he returned.

# Chapter 10

## The World Cup

*'I will make a commitment to excellence and to victory, and that is what life is all about.'*
AMERICAN FOOTBALL COACH VINCE LOMBARDI

It was a good thing, for the sake of Australian rugby, there was no television in the room.

Tim Horan and lock Rod McCall were holed up together in their tiny bedroom in the western wing of the Lensbury Club, a sprawling 100-hectare estate on the banks of the Thames in Middlesex.

The palatial establishment was the property of the Shell Oil company, which would take their employees out there on weekends for conferences and seminars. Well away from the bright lights and distractions of London, the club served as the perfect hideaway for the Wallabies to add the finishing touches to their World Cup preparation.

It had practically everything—accommodation for 120, rugby fields, cricket fields, hockey fields, tennis courts, a swimming pool and a gymnasium. Practically everything, bar television sets in the rooms.

Which is why Horan and McCall were lying on their beds—chatting. The conversation was meandering along about nothing in particular—who was in form, who was the team to beat, who had the best draw, did you see what happened at training . . .

Suddenly, Horan lifted his head off the pillow, propped himself up on his left elbow, and turned to his roommate.

'You know, I've been thinking . . .'

Two-metre-tall McCall, feet dangling over the end of the bed as usual, remembers looking across, almost startled by the sudden serious tone.

His young sidekick continued, slowly: 'I reckon . . . if you follow Campo whenever he's got the ball, just follow him as closely as you can, I reckon you're only one pass away from a try.'

McCall was quite taken back. The team room was normally the place for this type of exchange—it didn't seem right listening to such strategic dialogue unaccompanied by the sight of Bob Dwyer standing next to a whiteboard, marker pen in hand, frantically scribbling lines.

But Horan wasn't finished. 'I mean, Campo invariably finds space, doesn't he?' McCall nodded, like he thought he should. 'If he's in open space, and you're right there in support, there's probably a very good chance you'll outnumber the defence.'

McCall didn't quite know why Horan was telling *him* this—the only time he and Campo travelled at the same speed was when they were on an aeroplane together. But the big lock was impressed by the depth of thought and analytical approach of his 21-year-old teammate. Apart from anything else, Horan's theory made a lot of sense. In the duration of a game—*any game*—Campese was almost certain to find holes in the defence. The only problem was knowing which way the unpredictable winger would run when he did. He suspected Campese himself didn't know that. All the same, he gave Horan 10 out of 10 for effort.

Some 10 minutes later, the lights were out. The pair drifted off to sleep.

Ffffooomppp!

Right in the breadbasket, and over!

The 50,000 people at Dublin's Lansdowne Road would probably have cheered earlier, had they actually *seen* what had happened. But most hadn't. It had all happened too quickly.

David Campese, the Wizard of Oz, had just produced another piece of magic—the one which probably sent the New Zealand All Blacks disappearing from the 1991 World Cup.

It came in the 34th minute of the Cup semi-final after 33 of the most perfect minutes an Australian rugby team had ever played.

Flyhalf Michael Lynagh was the magician's assistant, punching a perfectly weighted grubber kick down the right hand side of the field, deep into Australia's attacking zone. Had he been faster across the ground, New Zealand fullback Kieran Crowley might have pounced heroically on the ball, and hoofed it downfield. But he wasn't. He was a little ponderous, a little tentative, the legacy of not having played for more than a month. The ball bounced once, then twice . . . suddenly Campese had it.

He went left, he went right, he went left again. So did the defence—except in the wrong order. They had no idea where he was going—Campese might not have either. Horan took a wild guess. He hooked to the outside, and trailed the Australian winger down the touchline, staying as close as he could without running the risk of tripping him. When Campese veered left, so did Horan. When he went right, Horan followed.

Just as Campese was running out of space, he veered left one last time, straight into the path of three New Zealand defenders. With scant regard for convention, while looking in the opposite direction, he hurled the ball over his right shoulder.

Horan was right where he'd told Rod McCall he would be—in Campo's jetstream. He calmly caught the ball, evaded the despairing dive of Kiwi winger John Timu and slid over for the try—right in front of the billboard he'd singled out to Anthony Herbert prior to the game. *There Herb, I'm going to score there, right in front of the Steinlager sign . . .*

There might have been one or two more spectacular tries scored in Australian rugby history, but not many. And certainly none as timely. Approaching the break the Wallabies had bounded to a 13–0 lead. For once in their collective lives, the Kiwis looked dejected. After Campese's magic act, there was panic on the faces of some, bewilderment on the faces of others.

Fullback Crowley, now retired from rugby and living in Takapuna, on New Zealand's North Island, was still picking himself off the ground 25m away, when he saw Campese's Midas touch bring a golden result. He recalls muttering under his breath something to the effect of: 'They've got to be kidding.'

'Maybe there was another word in there as well!' he says. 'I can't remember. Campese was just having one of those days. Everything he tried came off perfectly.'

Everything indeed. Some 20 minutes earlier, Campese had bamboozled four All Black players—on the other side of the field—but to equally devastating effect. In a ruck 20m out from New Zealand's line, Lynagh was trapped—a small pair of socks buried under a pile of dirty washing—so Campese, ever in search of opportunity, stepped into flyhalf.

As he took the pass from Farr-Jones, the maverick winger did what junior players from the age of six are told not to do, what coaching manuals say not to do, what Bob Dwyer says NEVER EVER DO IF YOU WANT TO BE PART OF THIS AUSTRALIAN TEAM . . . .

He ran across field.

Not just across field, but at 45 degrees across field, back around Richard Loe, past Sean Fitzpatrick, away from Grant Fox, leaving just one brick in the wall—winger John Kirwan. Afraid to take his eye off Campese, Kirwan started running backwards—four, five, six steps before speed made it unfeasible. He swivelled desperately around to his right, but as he did, Campese jinked left and flattened the accelerator, gliding in behind him to dive over in the corner. If he'd been a surfer, Campese would just have ridden the perfect tube, popping out the end a split second before the wave crashed on top of him. The man's sense of timing was impeccable.

That Australia led by just 13 points at halftime was strong testimony to New Zealand's character and courage. A lesser team would have drowned in the tide of gold jerseys which kept coming. And coming.

The All Blacks had time to retrieve the situation, but it was almost as if they didn't know where to start. The circumstances were totally foreign to them. When was the last time a New Zealand side had trailed 13–0 in a Test match? And in a World Cup semi-final. It seemed as if the All Black players were not equipped mentally to handle the turnaround.

As John Mason of the London *Daily Telegraph* observed in his match report the following day: 'It was uncanny to see the men in black panic. So rattled were they, it was hard to believe that here was the nucleus of the squad who have ruled the world for the better part of four years.'

As Kiwi scrumhalf Graham Bachop knocked on at the base of a maul, Scottish referee Jim Fleming looked at his watch and blew fulltime. 16–6 Australia.

The Wallaby players gleefully embraced. The All Blacks hung their heads. The reigning champions were out of the Cup—off to Cardiff to play in the consolation final—the 'who cares' fixture against Scotland, the other losing semi-finalists.

The Wallabies were off to Twickenham for the World Cup final. London had never sounded so inviting.

It was the penultimate chapter in the Wallabies' grand crusade, a crusade which had begun in earnest 29 days before, when the team had begun training in the fog and light misty rain of Middlesex, north-west of London.

Somehow, it seemed a lot longer than four weeks ago, but that was hardly surprising. The World Cup was hardly a regular tour, where leisure days and sightseeing are spliced in to break up the monotony of daily training. Under World Cup tournament conditions, Australia, like all of the tournament big guns, could expect to play four Test matches in 16 days—more if they advanced past the quarter-finals. Clearly, the focus needed to be sharply on rugby. The players trained, they ate, they slept, they waited.

On October 4, the moment arrived. On a surprisingly mild autumn afternoon, the Australians kicked off their campaign against Argentina at Stradey Park in Llanelli, Wales. Nick Farr-Jones stressed to his players before the match to retain their composure, to relax. Two days before, the Wallabies had huddled around a television set in their Swansea hotel, and watched England succumb to stage fright in their 18–12 loss to New Zealand. There was a lesson to be learned, the Australian skipper stressed—no matter what happens, let's just stay calm, and work our way into the match.

The policy could not have been more appropriate. Midway through the second half, the Argentine Pumas had clawed back to within four points, trailing 20–16. Composure was paramount. It arrived on cue. The Wallabies posted a further 12 points in the closing stages to win by the comfortable, though not entirely convincing margin of 32–19. The first rung on the World Cup ladder had been safely negotiated.

Horan helped himself to two tries at Llanelli, the second five minutes from fulltime, an early dividend from his policy of following Campese. Horan never suggested he was re-inventing the wheel by trailing the fleet-footed flyer. Michael Lynagh, he suspected, had probably been doing the same thing for years. But Bob Dwyer always spoke about getting that extra percent out of your performance: 'Striving for that smallest improvement which may mean the difference between winning and losing'. This was Horan's extra percent. While training at the Lensbury Club in the lead-up to the tournament, he had begun watching Campese—the angles he ran, the number of paces he took before stepping off his right leg, off his left. Which leg did he step off first, what lines did he run in this move, and that move. It might not amount to anything, he thought. But he would give it a try. In the 75th minute of the Cup, when he slid over beside the right hand upright for his second try, Horan allowed himself a wry smile as he fielded congratulations from his teammates. The extra one percent. It had already been worthwhile.

Rain. Misty rain, driving rain, torrential rain. At Pontypool Park, one also sensed it was equalising, underdog rain. If one team was going to benefit from the appalling conditions, it definitely wasn't the Wallabies. It would be their opponents, Western Samoa.

The second pool match, five days after the first, was one the Australians had been nervously awaiting since the Samoans' surprise 16–7 defeat of Wales at Cardiff Arms Park on October 6. The two countries had never before met in an international, but the presence of so many quality New Zealand-based players in the Samoan side guaranteed a close tussle.

Too close for comfort. Approaching fulltime, the Wallabies, having lost skipper Nick Farr-Jones with a knee injury early in the game, clung to a 6–3 lead. Not a single try to appease the 12,000 hardy souls who had braved the elements to watch.

There was nothing in it. The tackling throughout had been much like the kicking—high and often—with both sides defending on the cusp of legality. Only when Michael Lynagh steered over his third penalty goal with just minutes remaining was Australia's victory secure. The Wallabies had climbed another rung, albeit their wobbliest step since the narrow loss to the All Blacks in Auckland.

So back to Cardiff to prepare for the third and final pool game against their Welsh hosts at the Arms Park.

Following their team's 63–6 annihilation at Brisbane, the Welsh public were demanding revenge. They sought great solace in the fact that only four of the 15 who bowed at Ballymore remained in the team for the return match. On the darker side, Australia had 13 from the Brisbane bashing, with Farr-Jones and No 8 Tim Gavin—tragically injured in club rugby prior to the Cup—the only two absentees.

The new Welsh coach Alan Davies tried desperately to talk his players up. In the *Western Mail* on the morning of the game, the normally quiet reserved Davies was quoted as saying: 'There's no question of them (the Welsh players) losing—they're really fired up. We've done all the hard work. The players deserve to win.'

The gung-ho hyperbole seemed to be stretching Davies' credibility beyond breaking point, but at halftime, he wasn't far from the mark. Despite Australia's dominant first half, the Welsh were just 10–3 in arrears, the crowd of 65,000 willing a second-half revival.

As the teams wandered off to their respective huddles, Welsh flyhalf Mark Ring, taking a leaf out of his coach's book of self-belief, brushed past Little. 'We've got the wind, you're in trouble,' Ring muttered in a schoolboy tone.

Little at the time just smiled. 'What did he expect me to do? Go back into the dressing shed and not come out for the second half?'

Wind or no wind, the Australians moved up a gear in the second half, running in six superb tries to complete a stunning 38–3 victory. For the first time in the tournament the Dwyer engine had really hummed. And for the first time in the tournament Little believed Australia were capable of winning the World Cup. 'We were a little slow to get started against Wales, probably because most of us spent the first half thinking about Princess Di! (The Princess was introduced to the team just prior to kick-off.) She was more beautiful than anyone ever imagined. But in the second half, everything clicked. We played to the level that we'd reached in Australia earlier that year—against Wales, England and the All Blacks. It was an important mental conquest, because up until that time, we'd really struggled. I think we were all wondering if we'd peaked too early.'

Poor Wales, meanwhile, were almost back to where they were at Ballymore. And the local and Fleet Street press were hardly going to let them forget it. 'They were clueless and an embarrassment,' John Edwards wrote in the London *Daily Mail* on October 14. 'Wales weren't a team. More like 14 people off a coach trip to (nearby) Barry Island, called in at the last minute to substitute for the chosen side who'd gone down with food poisoning, and only Robert Jones survived.'

'The Welsh dragon has become a dragonfly—swatted at will by leading rugby nations,' The *Western Mail* reported. 'The only encouraging aspect of the Wales performance was their consistency—they won one lineout in each half.'

The Welsh hopes of survival now rested on the 2000–1 chance of Argentina defeating Western Samoa 3–0. It didn't happen. Wales were out of the Cup, Australia out of the country, and on their way to Ireland to play the quarter-final.

On any Wallaby tour, there is a very strict pecking order to the seating on the team bus.

As a steadfast rule, only senior forwards up the back, starting in the very back seat, with Rod 'Sergeant Slaughter' McCall, the 'bus conductor'. Either side of him, tighthead prop Ewen 'Link' McKenzie, and hooker Phil Kearns. In front of

McKenzie, on the right hand side, loosehead prop Tony Daly. Opposite him, it varies—normally Tim Gavin, but on this particular tour, when 'the Battered Sav' was ruled out with serious knee trouble, Willie O assumed the position. Only two backs were allowed into the inner sanctum. One was Anthony Herbert, Kearns' drinking partner. The hooker insists Herbert is a back trapped in a forward's body. The other was reserve half Peter Slattery, the ultimate rugby tourist, who is respected for having the constitution and imbibing prowess of a forward.

Clustered around the middle of the bus, you'll always find the midfielders—Horan, Little, Lynagh, and fullback Marty Roebuck. A little further forward Farr-Jones, then in the very front seat, immediately behind the driver, winger David Campese.

The seating positions never vary. They're always the same. Except on extremely unusual occasions.

Dublin was to be an extremely unusual occasion.

It was 11.30am. The Wallabies had just landed at Dublin Airport, and were about to start the 30 minute journey into town. Centre Anthony Herbert, before climbing aboard the bus, had slipped a Wallaby lapel pin to each of the two police escorts. 'Don't expect any delays getting into town do we fellas??'

'No SORR! Nought 'tat tall Sorr.'

A roaring of engines, and they were off. Herbert swears one of the motorcyclists hit the magic ton by the time he'd left the airport carpark.

The bus followed at breakneck speed, swerving all over the road, left side, right side, between lanes, up on the median strip, the footpath, overtaking on blind corners, running smaller defenceless vehicles off the road. It was entertainment not to be missed. By the time they'd travelled two kilometres—approximately 30 seconds—the entire team was crammed up the front, jostling for a better view of what they were going to narrowly miss next. If the Australian players were going to die, they at least wanted to see how it happened. The quips were almost as quick as the driver: 'Does this guy realise the game's not until Sunday?' 'Maybe he's got to have the bus back by midday,' came the response.

'It really was extraordinary—the scariest journey of my life,' Little recalls. 'I'd seen some kamikaze drivers in Italy, Spain and Argentina, but this guy took the cake.'

Some 15 minutes and 30 near misses later, the bus reached the top of Grafton St, a pedestrian mall which dissects the heart of Dublin, north to south. It was there the players expected to hear the hiss of the air-brakes for the first time on the journey.

Wrong.

*Oh no. He can't go down there . . .*

Yes he can! Up over the footpath, and down the mall, where no other heavy vehicle had ever ventured before. The late afternoon pedestrian traffic parted, like the Red Sea, a look of bewilderment on every passing face.

As the bus finally pulled up outside the Westbury Hotel, the Australian squad applauded like they had never applauded before. A standing ovation. Herbert was one of the first off. Before climbing down the steps, he slapped the driver on the back.

'Thanks champion, we were running a little late for lunch.'

So this is Dublin.

A bubbling metropolis of 1.5 million, the southern Ireland capital exudes vibrance. The moment people arrive in Dublin, they seem overcome with an eagerness to have a good time. The lively bars, friendly people and warm hospitality simply engender an attitude of fun. (Needless to say, in the much mentioned Rugby players' Bible of Popular Touring Destinations, Ireland would command at least two chapters, one on Dublin alone.)

Of the Australian playing contingent, only six—Farr-Jones, Lynagh, Campese, and forwards Steve Cutler, Cameron Lillicrap and Simon Poidevin—had been to Dublin before and knew what to expect. For the vast majority who hadn't, the love affair was about to begin.

So many stories abound about the Irish, it is difficult to decipher true from apocryphal. But it hardly matters. The ones which aren't true probably should be. The Irish attitude to life is best summed up by the story Grand Slam skipper Andrew Slack tells about his playing days with the Wanderers club in Dublin. Having drunk the clubhouse out of Guinness, the players decided it was time to wander off to an alternative watering hole. The only problem was how to get there. ''ere Slacky, you drive, you're too drunk to sing,' the former Wallaby captain was told. 'One way or another,' Slack says, 'you finish up with a headache—either from laughing or trying to work out the meaning of what's being said.'

In the first couple of days in Dublin, the Australian players would experience for themselves that quirky Irish approach to life. They would see the signs in shop windows: Haircuts while you wait. And in hotel foyers—Coffee Shop: Open 23 hours a day. Even the odd billboard by the side of the road—Keane, Mahoney and Smith. Flats to let. Previous turn right.

Little recalls heading out with Lynagh to meet Jack Ryan—the famed rugby players' host—and a couple of others for a quiet drink. They climbed into the back of a taxi: 'Ryan's Bar please.' The driver nodded: 'Certainly Sorr, but it might take us a while. Dere's 26 Ryan's Bars in Dublin.'

An evening or so later, skipper Farr-Jones sensing young Horan was a little homesick and pining for his fiancée, suggested the two of them go for a stroll and a chat. They walked and walked, so engrossed in conversation neither took any notice of where they were going. By the time they snapped to, they were totally disorientated. Horan collared a passing

local: 'Excuse me, can you tell us the way back to the Westbury Hotel?' 'Ay Sorr, it's nart dat difficult, but I wouldn't
be wantin' to start from here.'

There was one small downside to being based in Dublin. In
a friendly environment, the players were susceptible to losing
their sharp rugby focus and falling out of 'the zone' as the sports
psychologists might say. In Wales, where the Wallabies had
spent the first two weeks, such a digression was not possible.
No matter where the players went, they were constantly reminded by the fanatical Welsh fans of the seriousness of the task
at hand. *We're on the way back. We've turned the corner. We're
going to get you.* It was all pervasive. The solitary sanctuary was
the picture theatre. Little estimates he saw every movie in
Swansea twice in the time the team was based there.

Dublin was very different. People loved rugby, and they
loved talking about it. But only in a flippant, almost apolo-
getic manner: 'Oh you boys will beat us by turty points' they
were told time and again. The repetition was persuasive
enough to lure even the most militant forward to the verge
of disarmament. The Wallabies had to be careful, as once
bitten twice shy assistant coach Bob Templeton insisted.

'Tempo kept telling us about Ireland's tour of Australia in
1979,' Little says. 'The Irish kept on saying they were on a
learning curve, just looking to gain experience, but they finished up beating Australia in both Tests. He knew better than
anybody else that the Irish couldn't be trusted.'

On Sunday, October 20, the Australians would find out.

Willie Ofahengaue, Willie O, Willie Offen-has-ago, Willie
Offen-hungry, Aussie Bill, Woffa, The Tongan Torpedo . . .
call him what you like. But never *ever* whack him in the
mouth in the first 15 seconds of a Test match, especially a
World Cup quarter-final.

Irish captain Phil Matthews was the culprit, as the game
began in a flurry of flailing fists.

Horan, one of the first in to prise apart the truculent forwards, will never forget the look on Willie O's face as he shaped up to the Irish flanker. 'I'd never seen him angry before,' Horan says. 'He's normally such a passive person, even on the field. But when Matthews belted him, his eyes just widened. They were twice the size of (rugby league player) Laurie Daley's. It was like somebody had stolen a big bunch of bananas from his family village in Tonga!'

Matthews' aggression, however unwisely directed, typified the intensity of the Irish on that cold, misty October afternoon. Templeton was dead right. They were not going to lie down. Whatever the Irish lacked in rugby pedigree, they more than made up for in unbridled passion and vigour.

As much as Australia looked to have the game in their control, they simply couldn't shrug off the tenacious home side. Ireland hung on like a pit bull terrier to a postman's backside until the try which sent shock waves through every small corner of the rugby world. From out of the blue, Irish flanker Gordon Hamilton, a man who had been included in the side on account of his exceptional speed, galloped away untouched to score in the corner.

Some 200 of the 50,700 people in the crowd streamed onto the field to hug the heroic Hamilton. The remainder roared and stamped, and cried tears of joy.

Australia were behind for the first time in the match, and the tournament. This was not in the script. If they did not score in the next four and a half minutes, their World Cup campaign was over. They were on the first plane home in the morning.

Little momentarily thought of his mother and father, Pat and Ray, who at that minute were on a plane from Australia. Perhaps he would be able to wave to them out of the window of a plane heading in the opposite direction.

Horan was the same. His mother Helen and brother Matt had just arrived, having saved for the past 18 months to make the trip. What an incredible waste of money, he thought.

Some 60m away, sitting in stunned silence was the Wallaby coaching panel, Dwyer, Templeton, Jake Howard, and the rest of the mechanics who for two years had been fine tuning the engine. There was not a word being spoken. In front of them, the reserves, and injured skipper Farr-Jones, who'd once again been forced off with knee trouble. They checked their watches. 'I make it four minutes.' 'I make it three.' 'I make it six.' 'Good, we'll take yours.' Centre Richard Tombs, one of two players not to have taken the field at all in the tournament, didn't have a watch. He was questioning how he would get his laundry back if the team was on a 6am flight the next day. Not exactly the ideal time to be talking about a $25 bag of clothes but the remark offered valuable insight into the confidence of the Australian side going into the quarter-final.

Back down on the field, Lynagh, the stand-in captain, was not worried about Pat and Ray, nor Helen and Matt, nor for that matter Richard Tombs' T-shirts and football shorts. He was devising a plan to haul the Wallabies out of the mire.

He hustled the troops together, and set out in point form the course of action. It was clear in his mind what had to be done.

1. Everybody stay calm.
2. Kick deep to the left corner.
3. Get the ball back and secure possession.
4. The backs will do the rest.

Moments later, when they'd worked their way down the other end of the field, it was quite apparent Horan hadn't been listening.

'Are you going to have a shot (at field goal) Nod?'

Lynagh dismissed the question without so much as a cursory glance. Eighteen—all was not good enough. He called 'cut two loop' the simplest manoeuvre in the Wallaby backline's repertoire. The one they had already used to great effect four times in the match. Some 77 minutes gone, but the Irish backs were still none the wiser—the ball went gliding across the backline and Campese found space. When he was caught, Lynagh, the architect, was on hand to scoop up the ball and muscle his way over in the corner. As Horan picked Lynagh up off the ground, he could feel Lynagh's whole body shaking. 'I didn't hear him say a thing. There was no elation—just relief,' Horan says.

The view of the Australian reserves bench had been totally obscured—only by the deathly, eerie silence could they determine what had happened. They hugged and shook and slapped, harder than they ever had before.

There were still two minutes remaining, but the Irish were gone. Australia were home 19–18.

Pat and Ray were right, so too Helen and Judy, and most importantly of all, Tombsie would be able to collect his laundry at nine the next morning.

Everybody was happy, bar 15 Irish players, six reserves, a few coaches, and 50,700 fans.

At 7.30 that night, Little was curled up reading a book in John Connolly's sixth floor bedroom at the Westbury Hotel. So mentally and physically drained was he from the afternoon's unfoldings, he couldn't bring himself to go out and toast the Wallabies' finest hour, and their closest shave so far.

'It was like we'd played two games,' Little says. 'The last five minutes alone seemed to go on as long as a normal match. It was exhausting, undoubtedly because of the pressure we were under. I guess everybody was happy that we had got through. But it wasn't the same happiness as playing well and having a good win. It was just relief.'

The Australian players who did venture out that night were astounded at how well the Irish players—and public—had accepted their gut-wrenching loss. Ireland had gone within three minutes of barrelling the favourites out of the World Cup, and yet there were no 'could have beens' or 'might have beens', just endless variations of: 'I tort we 'ad you Aussies. Can I get ya a pint of Guinness.'

'They were amazing,' Horan recalls. 'I kept on thinking what it would have been like in New Zealand, if we'd beaten the All Blacks under the same circumstances.' At the post-match function, the only Irish player with any axe to grind was skipper Matthews, the initiator of the opening fisticuffs. Chatting to opposite number Simon Poidevin, a player he had confronted several times, and even played with on odd occasions, Matthews pretended to be a little indignant that Poidevin hadn't warned him about Willie O. 'If you'd told me he was like that, I would have hit somebody else,' the Irishman mused.

The convivial atmosphere which existed between the Australian and Irish players filtered down to the Irish public. As much as the Australians enjoyed being in Dublin, the Dubliners loved having them. The Wallabies could frequently be found in the Grafton St Mall, signing autographs and chatting with the locals. At night, the back-up side would be out in similar force, in bars, restaurants and coffee shops, while a couple of the more sedentary types, lock John Eales and reserve flanker Brendan Nasser, became popular locals at a pool hall they'd sniffed out, just across the Liffey River.

Ultimately, if the presence and polite manner of the Wallabies didn't win over the locals, the number of Irish names in the squad certainly did. Lynagh, Horan, Slattery, Dwyer, Kearns, Daly, Crowley and McCall served as a ready reminder of the rich Irish heritage in the Australian camp. Now that their own team was out of contention, the locals had no hesitation in switching their allegiance to the Australians. The

Wallabies had, after all, only beaten Ireland by a single point. Irish logic would suggest if Australia went on to win the World Cup, Ireland would be the unofficial runners-up, given that they finished so close.

When the All Blacks arrived in Dublin, direct from their quarter-final defeat of Canada in France, the locals had yet another reason to side with Australia.

While New Zealand were not without their own evidence of Irish ancestry—with names like Sean Fitzpatrick, John Kirwan, Bernie McCahill, and Kieran Crowley—what they lacked was a friendy public face, an overt sense of humility that the locals so much admired in the Wallabies.

While the Australians smiled and laughed, the All Blacks scowled. Before any time at all, the Irish press honed in.

'MEN OF STONE, HEARTS OF STEEL' screamed the headline on a half page feature article in the *Irish Independent*, the day before the game. Underneath, local rugby writer Vincent Hogan opened fire: 'Reassuringly, they rolled into town with all the charmlessness of old . . . Frowns of stone, eyes glazed with frosty indifference, All Black teams have never been known for courting niceties. They carry themselves with all the gaiety of grave diggers . . . What is it about these doleful souls from the southern hemisphere? How can they be so dour, so cold, so colourless when their Australian neighbours survive just as imperiously by extending the hand of friendship? . . . New Zealand's rugger men strut and scowl and generally imply a superior presence. It is as though, in their hostile silence, they are reminding you that God still wears a black shirt.'

Hogan even slipped into their skipper, Gary Whetton, suggesting he preferred prolonged periods on the lavatory to time spent in the company of newsmen.

It was music to the ears of the Australians, not only because it shored up their support for the Lansdowne Road semi-final, but because it helped confirm what they had already heard—all was not rosy in the All Black garden.

Rumours of a rift between New Zealand co-coaches, Alex 'Grizz' Wyllie and the more urbane John Hart, had been rife since the start of the tournament. Though ultimately working towards the same goal, Wyllie and Hart on the surface seemed polarised by both pride and theory, a division which their skipper, Sean Fitzpatrick, would later confirm in his book 'Fronting Up'.

Back at the Westbury, the Australians had a small smouldering issue of their own to contend with.

Four days before the Test, Little was sitting alone in his room reading, when John Connolly, the Queensland coach and Australian selector, came in shaking his head and swearing under his breath.

'I don't believe it, I just don't believe it,' Connolly said.

Little asked the only question he could: 'Don't believe what?'

'Guess who's just been dropped for the All Blacks game?' Little didn't know where to start. He, like all the other players, assumed the XV which beat Ireland would be retained for the semi-final.

'I give in, who?' Little said nervously, fearing Connolly may be trying to break some serious news to him in an up-front manner.

'Jeff Miller,' Connolly reported.

The news was hot off the press. Connolly had just come out of the selection meeting with Bob Dwyer and Barry Want, the third national selector who like Connolly had been travelling with the team for the entire World Cup tournament.

Connolly stepped into the meeting believing there shouldn't be, or wouldn't be, any changes. The selectors had tinkered early on with the back-row, but Connolly was convinced they had fielded the optimum combination against Ireland, with Miller and Poidevin as flankers, and Willie Ofahengaue at No 8.

Dwyer was not convinced, nor to a lesser extent was Want. When the No 8 position came up for discussion, the pair pooled their collective voting power: 'We reckon we should play Troy Coker.'

The big Queensland utility had been selected for the first two games at lock, but was then axed altogether—even from the reserves—for the match against Wales. Connolly in part accepted Dwyer's supposition about the need for height at the back of the lineout against the All Blacks, but at whose expense? If anyone was to go, he believed it should be Poidevin. Miller was faster and, in his opinion, had better hands and was more constructive at the breakdown. But Dwyer insisted Poidevin should stay. Want supported him, so Connolly was clearly outnumbered.

It was not the first time in his career Miller had been mysteriously dropped from a Test line-up. His most recent axing came just four months prior, after the annihilation of Wales at Ballymore. Miller was voted Players' Player, but that night was banished to make way for Poidevin in the Test pack to play England the following weekend.

Dwyer at the time strongly defended the decision, denying he had bowed to pressure from New South Wales. 'We were not appeasing anybody. There was almost as much flak in Sydney about Poidevin missing the Wales Test as there is now in Brisbane about Miller missing the England Test. The selectors have made an extremely brave decision. The easier decision would have been to go the other way and retain Miller but our job is not to appease the amateur critics. Our job is to pick the best XV to beat England.'

But many of the players didn't share their coach's view, with vice-captain Lynagh publicly criticising the decision: 'When you beat a side by 60 points and the best player on the field gets dropped, something is wrong. It just amazes me. Players will be thinking: Who's next? It seems no matter how you play on the field, you could go,' Lynagh was quoted as saying in *The Australian*.

Lock Rod McCall also spoke out: 'I wouldn't have been any more upset if I had been dropped myself. Team morale is a fragile thing. It has to be handled with care. I don't think this has helped team morale.'

But the issue had gradually been forgotten. Until now. As much admiration as the team had for Coker, there was a strong feeling that Miller had once again been badly short-changed. Horan and Little both subscribed to the view.

'You could sense it in the team meeting when the side was announced,' Horan recalls. 'The guys were just shocked. Rather than congratulating Troy, the first instinct everybody had was to console Nuts (Miller).'

Little agrees: 'Nobody could tell him why. That's what must have been so frustrating for him. It's a true measure of the bloke that he took the news so courageously. The temptation would have been to toss in the towel, but Jeff kept on training as hard as he always had.'

Coker himself was embarrassed by his selection, apologising to Miller at the first training run. After he had been dropped for the Welsh game, the rangy utility forward was convinced his playing commitments on tour were over, and had switched into party mode. He switched back in a hurry.

In relation to the choice of Poidevin ahead of Miller, Horan had no firm views. He had been rooming with the red-haired veteran right through their stay in Ireland, and respected his courage and determination. He also appreciated the support and guidance Poidevin had offered throughout his Test career. No matter where Horan is in the world, the now-retired Poidevin rings him the night before a Test to wish him well. But how could anybody go past Miller? In Horan's mind,

Nuts was the ultimate players' player—tough, supportive, skilful, and totally unselfish. That Miller, in his last tour before retirement, was once again being deprived of what was owed to him, was a source of great sadness to Horan. He wished at the time rugby teams had 16 players.

The matter went no further. With Miller manfully accepting the selectors' decision, the Wallabies settled down to prepare for what was arguably the most important game in Australian rugby history.

Although it was largely unspoken, there was an uncharacteristic confidence in the players' minds as they squeezed through the 400 rowdy supporters outside the Westbury Hotel, and boarded the bus for the 4km trip to the ground. The 21–12 demolition of the All Blacks in Sydney had stuck firmly in their minds, so too the 6–3 loss in Auckland, when they had played so badly and yet failed by a mere penalty goal. They just sensed the pendulum had swung their way.

History now shows that the confidence was well founded, with the Wallabies outplaying and out-thinking their opponents in every aspect of the semi-final.

While most of the accolades went to Campese, who totally mesmerised the opposition with his running skills, All Black flyhalf Grant Fox spared a couple for the Australian centre combination, who stood at the forefront when the Wallabies were called upon to defend in the second half.

'Going into that Test match, we believed that if the Aussies did have a defensive weakness, it was out wide. We weren't totally convinced with Little's abilities to close players down. But, in that Test, he changed our opinion completely. The two of them (Horan and Little) were a source of great frustration.'

In answer to the 'Men of stone, hearts of steel' allegations Fox has this to say: 'It might have appeared that way. But I don't think it's quite fair. The players were certainly very focussed on the task at hand. We probably didn't take into account the need for public relations exercises, the same way the Wallabies did. When training was over, it was over, that was it, on the bus and out of there. The bus waited for no-one. Only when we lost, people started to ask questions about what we did wrong. If we'd won, I don't think anyone would have batted an eyelid.'

When the Wallabies bumped into the All Blacks at Dublin Airport the following morning, they were heartened by the Kiwis' show of support for the impending final.

'They weren't exactly jumping up and singing 'Advance Australia Fair',' Little remembers. 'But after the way the quarter and semi-finals worked out, it became a bit of a northern hemisphere v southern hemisphere battle. I honestly think they wanted us to win the final.'

The All Blacks, and plenty of others in the rugby world. The alternative was England, who had bored Scotland to death the previous day to take the first semi-final 9–6 at Murrayfield. The match was a pitifully dour encounter, decided entirely on penalty kicks. *Mail on Sunday* columnist Patrick Collins crystallised the thoughts of most pundits by describing England as 'a team almost as difficult to defeat as they are to watch'. In contrast, the Dublin semi-final had been an enthralling encounter, offering the same intensity but with a bonus issue of attacking flair, panache and daring. New Zealand coach John Hart was quoted as saying that for 'the good of rugby' he hoped Australia went on to take out the final. Clearly, Australia were flying to London with the best wishes of every breathing rugby supporter—bar 15 million English supporters.

Weybridge, in Surrey, is the type of place you see middle-aged business executives pushing shopping trolleys through gourmet delicatessens, while talking on mobile phones. It is the very buckle of the London stockbroker belt, a sanctuary for the upper middle class, who reside most comfortably in their six-bedroom Edwardian style houses and commute daily, some 45 minutes by train to London. Entertainment types like Sean Connery, Phil Collins and Ronnie Corbett all have homes in the area, handy to exclusive golf courses such as Wentworth and St Georges on the Hill.

It was in Weybridge, at the luxurious Oatlands Park Hotel, the Wallabies would be based for the week leading up to the Cup final. A one-time hunting lodge of King Henry VIII, the Oatlands, with its sprawling gardens and nine-hole golf course, was the perfect place for the Wallabies to relax and contemplate the importance of Saturday's momentous occasion.

Having come so far and worked so hard, there was very little physical improvement to be made over the ensuing week. The Wallabies' final preparations were strictly mental. If there was one concern the team management had, it was the lingering effect the All Black victory might have had. In the eyes of most pundits, the Wallabies had cleared their highest hurdle in the semi-final, there was *only* the English left. There was clearly a refocussing required.

With just the two finalists remaining in the 16 team tournament, the media spotlight in the lead-up to Twickenham intensified. When the Wallabies turned up for their first training session at Richmond, there was a welcoming party of some 100 journalists, pens poised, cameras loaded. As they had done right the way through the tournament, the co-operative Australians honoured practically every interview request, with the team's fulltime media director, Greg Campbell, organising daily press conferences, and juggling the approaches for one-on-one fire-side chats. But two days before the final, the curtain came down—for the remainder of their preparation they had requested to be left in peace.

The next day, when Dwyer saw a white Jaguar parked beside the training field, the Australian coach went off his brain: 'Who the f . . . is that? Somebody tell him to get the f . . . out of here'.

Anthony Herbert put up his hand. 'Ah, it's OK Bob, he's here to see me . . .'

'Oh . . . OK . . . that's alright then.'

Dwyer understood. Herbert was the team bagman. A deal was going down.

The reserve centre stopped briefly at his kit bag, jogged over to the car, and climbed inside the front passenger seat.

Zzzzzzziiiiiipppppp. Electric windows up. Zzzzzzzziiiipppp. Electric seat back. A very brief exchange of pleasantries, then down to business: 'You got the money?'

'Yep. You got the tickets?'

'Yep.'

A swapping of envelopes, a handshake, and the man in the Jaguar was off.

Herbert jogged back to his bag, humming the 'James Bond 007' theme. He buried the cash and resumed training.

There was nothing illegal about the transaction. The Wallabies were simply off-loading their ticket allocation—at the going price. With the 60,000 capacity stadium officially sold out seasons before, seats were at a premium. Wealthy Londoners—particularly those in the stockbroking belt—were happy to carry a hefty freight just to get in the gate.

Room 338, where Herbert was domiciled by himself—a privilege normally extended only to the team captain—also became the Ticketing and Cashiers office. Calls would come in day and night. 'Hello, Mr Herbert, I'm told you may be able to help me . . .'

'It might sound like we were all swimming in bathtubs full of money, but at the end of the day, the ticket money hardly covered the cost of the drinks at the post-Cup party,' Herbert says.

Room 338 was not the only busy room in the Oatlands Park Hotel that week. Far busier still was a small office behind reception, where six fax machines had been temporarily installed to cope with the reams of incoming 'good luck' messages from Australia, and around the globe.

To make things easier for hotel staff and players alike, five tables were set up in the team common room, three for general faxes, the other two for messages addressed to specific players. Each player had a pile, which corresponded with their touring number.

Not until piles mounted, and tables were covered in black and white scrawl, did the players begin to fully appreciate the attention and focus the World Cup was commanding back in Australia—and just how much it meant to people.

'It was just amazing,' Horan says. 'I can remember getting one fax from a hotel proprietor on the Gold Coast. I'd stayed there once, about two years before, for three days. I was staggered. We suspected there'd be quite a bit of interest back home, but only among the rugby clubs, and the real sports fanatics.' Little had his own regional fan club. The Darling Downs—people he had never met—*never heard of*—writing to wish him well, just because he hailed from the same area.

However, of the thousands of faxes which arrived at the Oatlands that week, there was one which clearly stood alone in the minds of the players. It was a copy of an article which appeared on the front page of a Melbourne newspaper, welcoming into the world a baby girl called Harriet Elizabeth Nicola Farr-Jones Davina Wallaby Geddes. Bruce and Joanna Geddes, of Middle Park in Melbourne, had so named their daughter in honour of Australia's stunning win over the All Blacks.

It should be reported that almost four years on, Harriet Elizabeth Nicola Farr-Jones Davina Wallaby Geddes is a happy, well-adjusted little girl who attends kindy at South Melbourne. She has already met quite a few of the Australian players, been to three Test matches, wears a size two Wallaby jersey and jumps up and down yelling 'go Wallaby go' whenever she sees the familiar gold jerseys on television. 'It's been a very funny few years,' her father admits. To think the family came from Melbourne . . . the Australian Rules capital. The Wallabies had touched the hearts of Australia.

Saturday, 12 midday, November 2. At last the moment had arrived. It was almost time to get on the bus for the 45 minute journey to Twickenham. As the players assembled in the foyer, the hotel staff at the Oatlands, about 30 of them, formed the longest human tunnel they could for the players to walk through. The moment wasn't lost on either Little or Horan. The tunnels at high school matches were their earliest and most vivid memory of the game. 'Remember these?' Horan asked as they were walking through. A nervous 'yep' was all Little could muster. His stomach was churning. He could hardly talk.

When the Australian bus arrived at the ground, and eased its way into the Western Carpark, the players experienced for the first time the atmosphere reverberating around the stadium, the official home of rugby. Inside the bus, total silence, tension, sterility. Outside was exactly the opposite—a sea of people and cars, awash with colour, most of it red and white. There was the Rolls Royce and Range Rover set, slurping French champagne, while sitting down to their three course meals—smoked salmon, filet mignon and African strawberries—served on bone china by elegantly dressed waiters. The rank and file stuck to hot dogs, washed down by generous amounts of real ale and tepid lager. The cross of St George was everywhere.

So too were ticket scalpers. One of them did very well out of a Japanese tourist who paid 200 pounds ($450) on the understanding he would be sitting in the Royal Box with the Queen, after a sumptuous champagne lunch. No. It never happened.

There were painted faces galore, thousands of green and gold scarves, even a vibrant cluster of Irishmen, all kitted up in their emerald green jerseys and white shorts, proudly announcing they were there 'just in case one of da tooo teams don't turn up'.

In the minds of most players, the hour and a half between 1.30pm and 3pm is a blur. Little only really remembers how cold the dressing room was. With the long v-jay walls painted white, the shed reminded him of the interior of an old Queenslander. Horan recalls looking across to see prop Tony Daly hacking the sleeve off his jersey. Tim cut the sleeves off his jersey too, but very carefully. How could Dales frame that Australian jersey if—*not when but if*—the Wallabies won the World Cup? It looked like a singlet.

The moments ticked away. While the other players moved around the shed, Horan and Little as always stuck together, like velcro. Communicate. Talk. Defence. Communicate. Talk. Defence. If they had said it to each other once, they'd said it a zillion times.

Before they knew it, they were out on the field, standing face to face with their English foes . . . *I know who the lady in red is, but who are all those other blokes?*

Skipper Farr-Jones was moving along the jagged gold line, introducing Her Majesty, Queen Elizabeth II of England, to his players. 'Nice to meet you ma'am. How do you do. Nice to meet you your Majesty.' It was a real thrill, one of life's treasured moments, but long after the Queen had passed, the officials kept coming. And coming. On it went . . . 'Nice to meet you. Hello. Nice to meet you. A pleasure. Nice to meet you . . .' *CAN WE JUST START THE GAME? PLEASE.*

They'd been out on the field close to 20 minutes. As much as Horan had enjoyed walking slowly, deliberately, out through the tunnel and onto the pitch, just like his childhood hero—Parramatta league player Brett Kenny—he now wanted to run. Anywhere. Into anything. The wait was killing him.

Finally the whistle. The climb to the last rung of the ladder had begun . . .

In the general context of international rugby matches, the World Cup final will not be remembered as one of the classic confrontations. The tension and importance of the occasion made it almost impossible for the players to perform to the level they might in an ordinary, 'everyday' Test match. But the game did have its great moments. Like the Campese kick and chase, which so nearly resulted in a try. Like the Willie Ofahengaue charge after halftime. Like the shuddering tackle of Phil Kearns on Rob Andrew. Like the desperation of John Eales in cover, when an English try beckoned.

However, if there was one single moment which turned the game, it came in the 28th minute. Australia were leading 3–0 but were on the back pedal, like they had been for the bulk of the first half. England flyhalf Rob Andrew hoisted ahead, in the direction of Horan who had darted diagonally across field, sensing Australia was badly short on the right. He couldn't have been positioned more perfectly. He soared above Rory Underwood, took the ball and braced himself for Mick Skinner's big hit. But the huge English flanker bounced off, likewise halfback Richard Hill. As Horan spun to his left and set sail up the right hand sideline, English hooker Brian Moore ploughed across in cover but didn't have the speed. Horan's great rival, Will Carling, did. Knowing that the English skipper had him covered, and unable to position Campese for the pass inside, Horan kicked ahead, a 'banana' kick, which he hoped might turn and bounce into touch close to the English line. The result was better than he could have imagined. The ball bounced right and English fullback Jonathan Webb was still forced to take it across the sideline, giving Australia the lineout throw some 5m out.

The rest is history. Kearns a perfect throw to Willie O at No 5, a rolling maul, and CRASH! Down went Tony Daly and Ewen McKenzie, the ball squashed over the line under 230kg of front-row might.

Ahead 9–0 at halftime, Australia hung on in the second term, as the home side, possession aplenty, ran the ball stylishly, boldly, belatedly. Why hadn't they been playing this way throughout the tournament, muttered their supporters. The Australians didn't know either.

At 4.08pm, when England winger Simon Halliday went to ground, 15m out from his own line, Welsh referee Derek Bevan moved his left hand to his mouth. The Australians didn't hear the shrill sound, but his hand movement was enough. Australia had won the World Cup. The top of the ladder. At last. Little swivelled around and made a bee-line for his centre partner, who was already in the arms of Poidevin, his legs wrapped around the veteran flanker's waist in chimpanzee fashion. Joy was miles away. For the moment the feeling was simply relief.

Three-quarters of an hour later, having climbed the Twickenham stairs to hold the William Webb Ellis trophy, having hugged the rest of their teammates, and having belted out a most moving, misty-eyed rendition of 'Advance Australia Fair', Horan and Little were crammed together in a giant claw-foot bath, guzzling French champagne and savouring life's finest moment.

There, in the dressing shed of Twickenham, Rugby's hallowed home, the irony of the occasion would not escape them. Tim and Jason had been in the bath together at Jimbour some 10 years before, after a game of footy in Little's backyard. Same positions. Same inseparable friendship.

Except this time, no weeing!

For the two dozen or so who were heading straight home, it was not the ideal time for a flight. Bags had to be packed and in the foyer of the Oatlands Park Hotel at 9am. There were bodies everywhere.

The night of celebration had been a strangely subdued affair—the closing dinner for 1200 at the Royal Lancaster Hotel in London's West End, followed by a party with 200 or so close supporters back at the hotel in Surrey.

As reluctant as anyone was to come right out and say it, the winning occasion seemed at the time a little anticlimactic. There would be joy, of course, but it would come later, much later, when the enormity of the achievement filtered through their weary bodies.

David Campese sat soberly on a couch, waiting for his flight to Italy, while John Eales, still dressed in tartan pants from the night before, strolled around the foyer, bidding his teammates farewell. Eales, like Campese, was off to Italy, but not to play rugby, just to visit his Italian grandmother. World Cup hero one day, homebody the next.

On the right hand side of the foyer, just across from the concierge desk, a bleary-eyed Anthony Herbert was still coming to terms with the ungodly hour. Jug of Cointreau and ice in one hand, passport in the other, Herbert bent down and unzipped the William Webb Ellis Trophy from its bulky blue foam case.

He tucked the gold trophy under his arm. 'Come on Bill. We're taking you home.'

# Chapter 11

## Blacks and Boks Busted . . . the Crown Stays in Place

*'There is plenty of room at the top but not enough room to lie down.'*

AMERICAN HOCKEY COACH FRED SHERO

The opening question was launched across the room, like an Exocet missile.

'So Michael, now Australia has won the World Cup, do you expect the Wallaby players will become legitimate targets for the Sydney rugby league clubs?'

The hair on the back of Michael Lynagh's neck, still stiff from the 30 hour journey, bristled like that of an angry Alsatian who'd just caught a neighbouring dog digging for his best bone.

'Jeeeezus Christ, we've just earned the title as the best rugby team in the world, why can't you ask us something about that?' Lynagh barked.

Horan and Little, sitting side by side at the giant U-shaped table set up for the press conference at Sydney's International Airport, were glad the stand-in Australian skipper had made the point. They'd both thought exactly the same thing—though neither would have had the gumption to reply in the sharp, crisp manner of Lynagh.

There was no doubt the question was poorly timed and inappropriately delivered, for it belittled the magnificence of everything the Wallabies had achieved over the past five weeks . . . *all that climbing they'd done.*

But the newshound was on the right track. Just how were rugby union officials planning to keep the rugby league vultures away from the ripe pickings, now that the Wallabies had climbed to the top of the mountain, and had a look at the view?

As Queensland coach John Connolly so graphically pointed out in a television interview four months before: 'We'll have to build a 40 foot wall around Ballymore if we're going to retain the players after the World Cup.' There was no unnecessary doom and gloom about the statement—just cold hard reality. Some Wallaby players obviously had no appeal to the league talent scouts, but were the likes of Horan and Little, Lynagh and Campese, Ofahengaue and Kearns really going to stick around for another four years to achieve what they had already achieved in 1991? Australian Rugby officials simply couldn't afford to adopt a 'let's wait and see' policy. The issue had to be tackled front-on, before any ground was lost.

To a certain extent, their hands were tied by the myriad of rules and regulations relating to amateurism. But barriers were gradually being broken down. In 1991, the International Rugby Board, the game's ruling body, approved changes which allowed elite players to capitalise on their profile. For the first time in the game's 168 year history, players could benefit financially from the sale of books, the endorsement of products and invitations to address corporate functions.

Almost simultaneously, the ARU's Amateurism Committee was advancing the players' cause a step further. In consultation with senior players, the Committee was devising a scheme which could operate inside the new and less stringent amateur boundaries, for the collective financial benefit of the team. The ground work came to fruition in February 1992 when Wallabies Promotions and Marketing (WPM), a discretionary trust fund, was officially adopted by the Australian Rugby Union. The Test players were never going to become millionaires from the proceeds of the trust, but they would at last be recompensed for the huge amount of time they devoted to playing the game.

Rugby hadn't exactly declared war on its professional counterpart, but it had at least ducked into the ammunitions depot, and picked up a few bulletproof vests and a couple of crash helmets, in readiness for the battle ahead.

The role Horan and Little played in the hasty rearguard action by the game's top administrators cannot be underestimated. Of all the World Cup Wallabies, they were the two players Australian rugby could least afford to lose, given their age, ability, marketing appeal and attraction to the rival code.

Dick McGruther, the Chairman of the Amateurism Committee acknowledges that: 'Combinations like Horan and Little come along only once or twice in a generation. In 1992, they were as important to Australian rugby as (Dennis) Lillee and (Jeff) Thomson were to cricket in the 1970s. They had so much to offer. We had to do everything we could to retain their services.'

Queensland Rugby Union executive director Terry Doyle, another official at the coalface, and just as committed to keeping the pair in rugby, agrees: 'Of all the things we have done in Queensland rugby over the past 10 years, I regard the efforts to retain Tim and Jason as the most crucial. They epitomise everything we like to project about rugby—both on and off the field. Their on-field brilliance speaks for itself, but off the field, they both have this tremendous incandescence, this wholesome appeal. There's not a mother who sits in the grandstand at Ballymore who wouldn't like to have them as their son, or at least married to their daughter. They empathise with all sorts of people—they'll spend as much time talking to a seven-year-old boy as a corporate boffin. We've got a lot of great players in Australia, but it's Horan and Little as a duality which is so appealing. There's not a rugby union body in the world—a sport in the world—which wouldn't be proud to hang their mantle on the two of them.

'On the downside, having seized upon them for all the right reasons, the biggest mistake we could have made was to allow them to become similar promotional vehicles for our rivals. Not only would rugby be without them, but rugby league would then have two new superstars, two new marketing trump cards up their sleeve.'

'Repeat after me . . .'
'I Timothy James Horan . . .'
The last time Tim was involved in such a ceremonial clutch, he was standing in a crowded restaurant in Strasbourg, his right hand on his mother's head, peering up into the bloodshot eyes of the high priest Peter FitzSimons.

This time, the mood was infinitely more sensitive, the setting decidedly angelic. Horan's right hand was holding the left of his bride, Katrina Lucy Ferris, as they faced one another at the altar of Holy Spirit Catholic Church in Auchenflower, Brisbane.

The only common denominator was Jason. Like in France, he was standing on Tim's right, but this time performing the duties of best man.

It had been exactly a month since they marched up the steps at Twickenham and held aloft the William Webb Ellis Trophy. The World Cup was secure—time to attend to even more important things in life. As he and Katrina stood at the altar, surrounded by some 120 close friends and family—no media by request—Tim just savoured the tranquillity of their special moment. Ever since Twickenham, life had been frantic. Public appearances, team functions, dinners, media interviews, even a ticker tape parade through the streets of

Sydney—an occasion where an estimated 100,000 people turned out to welcome home Australia's World Cup heroes. In between it all, he had set up a family company, and he and Katrina had bought their first house, a cute colonial cottage at Gordon Park in Brisbane's inner northern suburbs.

But when he arrived at the church, with his customary punctuality, the storm seemed to subside. The mind stopped racing, the pulse rate slowed. He so much looked forward to sitting back with his new wife, relaxing, going to the beach, and getting rugby out of his mind altogether.

At the wedding reception at the St Lucia Golf Club two hours later, Jason would explain to the gathering how he thought Tim and Katrina were perfectly suited. 'Just look at all the different ways they complement each other,' he said, microphone in one hand, beer in the other. 'Trine loves to cook, Tim loves to eat, Tim loves to earn money, Katrina loves to spend it, Tim is messy, Katrina loves to tidy up, but most importantly of all, Tim can read, and Katrina can write. They're just the perfect match!'


It was Wallaby halfback Peter Slattery who phoned and told him. Little had just walked off the course in the Jack Newton Pro-Am Celebrity Golf Classic at Twin Waters, on the Sunshine Coast. The news hit Jason like a bolt of lightning.

Kerry Fitzgerald, Australia's leading referee—in Jason's opinion the world's best referee—was dead, the victim of a massive heart attack late that morning.

Little couldn't stop wondering why. Fitzgerald was just 42, a suntanned, fit, vibrant little bloke, who looked like he could run three marathons end on end without so much as a puff. Just six weeks before, Fitzgerald had officiated in the World Cup semi-final between Scotland and England at Murrayfield. Australia's presence precluded him from controlling the final, but there is no doubt in Little's mind he deserved to.

Fitzgerald had a feeling for the game that no other referee seemed to. He worked with the players instead of against them, by creating an on-field environment which rewarded skilful play, and punished negativity. The game was all the more enjoyable when Fitzy had the whistle in hand.

Jason felt sorry for Kerry's family, and just as sad for rugby. The code would not quite be the same without him.

For the newly crowned world champions, the challenges of the 1992 season could not have been more impeccably timed. A full scale tour of Australia by Cup semi-finalists Scotland, followed by a three-Test Bledisloe Cup series against the All Blacks, and a one-off Test in South Africa. The program was perfect. If ever rugby was in a position to dismantle its reputation as a boutique sport, and haul itself into the sporting mainstream, it was during the winter of '92.

With Australian rugby very much in vogue the world over, the early indications were that personal opportunities for players would be abundant. In the first week of March, Tim Horan received a phone call from Bob Templeton, Wallaby assistant coach and part-time international rugby mediator, asking him if he would like to play in a South African Barbarians XV against Currie Cup champions Transvaal at Ellis Park on March 24.

The idea appealed to Horan enormously. Not since 1969 had an Australian rugby player been on a sanctioned visit to the Republic. The Wallabies were scheduled to tour there in late August, but to get there first for a preview screening would be better still. The one hesitation he had was leaving Katrina, at the time seven months pregnant, at home by herself for seven days. Within a week, he didn't have to hesitate—the matter was taken out of his hands. Queensland Rugby Union officials, running the risk of being accused of heavy-handedness, declined to release Horan for the one-off game in South Africa because it clashed with the Reds' first hitout of the season—against New Zealand's Canterbury at Ballymore.

In what was arguably the first instance of a player benefitting from the newly relaxed amateur regulations, Horan had signed an agreement with the QRU to have his image used on all the union's promotional material—stickers, posters and invitations—for the 1992 season. But the early opportunity cost him a trip to South Africa.

'How would it have looked if Tim, the focal point of our marketing campaign, was in South Africa for the season kick-off? The first game sets the seal on the season. It was very important he play,' explains QRU Chairman, Dick McGruther.

Horan at the time was disappointed with the rebuttal, but copped it on the chin. It was a good thing he did. On Tuesday, March 24—the day of the game in South Africa—he arrived home at 9.30pm after one of the longest and hardest Queensland training sessions he could remember. Totally exhausted, he had a shower, a quick bite to eat, and slumped down on the bed. But not for long.

'Timmy, wake up, Timmy . . .'

'Huh . . . Who . . . What?'

'I think I'm going into labour.'

'No you're not. It's probably just growing pains . . . try to get some sleep.'

'No I think it's more than that.'

'Well maybe it's the Mexican sausages we had for dinner—maybe they don't agree with you.'

The drowsy 'Dr Horan' wasn't being sarcastic—there was good cause for scepticism because Katrina was not due for another six weeks. But to put her mind at rest, the couple started monitoring the contractions . . . 15 minutes apart . . . 10 minutes apart.

'Maybe I should ring the doctor . . .'

'SHE'S **WHAT**? EVERY **HOW** MANY MINUTES? GET HER IN HERE AS QUICKLY AS YOU CAN!'

By the time they arrived at the Royal Women's Hospital, the contractions were every three minutes. The sister's words were precise. 'You're going to deliver very soon.' The Horans became parents at 11.56am. A small but healthy baby girl they named Lucy Mary. The decision not to go to South Africa suddenly became one of the best Tim had made in his 22 years.

In the overall scheme of things, it was a miracle Tim was by Katrina's side for the birth of their daughter. Three days later, he and Jason flew off to Hong Kong for the Sevens. Tim might have withdrawn, had he not just been named captain of the Australian side for the first time. Back from Hong Kong, one night at home, then across to New Zealand for three weeks to play for the World XV in a three-Test series against the All Blacks. They came from everywhere—France, England, Scotland, South Africa, Canada, Japan, Argentina, Western Samoa. For Horan and Little to be syphoned out of such a deep pool of talent was clearly an indication of their lofty standing in the code.

The tour was also an interesting personal experience. Never before had either of them been tossed into such a cultural melting pot, with so many different languages and rugby ideals. It made for some absorbing on-field discussions. 'We didn't have names for the backline moves—we had numbers—one to five', Horan recalls. 'It was the only way everybody could understand.' The All Blacks won the series 2–1, but Horan earned world-wide acclaim, cementing with three stunning performances his reputation as the best midfielder in international rugby.

The Horan stocks would soar to a new high three weeks later when Queensland met New South Wales in the first interstate match at Waratah Rugby Park. The Reds won a memorable encounter 23–18 to clinch the Super Six championship, but after the game, all the talk was about Horan. He had produced several startling pieces of work, none more spectacular than his try in the 35th minute when he gave three of the fastest players in Australian rugby—Paul Carozza, Darren Junee and Peter Jorgensen—a sizeable start over 50m and beat them all to the ball.

'Tim has got to be one of the best, if not the best player going around in the world today,' NSW and Australian skipper Nick Farr-Jones trumpeted in *The Sydney Morning Herald* the following day. 'Who is the best is very difficult to judge, as different players play different positions. But as far as broken-play running, as far as being a structured player, as far as defence is concerned, Tim is right up there with the best.'

It was praise which hardly endeared the Australian skipper to one David Ian Campese, who just five months before stood alone, unchallenged on the world rugby throne. But who was going to argue with Farr-Jones now? Certainly not Little. 'Ever since we arrived on the Test scene together, Tim and I had been lumped together in double-barrelled dispatches. But in 1992, it got to the stage where I was embarrassed to be mentioned in the same sentence. His form was freakish. He'd not only pull off amazing things, but he'd manage to do it at the crucial stage of a game.'

Horan is very much a reluctant hero: 'I guess football is like anything else. When your confidence is up, things seem to go your way.'

On the field, maybe, but away from rugby even the inimitable Horan was prone to the odd mistake. Like the night he was sitting at home watching television. It was early May, the Scots arrival in Australia just a few weeks away. The phone rang.

'Hello Tim! Bill Lothian from the *Evening Post* in Edinburgh.'

'Hello Bill.' *Bill Lothian, my fat uncle.* He could recognise that voice anywhere. It was David Sole, the Scottish captain, with whom Horan had become quite chummy during their three weeks together in New Zealand for the World XV matches. But Horan was more than happy to play the game.

'What can I do for you, *Bill?*'

'I'm writing a preview of Scotland's tour of Australia, and I'd like to ask you a couple of questions about the Scottish team. First of all, how do you rate Sean Lineen and Scott Hastings as a centre pairing?'

Horan's mind was ticking over. *This was going to be fun.*

'I reckon they've got to be the worst centres in the world. Why Scotland can't come up with somebody better than those two mugs is beyond me. How many people play the game over the there—100,150? They're absolutely useless. They couldn't run through a wet paper bag.'

On the other end of the phone, stunned silence. 'Ohhh . . . Umm . . . OK, what about the rest of the Scottish team, what do you see as the strengths and weaknesses?'

*Keep it going, you're well ahead.*

'There's no strengths—just weaknesses. Particularly up in the front row where they've got that cream-puff captain David Sole . . .'

The conversation went on for a couple more minutes, with Horan delivering every derogatory remark he could think of. Finally, it seemed time to come clean: 'Come-on Soley, it's you isn't it?'

'No. It's Bill Lothian from the *Evening Post* in Edinburgh.'

Horan suddenly felt sick in the stomach. *What had he said? And how were the comments going to look in the Scottish press: 'Scottish skipper a cream puff, claims Aussie upstart'. This is the sort of thing Campo says from time to time!*

There was some hasty retracting to be done. 'Listen Bill, I hope you don't think I was serious when I said . . .'

It took a bit of explaining, but the damage was finally rectified.

However nauseous Horan might have felt after talking to Scottish journalists, it was well short of how poorly Little felt soon after the Wallabies assembled in Sydney for the first Scottish Test.

The players had been in camp no more than three hours when Little complained of a sore throat. The following morning, he was on a plane back to Brisbane, with blood tests confirming what the Australian team doctor had suspected—Little had glandular fever. The medical forecast was anything but bright. Depending on how entrenched the virus was in his system, Little would be sidelined for at least two months—long enough to miss the bulk of the All Black series. Another small, pesty pothole in Little's journey to success. Not enough to run him off the road, but deep enough to impede his progress.

Australia comfortably accounted for Scotland, winning the first Test 27–12 in Sydney before blitzing the World Cup semi-finalists 37–13 in Brisbane a week later. The five-try romp at Ballymore featured a try which stands alone in Bob Dwyer's mind as the most outstanding thing he has ever seen Horan do on a rugby field.

Horan took a pass from Lynagh some 35m out, weighed up his options then bolted, running around Scottish flyer Iwan Tukalo to score in the corner. 'There's no way a centre should be able to beat a quick winger in that situation, but Horan was prepared to back himself. He looked at Tukalo as if to say: I've got 40, you've got 40—come on mate, we'll see how we go! He beat him by a country mile. It was an awesome display of speed and vision. He knew exactly the line he had to run to stay out of reach.'

While Horan was working miracles at Ballymore, Pat Little was five kilometres away, weaving her own homespun magic in the kitchen of her son's house. Whether it was tender loving care or the accumulative effect of the 15 different magical cures Pat had sourced and assembled on the dining room table, nobody will ever know. But whatever it was, it worked like a charm. Just three and a half weeks after being diagnosed for glandular fever, Little was cleared to play in the first Test against the All Blacks.

The arrival of the Kiwis was met with great excitement and anticipation by the ever-expanding Australian rugby public. The series would be the first played under the controversial new laws designed to open the game up and make it a more appealing spectacle. Tries would now be worth five points instead of four, but even more significant were the changes to the ruck and maul laws. To discourage teams from engaging in slow, static forward exchanges, the onus was now on teams to get the ball out quickly—'use it or lose it' as the edict became known.

There had also been a significant changing of the guard in the All Black camp, with the public, the media and even the politicians, calling for heads to roll after the side's 'embarrassing' third-place finish in the World Cup. And roll the heads did. Those of coaches Alex 'Grizz' Wyllie and John Hart, followed by skipper Gary Whetton. Former Test fullback Laurie Mains was appointed coach, while hooker Sean Fitzpatrick took over the reins as captain. If the 1991 World Cup proved one thing, it was that the Kiwi public wouldn't tolerate a losing All Black side.

Little was further delighted to be back in the Test arena when he saw Va'aiga Tuigamala's name in the Kiwi line-up for the first Test in Sydney. Little had a small score to settle with Tuigamala which dated back to August 1989—the day Tim made his Test debut at Eden Park. Little that afternoon had played in the curtain-raiser for the Australian Under 21s against New Zealand Under 21s. The home side gave the young Wallabies a thrashing, with 'Inga the Winger' scoring three tries—a match statistic which didn't sit too well with Little, who had marked Tuigamala. Not once did the big

Samoan break through Little's defence, but the record books rarely delve into that sort of detail.

At the post-match function, as the two teams sat down for a meal, the affable Samoan parked himself in the middle of a group of Australian opponents—immediately opposite Little.

'Gidday. Howzit going?' Inga smiled, happy to strike up a conversation as he attacked a monstrous plate of ham and salad.

'Yeah not too bad,' Little replied.

*Chomp Chomp Chomp.* 'D'jou play today?' *Chomp.*

'Yeah.'

'Whereabouts?' *Chomp Chomp.*

'On the wing.'

*Chomp.* 'Oh yeah?' *Chomp.* 'Which wing?' *Chomp Chomp.*

'Actually I marked you.'

'Oh yeah?' *Chomp.* 'I didn't see you.' *Chomp Chomp Chomp.*

Mark Catchpole, the Australian Under 21 scrumhalf that afternoon, was listening in, and almost fell off his chair laughing. 'Gee Jas, heck of an impact you made—betcha he's dreading the next time he comes up against you.'

Little couldn't afford to allocate Tuigamala too much extra attention, but if the opportunity arose, he'd sink the shoulder in a tackle, just that little bit more fiercely than normal.

The series lived up to every expectation. After a colossal struggle in the first Test in Sydney, Australia emerged triumphant by the narrowest of margins—16–15. Grant Fox had a chance to snatch victory for New Zealand, but his 45m penalty goal attempt, five minutes from fulltime, drifted precariously across the face of goal. Not more than a metre between jubilation and despair. It was going to be *that* type of series.

To Brisbane, where dreams would come true, or nightmares would linger. Ballymore hadn't been a fertile pasture for Wallaby teams over the years. Ever since the infamous loss to Tonga in 1973, there had been a perception that the ground was not the luckiest venue in the country for critical Test matches. Rightly or wrongly, it was supported by the fact Australia had not beaten the All Blacks in the 11 encounters there since 1932. It was all about to change.

With Australia clinging to a 19–17 lead, and mere seconds remaining on the clock, Fox, so often the Kiwi saviour, launched an almighty field goal attempt from 40m out, directly in front. Little remembers seeing the whites of Fox's eyes, as the white Gilbert ball sailed up and up and up. Fox just knew the kick was going over. But as the ball neared the posts, it began to slowly drift left, almost as if blown off course by 5000 desperate Australian fans, exhaling in unison from the McLean Grandstand. No Australian player knows how, but the kick slid past the left hand upright, a clear 10m above the crossbar. Fox's head dropped, a look of resignation on his face. It was fulltime. Australia had won the Bledisloe Cup. Yes, it definitely *was* that type of series.

Sadly, the magnificence of the Wallabies' victory that afternoon was almost overshadowed by an on-field incident which over the ensuing week would incite a sports crazed nation.

It came just before halftime, as Wallaby winger Paul Carozza was sliding over in the XXXX Hill corner for his second try. The ball had already been grounded, but that seemed immaterial to All Black prop Richard Loe, who cocked his elbow and plunged, smearing Carozza's nose all over his boyish face.

French referee Patrick Robin was not in a position to see the incident, but some 8000 people on XXXX Hill were. And for the benefit of anybody who might have missed it, the incident was replayed on the giant screen which had been temporarily installed at the ground.

After the game, the Australian management, having thoroughly reviewed the incident for themselves, were totally outraged. Coach Bob Dwyer called on the New Zealand Rugby Union to take harsh action against Loe, who had narrowly avoided being cited for an alleged incident in the first Test which had left Wallaby flanker Sam Scott-Young requiring 15 stitches in a head gash.

But four days later, the NZRU cleared Loe of the charge, with chief executive George Very carefully explaining the incident: 'Loe had slid on his knees and pinned Carozza on his back in an endeavour to smother the ball and prevent it from being grounded.'

The decision brought an outcry, not just from the Australian media and public, but also from across the Tasman. Hundreds of New Zealanders telephoned the Queensland and Australian Rugby Union offices, dozens more wrote letters, apologising for their country's decision not to take action against Loe.

Former Australian coach, Alan Jones, writing in *The Australian,* had this to say: 'Those calling the shots in New Zealand rugby have betrayed a proud All Black tradition of fairness in defeat with their shameful failure to act over the (Loe) affair. It is a tragedy for New Zealand rugby in more ways than one. The most obvious concern is that New Zealanders are among the most informed rugby people in the world. They know their rugby. And in the business houses and on the dairy farms there will be rank embarrassment that New Zealand rugby and rugby adminstration can sink so low.'

For his part in the furore, Carozza, the Player of the Series, holds no grudges. He spoke to Loe just once, after the Third Test in Sydney a week later. 'He came up and whacked me in the shoulder, and said something like: "You're OK aren't you? The nose doesn't look too bad". I guess it was a front-rower's way of apologising,' Carozza says. 'The whole thing was pretty unnecessary, but I remember thinking at the time, I'd much prefer to have a flat nose and a Bledisloe Cup, than a good nose and no Cup!'

Horan looks at the incident a little more globally: 'If nothing else, it highlighted the inadequacies of rugby's judicial system. I don't think the New Zealand Rugby Union was right in dismissing the charge—the indiscretion was there for the whole world to see. But the system is also at fault. I don't think New Zealand rugby officials should be the ones passing judgement. It's a bit like asking a mother to sentence her child to jail. Natural instincts take over. There should be an independent authority set up to deal with instances of foul play which go undetected by the referee.'

It took a while, but the controversy gradually subsided. New Zealand went on to win the Third Test 26–23, in the process avoiding a whitewash which would have had the intransigent New Zealand public once again baying for the coach's blood. Not that such drastic action was necessary. At the end of the series, both teams had scored 58 points, both had crossed for six tries. But Australia, perhaps adapting a little faster to the new laws, had what really counted—the Bledisloe Cup.

Dublin wasn't a fluke after all. The Wallabies were worthy world champions.

Or were they?

Very few rugby people in South Africa seemed to think so. The Wallaby players were still splashing around in the Twickenham bathtubs when the first declaration of impending Springbok supremacy was made.

South Africa's revered flyhalf Naas Botha, after watching the Cup final from the grandstands at Twickenham, had the temerity to suggest he could assemble an informal, half-strength team from the South African players in the stadium, and give any of the semi-finalists 'a hell of a run' for their money. Nine months further down the track, the self-assurance in the Republic hadn't seemed to have waned. As the Australian team arrived at the Jan Smuts Airport in Johannesburg in early August to prepare for their historic one-off Test against the Springboks, there was an up-front confidence blended into the locals' hearty welcome. Yes, of course, they were absolutely delighted to have the Australian Wallabies back in the country after such a prolonged period of sporting isolation, but . . . *Do you really think you can call yourselves world champions until you've beaten the Sprinkgboks?*

The Australian players had it rammed down their throats wherever they went—the more polite middle aged lady version: 'You might have beaten England and New Zealand, but you won't beat our boys', right down to the boorish male youth: 'Hey Wallabies, Naas will kick your arse!'.

'Nobody in the team could believe the arrogance of the South African supporters,' Little says. 'Everybody thought New Zealand fans were parochial, but Auckland was a day at the beach compared to Pretoria.'

Unperturbed, the Wallabies went about their preparation with the usual urgency and purpose, squeezing in every bit of training they could, between the myriad of official team functions, welcomings and civic receptions. The tone of the tour had been set at Jan Smuts Airport, where 23 International Rugby Board officials, all wearing national blazers, had assembled to greet the Wallabies. It had been 22 years since an Australian team last set foot in the Republic—given that New Zealand were touring simultaneously, South Africa's rugby famine had suddenly become a feast. The time was right for pomp and ceremony.

And what highbrow ceremony it was. On August 11, four days after they'd arrived, the Wallabies found themselves in a room with the All Blacks, the Springboks, two dozen scantily dressed Can-Can girls, and a congregation of the country's most influential political figures—President F.W. de Klerk,

Inkatha Freedom Party leader Mangosuthu Buthelezi, and African National Congress heavyweight Steve Tshwete, to name but a few. The occasion would have commanded an entry in the trip diary of even the laziest rugby tourist, no matter where it was held. But given that the illustrious gathering took place 600m underground, in a disused mine at Gold Reef City near Johannesburg, there was cause for extra detail in the notation.

If the fervid fans and the gold-mine rendezvous with political leaders wasn't enough to convince the Wallaby players that this trip was not 'just another rugby tour', then the constant companionship of armed policemen certainly was. In the morning, when the squad assembled in the hotel foyer for training, it was not uncommon to see their secret police pals sliding around on skateboards underneath the team bus, searching the underbelly for bombs. There had been strong assurances from South African embassy officials, prior to the team's departure from Sydney, that the players would not be placed in any danger during their two weeks in the Republic. The bomb searches, the players suspected, were probably nothing more than routine precaution in such an unstable political environment, but they put the players on edge nonetheless.

The bomb searches were just one form of reminder as to where they were—there were plenty of others. Little remembers one afternoon being escorted to the gym by one of the policemen, who was carrying a small but well-stocked rucksack. Jason just assumed it was filled with the usual: shoes, shorts, T-shirt, and towel.

'Are you going to join in,' he asked in polite conversation.

'No, I better not,' came the response.

'Well why did you bring your gear?'

'I didn't. It's not for the gym.' The policeman emptied the contents of the bag: sub-machine gun, grenades, tear gas, riot baton.

'OK, you're the boss. Just tell me when you'd like to go back to the hotel—I'm not going to argue,' Little quipped.

The final trepidation the Australians had centred on their opposition. On any other tour of a major rugby playing country, the Wallabies knew exactly what to expect when they ran onto the field: hard, combative driving play from the All Blacks, flamboyant improvisation from the French, conservative percentage rugby from the English . . . but the Springboks? How would they play the game? They had just three preliminary provincial matches to get a handle on the South African style and standard.

The first match, against lowly Western Transvaal at Potchefstroom, two hours south of Pretoria, didn't unveil any monumental mysteries about Springbok rugby, as the Wallabies outclassed the second division side 46–13. But what the outing did provide was an insight into the problems associated with playing at altitude, given a shortage of time to acclimatise. Prop Matt Ryan crystallised the thoughts of most players when he said to Tim Gavin just before the resumption of play in the second half: 'Timmy can you help me get this plastic bag off my head so I can breathe?'

'It was bloody awful,' Ryan recalls. 'Your legs feel really heavy, and your lungs burn.'

Four days later, the Australians had to contend with a different 'heaviness' as they tackled the Northern Transvaal 'Blue Bulls', one of the proudest and arguably the best performed provincial teams in the land. It was of little relevance, given the extended period of isolation, but Australia had never beaten the Bulls, and when they ran on to Loftus Versfeld they had some appreciation as to why. The Bulls forwards per man were, on average, 6kg (almost a stone) heavier than their Australian counterparts. Irrespective of how skilful the locals were, the Wallabies sensed a struggle.

And that's what they got. There are mornings after rugby matches when players wake up thinking: 'What the hell do

I play this game for?' August 14 would be one of those mornings. Australia had won the game 24–17, but the locals put up an awesome fight. Had their goal kickers landed a few more of the eight penalty attempts they missed, the result may well have been different. It was good to win, even better to silence the obnoxious throng who had gathered to watch the match, but the Australians now had no illusions as to the enormity of the challenge they faced in their one-off Test against the Boks.

It was a mental picture which developed further the following day, when the Australians were guests at Ellis Park for the Test between South African and New Zealand in Johannesburg. The atmosphere was war-like, even before the outlawed Afrikaner anthem 'Die Stem' had been blasted across the public address system. The Australian players were not exactly well versed in South African tradition, but it did seem strange to be breaking an agreement not to play the national anthem during a minute's silence for victims of political violence. Horan recalls sitting behind the tryline with the bulk of the Wallabies, squirming uncomfortably in his seat at the irreverence of the gesture. New Zealand won the Test 26–23, but two late tries by Danie Gerber had given the Springboks hope, and the Australians a sample of how much noise the local fans make the moment they sniff a scent of victory.

The flight to Port Elizabeth the following day came as welcome relief for the Australian camp, who for 10 days had been holed up in the Afrikaner heartland of Pretoria. Down on the coast they found the people more convivial, and the scenery eye-catching.

Horan also remembers being stunned and saddened by the down-trodden nature and appearance of the black people they encountered around their first 'home base'.

'You could tell by looking at them they'd had very hard lives,' he says. 'And their jobs were always so menial. I'll never forget the two guys at Loftus Versfeld (the stadium in

Pretoria)—they were working their way around this giant stadium, cleaning 40,000 individual seats. I felt so sorry for them. When I went across to give one of them my cap, he shied away. It looked like he thought I was going to hit him. But to see his face light up when I handed him the cap was worth a million dollars. He put it on wearing the biggest smile I'd ever seen.'

A couple of days after their arrival in Port Elizabeth, the Wallabies would be greeted by not one, but a sea of smiling black faces. Australian team manager John Breen had asked for volunteers to attend a coaching clinic in a black township outside the city, and there was no shortage of takers. Two years on, the afternoon is still remembered as one of the most uplifting and rewarding ever spent on any tour. 'The kids were just fantastic,' Horan says. 'I'm sure they had no idea who we were—they just knew we had these silky bright tracksuits that felt nice to touch. But they were so enthusiastic and skilful. There was one kid Michael Lynagh had in his group—he must have been 15 or 16. He kicked seven or eight goals from the sideline in a row—barefooted. Heaven help the sporting world if South Africa ever manage to develop all their talent. There was probably a world class rugby team, and a world class cricket team in the making, right there in that single township.'

Horan neglects to mention that his own coaching skills that afternoon were the source of much ridicule as the jubilant Australian party made their way back into Port Elizabeth on the bus. Having run out of drills for his kids to practise, the apprentice coaching guru had sent them on a 3km run around the Dan Qeqe Stadium, just to fill in the final 20 minutes. 'Did you think they were Kenyans?' Little sniped from his usual seat in the middle of the bus.

Some 12 hours later, the mood back in Port Elizabeth was far more serious. As the Wallabies prepared for their final preliminary match against Eastern Province, they did so not knowing if Saturday's Test would go ahead. The decision by Dr Louis Luyt, the SARFU President to play the Afrikaner national anthem at the Test in Johannesburg had so incensed ANC leaders, they were now threatening to withdraw their support for the tour.

It took several days of delicate negotiation, commencing with a crisis meeting between Farr-Jones, Dwyer, and Australian Rugby Union officials at 2am, before the situation was retrieved. 'We really thought we were on the plane home,' winger Paul Carozza says. 'Bags were packed, players were ringing their wives and girlfriends, telling them to expect the team home in a couple of days.'

Horan always had great personal respect for Farr-Jones, both as a player and as a person. But his appreciation of the ever-diplomatic Australian captain heightened during those tumultuous few days in the republic. 'I'm sure there were a lot of other people who contributed to solving the problems but I really admired Nick for the role he played. It showed him to be the complete leader, even well away from a rugby field.'

Political turmoil behind them, and a third successive victory under their belts—this time over first division Eastern Province—the Wallabies flew across to Cape Town. The preliminaries were at last over. They could focus now on the real reason they were in the country—to beat the Springboks.

As much as the Australians had loathed the incessant chant of *'Wait 'til the Boks get to you . . . you're not world champions until you beat the Boks'*, the boorish local supporters did have a point—South Africa at the time *was* the only International Rugby Board country the Wallabies hadn't hurdled in their march to World Cup glory. Sitting in the dressing shed at Newlands Stadium, waiting to run out onto a boggy pitch, into a cauldron of 50,000 screaming South Africans, there was a nervousness which neither Horan nor Little could remember before.

'There seemed to be so much to lose,' Little recalls. 'If we'd gone down to the Springboks, everything we'd achieved in the past 12 months would have quickly unravelled. We simply couldn't afford to let it happen.'

Why Horan was there to take the kick, he cannot remember. Call it good luck, call it good management, it doesn't matter. He was there all the same, deep in Australian territory, a wall of South African defenders in front of him. There wasn't exactly time for a head count, but at first glance, it looked like most of the green jerseys were being worn by forwards—quite a bit bigger, but quite a bit slower than he was. He would soon see. He ran up and around and through and over and past the lot of them, his legs pumping so hard there was Newlands mud being sprayed in the direction of would-be defenders.

When confronted by a smaller but more mobile secondary wall, Horan put boot to ball, hoping at worst to pin the Boks on their own muddy tryline. But it was better than that. As Springbok veteran Danie Gerber fielded the kick, Horan in the one adroit movement tackled the monstrous midfielder and dispossessed him of the ball, a mere five metres from the line. Out of the corner of his right eye Horan could see him coming . . . Campese . . . standing out like a beacon in the only remaining unmuddied gold jersey. Horan's desperate low level pass hit the winger on the chest, a split second before Campese fell across the line for his 50th Test try. A magical moment shared by the same two who had created similar havoc for the All Blacks in Dublin. 'You still owe me a few,' Campese said, after Horan had picked himself up and rushed over to offer congratulations.

Seventy-four minutes had gone. Australia were ahead 19–3. The Wallabies knew it, so did the Springboks, and so too did the crowd. The result had been decided. That moments later Paul Carozza would fly down the touchline—his new-look flat nose nonetheless aerodynamic—to score his second try of the game, was totally immaterial. The Test match, and the title of world champions, rightfully belonged with the Wallabies. If not in 1991, in the August of 1992, they were clearly the best team in world rugby.

After a brief but boisterous dressing room celebration, the Wallabies made their way up to the post-match function, happy for the first time on tour to talk rugby with the rabid local supporters. Australia, the supposed imposters, had just whipped the Springboks—the aspirants to the crown—by the record margin of 26–3. What could they possibly say now? The silence would be golden.

It was, but not for very long. An hour later, as the Wallabies were climbing aboard the bus to go back to the team hotel, there was one parting plaintive cry from an overweight male supporter, wearing a green Springbok cap: 'You might have beaten the Springboks, but you wouldn't have beaten Transvaal'.

'Quick, where's the airport?' Little thought to himself. 'Let's get the hell out of here.'

'LEAGUE TARGET RUGBY TWINS'

What a surprise! There it was again.

After every major tour, it seemed to be exactly the same . . . newspaper headlines foreshadowing the defection of Horan and Little.

'Now? What about now? Are you going to switch now?' the journalists would ask, in anticipation of being able to write the story they'd been waiting on for a good four seasons.

Once again, the league scouts would be disappointed, although their failure was related in no way to lack of effort. Within three months of returning from South Africa, Horan fielded two serious league offers, and phone calls from numerous other clubs, which he immediately declined. Katrina wanted to put a new message on their answering machine:

*'Hi, you've reached the home of Tim, Katrina and Lucy Horan. We're not home right now but please leave a message after the beep. Oh . . . and by the way . . . Tim's quite happy with rugby union at the moment! Thanks for calling.'* 'The phone calls just didn't seem to stop,' Katrina says.

Manly and North Sydney were the two serious pursuers. Manly coach Graham Lowe was put in touch with Horan by his close friend, Kevin Roberts, the chief executive of Lion Nathan, the New Zealand based company which owned Castlemaine Perkins. The deal was attractive—a package of $200,000 a season for three years, plus a car. The seriousness with which Horan considered joining Manly is best illustrated by the extensive inquiries he made about working in Sydney for Tooheys, Castlemaine's sister brewery. Yes, it was possible, Roberts told him. But Roberts was nonetheless keen for Horan to stay with rugby, irrespective of his strong allegiance to the All Blacks.

Horan agonised over the Manly offer for weeks, sitting down with Katrina and drawing up a list of pros and cons. Ultimately, lifestyle considerations won—but only on a countback.

'I was very close to signing,' Horan says. 'I guess in the end, I didn't want to be owned by anybody—to be told what to do all the time. Rugby league would have been such a total commitment. In many respects rugby union is a bit the same, but at least every now and then, there's a break. You can have a weekend off, or go back to club football, and just enjoy running around with your mates without the pressure of being watched by 20,000 people. From a family viewpoint it was also better we stayed in Brisbane. Lucy wasn't even one at that stage, so it would have been a huge upheaval, selling our house, moving to Sydney and starting again.'

Having declined the Manly offer for those very reasons, he could hardly about-face a couple of months later and join Norths for much the same money. Or could he? It was almost as if he was being given a second bite at the cherry—a rare chance to correct what was wrong—to banish any regrets he might have had in turning down the Sea Eagles. But he still wasn't 100 percent sure. He had been very impressed with the Norths officials who, unlike so many of the previous talent scouts, seemed genuinely prepared to listen and find out what *he* wanted. The club had even gone to the trouble of printing out their proposed first grade side for the 1993 season. They showed him the impressive line-up of names. Beside No 3: Tim Horan.

Another four or five days of agonising followed, but once again, lifestyle narrowly won out. He rang Norths and delivered his verdict, genuinely disappointed that he hadn't been able to give them the decision they'd wanted.

'It might sound strange but by the end of 1992, rugby league didn't hold the fascination it once did,' Horan says. 'Early on in my career, I was very keen to prove myself, even to the rugby league public. But after we'd won the World Cup, there was far greater acceptance of rugby. Union players were no longer the second class citizens. People might have still wondered when you were going to give league a go, but they respected you as a rugby player in the meantime.'

It had been a long year—an interminably long year—and still it wasn't over. Just eight weeks after returning from South Africa, the Wallabies were off again, back to Ireland and Wales, the two places the players enjoyed most and least during their four-week World Cup campaign.

They probably would have preferred to save Dublin until last—that way, they would have something to look forward to for most of the trip. But Dublin was first, Swansea last. The murky grey seaside city didn't hold quite the same fascination. But they would get by. 'There should even be different movies screening at cinemas by now,' Little thought hopefully.

Dublin was every bit as good as they remembered, even better for some, like No 8 Tim Gavin who in 1991 had visited as a frustrated spectator, his left knee still weak from the reconstructive surgery he'd undergone a month before. But now Gavin was back in the full swing of touring. As thousands of Irish teenagers loitered outside the front door of the Westbury Hotel, trying to get a glimpse of their idols from rock group Metallica (the heavy metal band were also staying in house), Gavin—long brown wig on his head—dangled out his fifth floor window, guitar in one hand, waving with the other. The crowd went wild.

It was good to be back in town.

This time round, the tour took in all the sights of Ireland, even a brief foray into war torn Northern Ireland. There was a distinct uneasiness among the players when two heavily armed guards climbed aboard the bus at the checkpoint on the fringe of Belfast. But there was no cause for concern.

'Hello boys, would you mind signing these for us?', asked one, some lethal looking weapon slung over his shoulder. The two footballs went through the hands quicker than the legendary Ella brothers could ever have imagined.

When the Wallabies finally returned to the sanctity of Dublin, to prepare for the Test against Ireland, most were overcome with that strange feeling of deja vu. The closer they got to the Test match, the harder it was to block out memories of October 1991—the deafening roar of the crowd as Irish flanker Gordon Hamilton galloped away for the try which almost cost Australia so dearly. As he boarded the bus for Lansdowne Road, a cold shiver ran through Jason Little's body. 'I often think about that quarter-final,' he admits. 'I wonder just how different the whole game in Australia would be now if Noddy (Lynagh) didn't score that try. There would have been no All Black semi-final, no World Cup victory, no ticker-tape parade. Nothing. The All Blacks probably would have gone on to win, and we'd have been back where we were five years ago.'

Much to the relief of the Australian party, there would be no close call in 1992. Little and Horan both helped themselves to tries as the Wallabies romped away to a comfortable 40–19 victory. In the pubs around Dublin that night, the hospitality was as hearty as it had been 12 months before: 'I tort we had you Aussies. Can I buy you a pint of Guinness . . . '

The little Irishman at the baggage check-in at Dublin Airport nodded knowingly: 'Swansea? Ah, I know it well. I spent a week there one afternoon.'

With the weather cold and wet, there was little else for the players to do in the Welsh harbourside city but go back to the movie theatres they'd frequented during the World Cup, when they'd stayed at the same Holiday Inn hotel.

There was at least one new attraction—the go-karts. In between training sessions and games, frustrated Formula 1 drivers would spend hours on end weaving the machines around a tight track, which was just a short walk from the hotel. Their generous Welsh hosts even put up a trophy for the 'Drivers Championship', which was duly won by Fangio Horan. The victor climbed upon a wooden box, held the trophy aloft, and sprayed his fellow drivers with a can of Coke. Another 'ugly Australian' award in the bag.

On the field, things were running a little less smoothly. Adding to the pressure of midweek losses to Llanelli and Swansea was the squad's mountainous injury toll. Skipper Michael Lynagh was now being called Neale Fraser (in honour of the non-playing Davis Cup tennis captain), after badly dislocating his shoulder in Dublin. Loosehead props Tony Daly and Cameron Lillicrap had both flown home with injuries, as had centre Anthony Herbert. (All three were said to be victims of the jinxed bus seat—one from the back on the right hand side. When Daly was injured, Lillicrap assumed the position. When he was injured, Herbert moved in. When Herbert was injured the seat was ruled off limits for the rest of the trip.)

Of the players still in the country, lineout ace John Eales had his left arm in a sling, having landed awkwardly on his shoulder in the game against Llanelli, and three or four others, including wingers Campese and Carozza, were sitting out training sessions, nursing niggling injury concerns.

For the first time since New Zealand in 1990, Bob Dwyer was clearly feeling the strain. After the loss to Swansea, he shut in a room the playing XV, plus an unfortunate reserve who'd run on in the second half, and gave them a verbal shellacking. It came just two weeks after a similar tirade after the midweek side had lost unexpectedly to Munster in Ireland. But this time, it was even more vicious, according to the five or so players who'd been part of the Munster Massacre, and were now listening in from Greg Craig's physio room next door. 'We didn't have to be in the next room—we could have heard him (Bob) from the next hotel,' hooker David Nucifora says. 'He was just going off.'

A couple of days later, the players heard back from Australia that the national coach had rated their tour performances with A's, B's and C's in a Sydney newspaper. Dwyer had played the rating game with Sydney journalist Terry Smith, who was covering the tour for a group of Murdoch newspapers. It was a potentially dangerous and divisive exercise.

For the likes of Horan and Little, it mattered not. As Horan says: 'I didn't mind, I got my first A since Phys Ed in grade five!' But what was the exercise going to do for the confidence of Queenslanders Paul Kahl and Matt Ryan, both of whom got Cs on their report card?

'It definitely wasn't the smartest thing Bob has ever done,' Little says. 'He tried to justify it to the players by saying he was merely trying to motivate people through the media, but I think if he had his time over, he would have refrained. The players know themselves how they're playing without that sort of public scrutiny.'

The full irony of the situation came some seven days later, when Kahl was named in the Test side, in place of the injured Lynagh. Earlier, there had been speculation that Horan would be moved to flyhalf, but the tour selectors deemed it unwise to break up the established centre combination.

Horan had pushed hard for Kahl's inclusion. He had played regularly with the gifted left-footed pivot at state level and was confident he'd make a Test debut which belied his C class rating. He was right. Kahl gave a polished display as the Wallabies scored a 23–6 victory over a determined but out-classed Welsh side.

Oddly, of the eight Tests Horan played in 1992, he cannot remember being more determined than he was when he ran on against Wales. 'We all were,' he says. 'The eye gouging and biting and ball grabbing which had gone on in some of the lead-up games had really irked a lot of the players. To lose would have been totally unbearable.'

It seemed like no time at all before the players were back at Ballymore, in a giant marquee surrounded by caged African animals, helping to launch the 1993 season. 'They're Back' screamed the promotional posters, dangling from the elaborate ceiling. Well not quite yet, but they would be soon—for the first time in 22 years. The Springboks were heading back to Australia for another shot at the title—a three-round main event which would surely prove a knock-out with the Australian sporting public, and ensure rugby continued its roll-on through the 90s.

When the Springbok party landed in Perth in early July, they did so bearing a little more humility than when they first returned to the international rugby arena. Not that the South African players ever shared the arrogance of their fans. But they had been quickly brought to earth by the giant strides of progress the rugby world had made in their absence. South Africa's Test record since their readmission to world sport 12 months before had been anything but impressive, with away losses to France and England, and a further loss and a draw with the French on home soil. Clearly, it was not a time for thumping chests.

The Springboks impressed early, scoring a remarkable 239 points in their first three matches, albeit against sub-standard opposition. The momentum was checked when they lost, by a mere point, to New South Wales. But they were entitled to go into the first Test at the Sydney Football Stadium with confidence, particularly in light of the Wallabies' 25–10 Bledisloe Cup loss to New Zealand in Dunedin a couple of weeks before.

It was the first rugby international played under lights in Australia. But the Wallabies' performance anything but mirrored the brilliance produced by the four giant light poles which make the ground such an identifiable inner-city landmark. The Australians, without injured stars Lynagh, Ofahengaue and Eales, were as awful as the Springboks were determined. The result, a well deserved 19–12 victory to South Africa.

There was no cause for alarm, but the Wallabies clearly had some work to do. And work they did. They trained and trained, harder than they ever had before, adjusting this, fine tuning that, scrapping something else altogether. Bob Dwyer led the way, examining the performance of his own side, and the opposition right down to the last microscopic detail. Little can never remember the Australian coach more thorough or methodical in his approach to a game. Down 1–0 in this series, and having already been belted by the Kiwis, a win was becoming pretty important.

'Oh no . . .'

Tim had heard Jason say it a thousand times. Whenever he sliced a ball on the golf course, out the words would come . . . 'Oh no.'

But this time the stakes were a lot higher than the $2 'skins' they played for on the golf course. They were 20 minutes into a Test match—a *crucial* Test match—and Little had just thrown a pass which gave South Africa a converted try, and a 10–3 lead.

As the Australians were huddled underneath the goal posts, being reminded by their skipper Phil Kearns to stay calm, not to panic—'we've got these guys' measure'—Horan was to one side, pulling faces at his best mate, making him feel even worse. 'What did you do that for you idiot?'

It hardly seemed the right time to be fooling around, 1–nil down in the series, 10–3 down in the the match, but Horan for some reason felt supremely confident. He just *knew* Australia were going to win. Even when he was being admonished by English referee Ed Morrison for clipping Springbok winger James Small across the ear—his first and only caution for foul play in 35 Tests—he couldn't resist sending a cheerio call to Channel 10 television commentator David Fordham, via the small microphone pinned to Morrison's chest. 'I just wanted to Test it out to make sure it was working.'

The Horan confidence proved to be well founded, but for once, it was Little who assumed the position on centre stage. With two stunning individual tries, one in each half, Little swayed the match, as Australia romped away to win 28–20. Had it not been for a remarkable Test debut by Fijian flanker Ilie Tabua, the 'Human Skewer', Little would surely have clinched man of the match honours. But he could feel justifiably proud of the standing ovation he received from the patrons in the McLean Grandstand as he left the field with a head gash, a couple of minutes from fulltime. The moment remains Little's fondest memory in rugby.

When Horan finally reached the sanctuary of the dressing shed, after fighting his way through the throng of fans on the field, he headed straight for his centre partner who by that stage was sitting on a bench, icing his forehead.

'Well done mate, three tries. Fantastic effort,' Horan said, extending a hand of congratulations.

'No . . . I only got two,' Little modestly corrected him.

'No. Three—two for us, and one for them.'

Horan always seemed to have the last word.

A week later in Sydney, the Wallabies clinched the series, defeating the South Africans 19–12 in another torrid, physical encounter. As the Sydney fans waved goodbye to the popular Springbok tourists, they also bid farewell to one Nicholas Campbell Farr-Jones who, for the second time, was making his last Test appearance. The World Cup skipper had hung up his boots in Cape Town 12 months before, but at Dwyer's request returned to the fray when his replacement, Peter Slattery, had been poleaxed by a Tongan forward in the first international fixture of the season. After all Farr-Jones had contributed and achieved in his 63-Test career, Tim and Jason were delighted to be able to assist in sending him out a winner.

'What are you doing Kearnsie?'

Australian team manager John Breen stood and watched in bewilderment as hooker Phil Kearns rummaged rudely through his bedroom, on the second floor of the Blackfoot Hotel in Calgary, Canada.

'I'm looking for it. It's got to be here somewhere,' Kearns said, pulling open drawers, lifting up sofa cushions and peeking under beds.

'What's got to be here somewhere?' Breen asked.

'The plot. We've lost the plot. I'm sure we had it with us when we were in the (United) States, we had it when we arrived in Canada, but now it's gone. We've lost it. We've lost the plot.'

It was the vice-captain's extravagant way of letting the team manager know not all was well in the Wallaby playing ranks.

And he wondered why. The squad had kicked off their 11-match tour of North America and France with three straight wins—the first in 40 degree heat, the second in snow, and the third, the Test scalp of World Cup quarter-finalists Canada. But the national coach was far from satisfied. When flanker Ilie Tabua turned up late for the bus at the start of training, the day after the 43–15 win over Canada, Dwyer gave the squad a dressing down not dissimilar in volume to the haranguings of Munster and Swansea. 'I've forgotten the exact words, but it wasn't pretty,' Little says.

The cause of Dwyer's annoyance was his belief that the team was not playing to its potential. Yes, Australia were winning, but not winning as well as they should be. Dwyer had always possessed a strong perfectionist streak, which in part explains why he had been so successful as a coach over the years. But in this particular instance, the players sensed he'd lost a little perspective, or, as Kearns so graphically illustrated, 'the plot'.

Horan and Little have never involved themselves in team politics, preferring instead to stand back and play the hand they're dealt. But on this occasion both felt quite strongly.

'I've got great admiration for Bob as a coach,' Horan says. 'He's very thorough and I think he's got a lot of good ideas. But every now and then, his people skills let him down. I can appreciate that coaches have to keep a distance between themselves and the players, but he went over the top in Canada and France. I felt particularly sorry for the young guys—Barry Lea, Ryan Constable, even Mark Catchpole—who were on their first Wallaby trip. Bob rarely spoke to them. On the few occasions he did, it was to criticise them. On your first Wallaby trip, you need encouragement more than anything else.'

If Dwyer was disgruntled before the side reached France, his mood and tolerance slipped a further couple of notches in Bordeaux, where the world champions lost the first of the two Tests 16–13. It was a match they should have, and would have won, had it not been for a catalogue of squandered opportunities. So perhaps Dwyer was right—perhaps they had been settling for good, instead of striving for better. In any case, it primed the Wallabies for revenge—a revenge identical to the one the French had exacted against Australia back in 1989.

The Test at the famed Parc des Princes in Paris would be Marty Roebuck's last. The perky little fullback had given the Wallabies outstanding service since arriving on the international scene in 1991. But now, aged 28, he felt it was time to hang up the boots. Australia had never beaten France in Paris. What a fairytale ending it would be, he thought to himself, if he could walk away from Test rugby a winner on one of the great grounds of the world.

The machinations were swirling around in Roebuck's head as he sat alone in the back of a cab, which was speeding across Paris under police escort, towards Parc des Princes. It was the eve of the Test. Roebuck, having been secretly handed the goalkicking duties for the game by skipper Lynagh, was anxious to get in some last minute practice, just to get the feel of the stadium.

Tomorrow afternoon, there would be 55,000 people in the ground, but now, late on Friday afternoon, there were just three—Roebuck and two gendarmes, who were happily retrieving balls from behind the posts, and kicking them back to the Australian fullback. At the completion of the brief practice session, the French policemen watched Roebuck run over to the far southern corner, and bury a 10 franc piece in the ground.

'Bon chance—for good luck,' Roebuck explained, as the trio headed for the gate.

An hour or so later, Roebuck was back at the hotel, lying on his bed waiting for dinner. He turned to his roommate,

Horan, who not for the first time in his life, had his face buried in a racing form guide, trying to find a winner. He told Horan about the coin, how he'd buried it for good luck, but his young sidekick seemed to take little notice. He was too engrossed in the form guide. Roebuck left him in peace. He knew how tough it was to pick a winner at home, let alone when the guide was in French.

There was just five minutes to go. The Wallabies, though under enormous pressure from the giant French pack, looked to have the game well and truly sewn up. But the home side was not going to give in without a fight. As Phil Kearns and the other seven jelly-legged Australian forwards prepared to pack their fourth consecutive five-metre scrum, they could hear the commotion behind them.

'Whaddya mean you've found it? You couldn't have.'

'Mate I have. Look. Here it is. You owe me a million francs.'

'I don't believe it. How'd you find it?'

They could only guess at the time, but it sounded like Roebuck and Horan. *What the HELL were they on about?*

In six minutes, after Australia's emphatic 24–3 victory had been confirmed, all would be revealed.

Roebuck had made the fundamental error of challenging Horan to a bet offering a large cash reward to the winner.

'This coin you've buried on the field, how much will you give me if I can find it?' Horan had asked his unsuspecting victim in the dressing shed, minutes before they took the field.

'Mate you won't find it.'

'You never know. How much?'

'A million francs.'

Perfect. Horan had a live one on the line. He slipped another 10 franc coin into the right pocket of his shorts, and ran out to do battle.

Horan waited patiently, and when the right moment arrived, he reeled him in, showing Roebuck the coin he'd been carrying in his pocket for 75 Test match minutes.

At fulltime, Roebuck could not be seen for dust. Avoiding television reporters trying to award him man of the match honours, the panic stricken fullback hared off down the other end of the ground, back to where he'd planted his good luck charm the day before.

Much to his relief, there it was, caked in mud.

As Horan has always maintained, it's serious business this Test match rugby.

# Chapter Twelve

## Little on Horan

*'The human brain starts working the moment you are born and never stops until you stand up to speak in public.'*

SIR GEORGE TESSEL

Having known Tim for more than a decade—as a rival, a teammate and a friend—I think I understand him better than most. So, to give an insight into the guy, and both his personalities, I thought it fitting to list 'The 10 Things You Might Not Know About Tim Horan'. I could tell of the time in 1994 when the Argentine daily, the *Buenos Aires Herald*, had Tim listed in the obituaries column. According to the newspaper, Tim had been killed in a car accident, not long after the Queensland tour to South America in March. A journalist on the paper had been contacted with all the details of the fatal crash, and tipped headlong into the trap, set up by persons unknown.

But with this list limited to 10 personal insights, I'll look for other subjects . . .

### 1. THE GAMBLER
Helmet (the nickname is derived from the size and the shape of his head) doesn't have a lot of vices in life, but gambling

is definitely one of them. It's his No 1 passion (after Katrina and Lucy of course). In fact, I reckon if he had to choose between rugby and gambling, he'd be back sitting in a chair studying the form guide, before his size 10 boots hit the bottom of the bin. He'll bet on anything—not just formalised events like the horses, dogs, trotters. Like on tour, when we get issued with our boarding passes at the airport: 'I'll bet you I'm further down the back of the plane than you', or 'I'll bet you I'm closer to the left wing than you'. In the hotel, he makes me nominate which of the elevators I think will arrive first. Eveything's got to be a game. I can imagine him in the hospital when Lucy was born: 'Come on Trine—nominate what you think the baby will be—you take boy, I'll take girl.'

Golf is no different. Whenever we play, there's got to be 25 bets in place before the first tee shot is struck—best front nine, best back nine, best total, longest drives, most pars, least balls lost. It takes us four hours to play 18 holes, and another six hours to work out all the wagers. And if I win, I almost have to fly Tony Daly, Phil Kearns and Ewen McKenzie up from Sydney to help me get the money out of him. Tim doesn't take losing on the golf course very lightly.

Michael Lynagh used to have great fun with Tim when he first arrived in the Wallaby squad. In the week before every Test on tour, Noddy would challenge Tim to nominate the Test line-up—the starting XV plus the six reserves. It was winner take all—the person with the most right got the money. It was always the same result: 'How'd you go Timmy?' 'Pretty well—I got 18.' 'Ah. That's not bad, but I got the lot right. Sorry. I guess I win again.' Not until the fourth or fifth tour did Tim realise that Noddy sat in on selection meetings and knew exactly what was going on!

Tim and I have spent quite a bit of time together at the races over the years. I'm not a mad keen punter, but I really enjoy a day at the track all the same. I might have five bets in the afternoon. Tim will have 500—at least one on every race in every state. When Brisbane's finished, it's Melbourne and Sydney. When they're over, he starts flicking through the guide to find Adelaide, or Perth or Muswellbrook or Moe—wherever they're going around. The funny thing is he normally finishes ahead, except for this one afternoon at Eagle Farm. He'd had an absolute shocker. He wanted to back the favourite in the last race, but he had run out of money, so I foolishly agreed to lend him $100—providing he put it on each-way. When he came back from the tote, I looked at the ticket—sure enough, he'd put it on the nose (win only). 'I thought I told you to back it each way,' I told him. As usual he had an answer: 'Mate, if it wins we go out, if it loses, we still go out. That's each way.' As luck would have it, the horse won. Everybody was happy.

## 2. THE LARRIKIN

On tour, I might have a mortgage on the 'Jason Little Award' for saying stupid things, but Tim definitely dominates the ugly Australian. Every team happy hour we have, there's always a plethora of allegations against Tim—and sadly, all of them are true. I remember on the Queensland tour of Japan in 1991, John Brass, who was manager at the time, gave the team a long talk about propriety. It was the first tour to Japan in decades, and he stressed how important it was for the behaviour to be exemplary. The next morning he walked out of the team hotel to see Horan being chased up the street on a stolen pushbike!

There was another occasion on the Wallaby tour of Ireland in 1992. About eight of us were playing golf in Dublin. The members had been good enough to lend us their clubs. On about the 14th hole Tim was mucking around with the putter, swinging it around like a cricket bat when the putter head flew off over a hedge. Tim panicked, not knowing how he was going to get himself out of the bind. Anthony Herbert

RIGHT: Sharing a bath after a game of footy in the Little's backyard at Jimbour...

BELOW: 11 years later, back in the bath, this time after the World Cup final at Twickenham...except this time no weeing!

ILLAWARRA NEWSPAPERS HOLDINGS

ILLAWARRA NEWSPAPERS HOLDINGS

LEFT: The inspirational leaders Michael Lynagh and Nick Farr-Jones, show-off the Wallabies' World Cup spoils to the Sydney public.

ABOVE: The ticker-tape parade through the streets of Sydney. Wallaby coach Bob Dwyer and team manager John Breen, in front of the centre pairing. Little still hadn't got rid of that mascot!

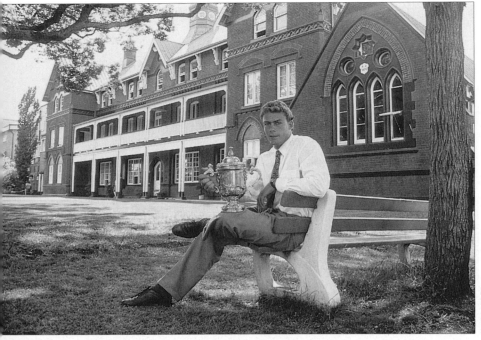

MIKE LARDER

MIKE LARDER

ABOVE: Little in the grounds of Toowoomba Grammar, the scene of his early heroic sporting deeds.

LEFT: Pat Little serves up a well-earned tea break during the World Cup promotional tour of south-west Queensland in 1992.

RIGHT: The World Cup trophy doesn't look totally out of place on the bonnet of Ray Little's 1945 farm truck.

MIKE LARDER/SPORT. THE LIBRARY

ABOVE: Back to back.

TOP RIGHT: The Wallaby World Drivers' Championship in Swansea, Wales. From left: Marty Roebuck, Willie Ofahengaue and Fangio Horan.

BOTTOM RIGHT: If I bend it a little more, maybe it will come back... Horan prepared to demonstrate his boomerang throwing skills to Wallaby teammate Brendan Nasser, and strength trainer Brian Hopley.

ACTION PHOTOGRAPHICS

ABOVE: Try-scoring record holder David Campese. He was a hard task master for the young centres when they first arrived on the scene in 1989.

RIGHT: The influential figure of backline lynchpin Michael Lynagh.

ACTION PHOTOGRAPHICS

LEFT: Lucy Horan meets uncle Phil Kearns for the first time.

OPPOSITE: At Tim's 21st birthday party in Toowoomba, with Rod McCall, Annabel and David Nucifora, and Greg Martin.

RIGHT: Horan tackles a different sporting discipline during the Allan Border Testimonial match at the Gabba, January 1994. Test wicket-keeper Ian Healy is behind the stumps.

MIKE LARDER

LEFT: An illustrious collection of sporting celebrities at the Allan Border Testimonial cricket match.

Front row: Dermot Brereton, Paul Vautin, Sir Richard Hadlee, Allan Border, Rod Marsh, Greg Chappell, Mike Proctor, Allan Langer, Tim Horan, Wally Lewis, Peter Sterling, Ian Healy. Back row: Jeff Thomson, Craig McDermott, Joel Garner, Carl Rackemann, Geoff Lawson, David Boon, Greg Ritchie, Doug Walters, Trevor Hohns, Hansie Cronje, Martin Kent, Barry Richards, and Mel Johnstone.

LEFT: The rugby union Sale of the Century. Horan, John Eales, and Michael Lynagh with Jo Bailey and Glenn Ridge.

ABOVE: Tim with Channel 10 commentator David Fordham, Greg Norman and John Eales during a Sportsmans' dinner in Brisbane.

Opposite: Trying to find a flat place to rest the Bledisloe Cup!

Right: Little lends a hand a hand as Reds' winger Damian Smith runs into Auckland traffic at Ballymore.

Below: Queensland's 20–14 win over England at Ballymore in 1991 was one of the most memorable of the John Connolly coaching era.

GARRY TAYLOR

GARRY TAYLOR

LEFT: Souths on the way to another club victory. In 1991 the victims were Wests.

BELOW: Little proving a handful for the Scots at Ballymore in 1992.

OPPOSITE: On the way for the match-winning second try against the Springboks in the second Test at Ballymore in 1993.

GARRY TAYLOR

GARRY TAYLOR

GEOFF McLACHLAN

LEFT: The knee nightmare of Natal. The injured duo outside the team hotel in Durban, the morning after the fateful Super 10 match in May 1994.

BELOW: The reality of the trouble sinks in as they arrive at Sydney airport.

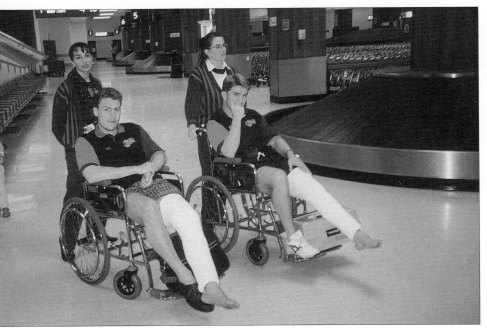

spelt out the options—either he could be honest, or he could fling the shaft in the bushes, and tell the club manager most apologetically, that he'd left the expensive 'Ping' putter out on the course. No prizes for guessing which option he chose. Tim felt bad enough already, but worse when the manager sent three greenkeepers out on the course to look for the 'missing' club. Tim by this stage was offering to pay. The manager told him: 'No it's not a problem—it'll turn up.' Tim thought he'd got away with it, but the next day, an elderly man who lived across the road from the golf course, wandered into the clubhouse with a putter head he'd found in his front yard. You can imagine how happy the manager was. He rang the team hotel and gave Tim an awful mouthful. Tim in turn phoned the owner to apologise. He wouldn't accept any money so Tim left him a Wallaby shirt to pick up at the hotel for his trouble. Another well thought out Horan episode to help Australia's diplomatic relations!

## 3. THE FOOD FIEND

Tim's eating habits are legendary among his rugby peers. That's how he got the nickname 'Truckie'. He eats nothing but 'truck driver's breakfasts'—steak, sausages, bacon, eggs and chips. And every bit of meat on the plate has to be burnt to a cinder. He won't touch anything that's green. When he was really young, he used to stuff his vegetables in the pocket of his dressing gown and when his mother wasn't looking, flush them down the toilet. He got away with it for about two years until one night Helen found all these peas floating around in the bottom of the bowl.

I'm sure that when the Queensland and Australian teams enlisted the services of dietitian Holly Frail a few years ago, it was mainly for Tim's benefit. It's made a huge difference too—he now puts green things on his plate to show Bob (Dwyer). He still doesn't eat them, but it looks a lot healthier.

I guess if there's one story which best sums up Tim's eating habits, it's the one Paul Carozza tells about the afternoon he was in the gym with Tim at Ballymore. This guy he'd never seen before walked into the shed and started chatting to Tim. When he'd left, Squabba (Carozza) asked Tim: 'Who was that, your personal trainer?' 'No, it's my butcher!' Helmet was obviously such a good customer, this guy was prepared to follow him all over Brisbane, just to make sure he had enough meat!

## 4. THE PRANKSTER

I'm tempted to use the phrase compulsive liar, but prankster is probably a little more accurate. If there's a leg to be pulled, Helmet just can't help himself. One night Tim, myself and Brendan Nasser were out in London, having a cup of coffee with some people we'd met after the theatre. Tim was up getting another piece of chocolate cake when this girl turned to Brendan and said: 'It sounds like Tim's doing well out of his surf shops?' Brendan just looked at her: 'His *what*?' 'His surf shops—he told me he runs a chain of surf shops. He's got them dotted all over Australia.' Brendan and I just looked at each other and shook our heads. It was vintage Horan.

Tim's other favourite toy is the telephone. There's no end to the number of bogus phone calls he makes during a tour. He stung Georgie Gregan badly in 1994, when he came into camp to see Greg Craig the night before the Bledisloe Cup Test. I was rooming with Webster (Gregan) at the time—the conversation went something like this.

'George Gregan please.'

'Speaking.'

'Oh George, Hi, my name's Barry Thompson, ringing from radio 2CB in Christchurch, Noo Zeeeland.' (Tim had been honing his Kiwi accent!)

'Hi Barry.'

'George, I'm wondering if you wouldn't mind doing a quick interview about the Aussies' chances on the weekend.'

'Yeah no problem.'

'OK, great, I'll just get the tape rolling . . . .'

'So George, you're first Teeeest against Nooo Zeeeland, how do you think the Aussies will go.'

It went on and on. At first, I had no idea it was Tim, but then the questions started getting really ridiculous—Tim was asking Georgie if he'd mind coming across to Christchurch for a celebrity bowls tournament, the day after the Test, whether there were any homosexuals in the Australian team, all sorts of stupid stuff. But Georgie didn't catch on. He was like Tim's new toy when he came into the team. He was so polite and innocent. Tim could get away with murder.


## 5. THE BUSINESSMAN

Irrespective of how well or poorly Tim did at school, there is no doubt he's got a very good head for business. Even at a very young age he knew exactly where he was going, and how he was going to get there. He invests his money very wisely, and is always on the lookout for new and different opportunities, which explains how he came to be involved in the Monkey Bar, a tavern in the city, with rugby league players Bob Lindner and Mal Meninga.

He's also a very hard negotiator. I remember talking to his father after he and Tim had met with Manly officials towards the end of 1992. Tim had asked Mike to come down to Brisbane from Toowoomba, to help him with the negotiations. During the meeting Mike was stunned at how ruthless Tim was. He thought at the time: 'I don't know what he wanted me here for—I would have given in half an hour ago.' Tim's very, very persistent. Any deals we've done together, I just let him look after them.

## 6. THE RACEHORSE OWNER

I'll balance up the comments about Tim being an astute busi-
nessman by revealing that a couple of years ago he bought
into one of slowest horses in the history of racing. John Connolly can testify to that. Tim talked Connolly into buying a
share—'Knuckles' reckons he's wasted some money in his
time, but none as badly as the 'hard earned' he poured into
that horse. One morning, he and Tim went up to the
McLachlan stables at 5 o'clock to watch their magnificent
beast run a time trial. When they arrived at the huge complex,
they were greeted by the sight of 80 stables. There were 79
horses, all standing alert and ready to race, but when they
got to their stable—empty. 'Where is it? There's no horse,'
Connolly said with great concern. They looked inside to see
this slovenly creature fast asleep in the corner of the stable.
The stable hand kicked it and pulled its tail, but no matter
what he did, the thing wouldn't wake up. 'Knuckles' wanted
to rename it 'Standing Still' or 'Fast Asleep.' The nag had
about 10 starts and never finished better than 13th. McLachlan rated it among the five slowest racehorses he has ever
trained—and he's trained plenty!

## 7. THE ROOMMATE FROM HELL

Out of all the Queensland and Australian players, Tim would
have to rate as one of the worst roommates, particularly if
you get caught with him for a long period of time. He has
so much energy, it's exhausting. There's never any peace and
quiet. There are a couple of people, in particular, he preys
upon—Willie Ofahengaue and Paul Carozza. When Willie
O first came into the Test team, he never said 'boo'. Tim
would lock him out of their room for an hour at a time, just
to get him to talk. But Willie would stand there smiling, and
wait until Tim let him in.

I don't know what it was about Squabba, maybe because
he's pretty quiet and shy too. But Tim would never let him

rest. Squabba tells the story about the time he was rooming with Helmet before an interstate game in Sydney. He got up to go to the toilet at 3am. As he was stumbling wearily back to his bed, BOOOOOOO! Horan leapt out from behind the wall with a knife. Carozza must be the shortest player in world rugby, but he almost hit the ceiling. As Squabba points out, who else would have the energy to get up at 3am, just to scare the hell out of somebody? 'It wasn't even as if he was doing it for the benefit of an audience—he was doing it totally for his own amusement,' Carozza says.

## 8. THE PUBLIC SPEAKER

Public speaking is probably the hardest thing you're expected to be able to do when you start playing representative rugby. Most of the guys find it very intimidating at first—I still don't like doing it.

Early on, it certainly wasn't one of Tim's strong suits either. I remember when he made a speech at his 21st birthday up in Toowoomba, all the guys were down the back heckling, calling him Jeff Fenech. He's improved a lot since then, but there's one speech he made up in Hong Kong in 1992, the first year he captained the Australian Sevens team, that people are still talking about.

Every year, the Australian Trade Commission puts on a cocktail party to welcome the team, and it's traditional for the captain to say a few words. Tim was really looking forward to it, telling me beforehand how he was going to impress the bankers and financiers by using all these big words. I told him it was a dangerous thing to confuse ambition and ability, but he wouldn't listen.

His opening gambit went something like:

'I'd like to incinerate what Bob (Dwyer) said . . . Sorry retriculate . . . interperate . . . artriculate . . . I'd like to say what Bob said!' But it just got worse and worse. The Australian players were rolling around on the floor laughing, as were the rest of the guests.

Every year we go back, somebody will ask Tim: 'Are you speaking today? I hope so. I remember last time you were hilarious.'

The really funny thing is, Tim was being serious!

## 9. THE FAMILY MAN

All the fun and frivolity Tim seems to engage in might make him sound irresponsible. Far from it. When he needs to be, he is the consummate family man—very sensible, even serious at times. He's an excellent husband to Katrina, and a very good father to Lucy. On the flip side, Tim is also very lucky to have Katrina. She's such an enthusiastic and even tempered person. She's been a tower of strength to Tim during all the dramas they faced in 1994.

I have to admit I was very happy when Tim got married. I think some people were starting to cast aspersions on our sexuality!

It definitely took the pressure off!

## 10. THE CULTURE BUFF

Tim is so keen to broaden his horizons, he's established what he calls the 'Culture Club'. There's about six of us, mainly rugby players, and we take it in turns to organise a social function totally removed from the norm. Theatre, comedy, opera, ballet—anything, just as long as it's not sport. It's a really good idea—it encourages you to try things that otherwise you might not. I don't think Helmet will ever be a true culture 'buff' but at least he now knows that The Nutcracker is not about a head-butting competition!

## 11. HE THINKS THE SAME WAY I DO

# Chapter Thirteen

## Horan on Little

*'The only people who never make mistakes are those who never do anything.'*

While reports of my death in 1994 were grossly exaggerated, there have been times when I've almost died laughing at the mishaps, mistakes and misfortune that have befallen Jason over the years. But with this being a family publication, I'll have to stick with topics suitable for the consumption of all ages.

### 1. THE CHEF

Jason has got to be in the top 10 worst cooks of all time. I'm sure that whoever offered the Queensland players cooking lessons a couple of years ago, they had been around to Jason's place for dinner the night before. He probably served up one of his famous pizzas—in a glass!

When it comes to preparing meals, he's actually a very strange mixture: he only shops at delis—I doubt he's ever set foot in a supermarket. In fact if you gave him a shopping trolley, he'd probably try to put his suitcases in it. He hates chopping up vegetables—he wears swimming goggles anytime he has to slice onions—but once all the vegetables are prepared, and the necessary ingredients laid out on the bench, he loves the challenge of putting them together in culinary fashion.

Not that it happens terribly often. Most times Katrina and I are invited over to Jason's house for dinner, it's the night after his Mum has been to stay for a couple days. Invariably, Pat has left a couple of large quiches or a lasagna in the fridge, just waiting to be heated up.

On the odd occasion, even the heating process gets a bit tricky. One night, he and flatmate Damian Smith set off the smoke alarm in the kitchen when they forgot they'd put a frozen pizza in the oven. I'm not sure, but I reckon if somebody bought the house next door and set up a takeaway restaurant, they'd make a lot of money in a short time!

## 2. THE UNI STUDENT

By my calculations, over the last six years, Jas has had almost as many career starts as he has girlfriends—and that's no small feat! I'll never forget his first job—he was 17—Souths promised to find him work when he came to Brisbane, and they did—as a storeman and packer. Pat and Ray must have been so proud! He only lasted about three hours. He worked until lunchtime and never went back. After that, there were banks, insurance companies, building societies, Queensland Cotton. I learned very quickly to use a pencil—not a pen—to write his work numbers into my telephone book!

It took Jason a long time to decide what he wanted to do, but I think he's finally found his niche at Bond University. I know study weighed heavily in his decision not to go to the Crushers. He would have had to start another career path after he'd retired from football, so in that regard, he's definitely made the right decision.

It's also handy being a student as far as training is concerned. Going on how many sessions Jason has missed, John Connolly reckons he's either the dumbest university student in south-east Queensland, or he is going to be the smartest. He says he's never before come across a student who has eight hours of lectures on Sunday, and exams at 6 o'clock in the morning!

## 3. THE RELUCTANT COMIC

Jason was the happiest man in Australia when Garrick Morgan arrived on the Queensland and Australian scene in 1992. It really took the pressure off him. For four years he'd been the figurehead of the award for the silliest thing said or done on tour. All of a sudden there was a new contender.

He still features every now and then, but he's not nearly as dominant as he was when we first started out. I stuck more to the principle of being thought a fool, rather than opening my mouth and removing all the doubt, but Jason was a lot more honest. He'd say the first thing that came into his head, often without engaging the brain. I remember on the plane across to Canada in 1989, Peter Slattery asked him whether the book he was reading was any good. Jas said it was OK, but it didn't have much of a plot—it was jumping around all over the place. When Slats turned the book around, he saw the title: *Frederick Forsyth's Book of Short Stories!* That was one certain penalty skull! There's also the famous story about the dog in Japan. When we arrived at Tokyo Airport in 1991, there was a black labrador up on the luggage belt, sniffing the luggage as it came around. Legend has it that Jason was heard to say: 'Look at that guide dog, up there looking for the blind man's luggage.' If it's not true, it probably should be!

(RIGHT OF REPLY: Nobody appreciates my sophisticated sense of humour. J.L.)

## 4. THE RELUCTANT HERO

It's doubtful there's an international player in the world who hates talking about rugby more than Jason does. When training is over, that's it until the game. When the game's over, that's it until the next training. He was exactly the same at school—he was captain of rugby, cricket and athletics, and yet he never mentioned sport. Even when teachers or other kids asked him questions, he would quickly change the subject. He's incredibly modest. You wouldn't even know, walking through Jason's house, that he played rugby. There's one small group photograph of the 1989 Queensland team in Argentina, sitting on a book shelf next to his desk, but that's it. Not a World Cup souvenir or a piece of rugby memorabilia anywhere to be found. His mother and father are exactly the same. Not so long ago, Pat and Ray billeted three schoolboy players who were in Dalby for the regional state championships. They were staggered by Pat's knowledge of the game, but they had no idea they were staying in the Little family home—until Jason rang up one night. *'You're Jason Little's mum and dad?'* They couldn't believe it. They kept Pat and Ray up all night asking questions—where did he sleep, what did he eat for breakfast, what did he watch on television—it went on for hours.

## 5. THE NON-CONFORMIST

This may well tie in with his reluctance to talk about rugby, but Jason also hates to wear any piece of clothing which identifies him as an Australian rugby player. He'll happily dress in the official team outfit when he's in camp, or when he's doing a public appearance with the rest of the team, but that's it. When he's out by himself, shopping or just killing time, there's not a Wallaby logo in sight. Most Australian players have got cupboards and cupboards full of rugby clothing. Apart from a couple of Test jerseys, Jason hasn't kept a thing. He's given it all to charity or to friends. He'll tell you his objection to wearing team 'uniform' is a hangover from his boarding school days, when he had a uniform for every time of the day—class, sport, study, church, dinner, even weekends. But I tend to think it's because he is essentially a very private person who feels uncomfortable when other people make a fuss over him. He has never been able to understand what the big deal is about. He plays rugby because he enjoys the game, the friends, and the lifestyle that it provides. But that's where it stops. He's not interested in breaking records, or reaching milestones. He couldn't even tell you the score in the World Cup final. Once a game is over, it's history.

## 6. THE HAIRLESS ONE

I don't want to pull the cape off Superman, but Jason's got two very strange fixations—one about facial hair, and another about people touching his ears.

The first one is to explain—Jas is the least hairy male I've ever seen. He didn't start shaving until he'd played about six Tests. His lack of body hair has been an ongoing joke since we were at school. He's always trying to grow moustaches and beards, but after an hour in the sun, you can't see any evidence of any facial growth. I remember once back in 1991, on the Queensland tour of Japan, fullback Greg Martin actually caught Jason rubbing mud into his 'trainer' moustache during a game, just to make it more visible. No doubt he would have earned another Jason Little Award that night.

The ear phobia dates back to when he was really small. One of his father's friends was always trying to get Jason to shake his hand. When Jason didn't grip it firmly, this fellow would rub his ears vigorously, or even put his tongue in Jason's ear. Ever since then, Jason can't stand having his ears touched, which is very unfortunate, particularly when you've got people like Cameron Lillicrap and David Nucifora in the Queensland and Australian teams. They'd sit behind Jas on the team bus and torment him for hours. Who said rugby forwards didn't know how to have a good time?

## 7. THE HOPELESS HANDYMAN

It's a good thing that Jason can run fast and tackle, because
he's never going to carve out a name for himself as one of
the world's great handymen. The skill level he shows in the
kitchen is rivalled only by the one he shows around the house.
Jason is the only person I know who would pay $55 to have
a plumber turn the tap on under the sink, as happened about
12 months ago. I wouldn't be at all surprised if he also paid
an electrician to change his light bulbs.

I'm sure it comes from having Ray as a father. Ray is the
original Mr Fixit—there's nothing he can't repair or build or
install. He's set the house up perfectly for Jason—every bit
of garden has been landscaped or bricked. There's not a blade
of grass to mow, or garden to attend. All Jason has to do
when he gets home is park the car.

## 8. THE FASHION KING

A couple of years ago, Jason was responsible for starting what
has become one of the great traditions of Queensland Rugby.
To break up the monotony of training, he started wearing
his worst T-shirts to training on Friday nights. Before any
time at all, it had become a competition among the backs to
see who could arrive with the ugliest T-shirt. Even if it's 30
degrees, players now turn up with a tracksuit top on, just to
conceal the week's entry until the judging starts. I'm pretty
sure assistant coach Andrew Slack thinks the competition runs
every night, judging by the clothes he wears to training!

Ugly shirt night even extends to overseas tours. Guys will
cart their worst garments halfway around the world, just to
wear them once at training on Friday night. As far as victory
goes, Jason was very hard to toss early on, but in recent times,
Peter Slattery has dominated. Slats has unearthed a secret supply—he's found a shop on the Gold Coast which he says is
a gold mine for Friday night shirts. But he won't tell anybody

where it is. At last report Barry Lea was thinking of enlisting the services of a private investigator.

## 9. THE ELIGIBLE BACHELOR

Somebody finally got it right when they included Jason in Australia's Most Eligible Bachelors list of 1993. I just can't work out why he was dropped from the list in 1994—I reckon his form had been better than ever.

He makes out he's really embarrassed by being included, but I'm sure he's secretly honoured. He always looks the part. He spends a squillion dollars on clothes every year—he and David Wilson are the two fashion plates of the Wallaby team. They're as bad as each other. They'll spend days hunting around the shops in foreign cities looking for clothes to buy. Jason's going through a vest phase at the moment. He seems to come back with a different one from each trip.

Complementing Jason's bachelor image is his obsession with having a suntan. He hates being white and pasty. Whenever we come back from an overseas tour at the end of the year, Jas will duck off to the beach by himself for a few days, until he looks healthy again. I remember in Hong Kong a few years ago, Jason flew over from Italy to link up with the Australian team. He knew he'd be the laughing stock if he turned up really white, so he paid about a million lira at a Milan health club to lie in the solarium for three hours. The only problem was he didn't realise you actually had to lower the sun lamp on top of you. He might as well not have switched the apparatus on. Another great example of Jason's knowledge of all things technical!

## 10. THE WHITE FIJIAN

On the subject of looking white in Hong Kong, there was one year he couldn't help it—he was surrounded by Fijians. Of all the great memories I've got from Hong Kong, the sight of Jason standing in the middle of the field, in a huddle of Fijians is probably my favourite.

It was 1992. We'd already been knocked out, and Jason and I were sitting up in the players enclosure, having a few beers to celebrate the end of the tournament. We were well into it when Waisale Serevi, our mad little mate from Suva, came up and asked if one of us would mind sitting on the line for Fiji in the final. Which one, he didn't really care. The decision was easy. I'd had four giant mugs of beer, Jason was still on his third. Jason was up. He swilled down the remainder of his beer, and rushed downstairs to join his new teammates.

It's one of my few regrets in life that I didn't have a camera to get a photo of Jas in a close circle, saying prayers with eight Fijians. I think I know what he was praying for, too—a toilet! He didn't have time to go before, so by halftime, he was feeling very uncomfortable. He could hardly run into the stands in his football boots, so he had no choice but to empty his bladder, oh so secretly, in front of the dugout. He felt better for a while, until the giant Fijian manager came back from the halftime talk and sat in the puddle. I swear it could only happen in Hong Kong.

## 11. HE THINKS THE SAME WAY I DO!

# Chapter Fourteen

## Brought to Their Knees

*'He jests at scars, that never felt a wound.'*
WILLIAM SHAKESPEARE

Even before a ball had been kicked, Tim had caught Jason out.

The pair were just 11, roaming around in the canefield behind Ron and Gloria Kelly's house in Bundaberg, the day before the start of the State Under 12 zone championships. Horan had quietly broken off a piece of cane, and when Jason wasn't looking, gently prodded him in the back of the leg. 'SNAKE, SNAKE' he yelled, and Jason was off, as fast and far as he could go. By the time he stopped, he had no idea where he was. It took him and Tim 20 minutes to find one another, and a further 40 minutes for the pair to find their way out of the canefield and back to the house of their billets.

That's the way it had always been—Horan, the scheming prankster, preying on Little, the unsuspecting victim. It was all about to change.

Arriving home at his sister Janelle's house one Friday afternoon in May, 1991, Jason saw what looked to be a large carpet snake lying on the front lawn. He took the appropriate evasive action, tip-toeing in a large semi-circle to the front door of the house. But when he got inside, his distraught sister requested he move the snake, and QUICKLY PLEASE. Jason reluctantly ventured outside, crept up on the snake and jabbed it with a stick. Nothing. He jabbed it again a little harder. Still nothing. While he didn't know a lot about snake behaviour, it didn't take him too long to work out that this particular carpet snake was dead. The 'bright idea' light bulb immediately lit up. He put the deceased reptile in a large plastic bag, and dumped it in the boot of his car.

The next day his club Souths were playing competition leaders Sunnybank at Yeronga—the timing couldn't have been more perfect. As the rest of the team made their way onto the field, Little feigned the need for some additional last minute strapping, and ducked back into the dressing shed to set the trap.

Souths blitzed Sunnybank that afternoon, no thanks to Little, whose mind was anywhere but on the action, in anticipation of what Tim would do when he found the snake. The thought occurred to him what coach Phil White might say, if Horan was unearthing dead snakes in his kit bag, five minutes after the team had lost. *No, it didn't matter. It was a risk worth taking.*

After the game, there were more people in the Souths dressing shed than there were back in 1986, when the club won its first premiership in 28 years. As Horan approached his kit bag, the teeming mass closed in.

He pulled out his towel, his shirt, his . . . 'YAAAAHHHHHHHH'. Horan leapt in the air—reaching heights the Russian pole-vaulter Sergei Bubka would have been proud to scale. The dressing room erupted in laughter as Horan, realising he'd been nabbed, poked his nose into his bag to take a second look. 'Yeah good one mate . . .' he said to Jason, who was already on his way out the door at high speed. At last, Little was on the board. Horan still led, two hundred and something to one, but Little's was a good 'un.

Over the ensuing years, there would be plenty of other occasions to illustrate just how close their relationship was, and how similarly they thought.

Like in New Zealand in 1993, the day they were to play the All Blacks for the Bledisloe Cup in Dunedin. The team was on the bus, heading for the Carisbrook ground when Horan was struck by a horrible realisation: 'Hang on—I think I've forgotten my mouthguard,' he said to his centre partner who, as usual, was sitting beside him.

As Horan started rummaging frantically through his kit bag, Little began to think: *Hmmmm. I can't remember packing mine either.* It turned out both had left their mouthguards back at the hotel. The coincidence mightn't have been so strange, had it not been the first time in 29 and 27 Tests respectively that either had forgotten to pack the piece of protective equipment.

On another occasion, while preparing for the third Test against the Springboks in 1993, Horan and Little were required to do a joint interview with Channel 9's 'A Current Affair'. Arrangements were made to meet reporter Chris Smith in the foyer of the Holiday Inn Crown Plaza hotel at Terrigal straight after training. Jason walked out of the lift and thought he was looking into a mirror. There was Tim in green and white striped shirt, blue jeans, brown deck shoes and white socks—identical garb to Jason, right down to the brown plaited belt. They had trouble convincing Smith they were not hamming it up. 'You would have sworn the whole thing was planned,' the reporter says. 'The two of them looked like the Bobsie twins.'

Their telepathy even extends as far as travel documents. Prior to the French tour in 1993, Jason had all but resigned to the fact he'd lost his passport, and was making last minute arrangements to have it replaced. But while explaining his carelessness to Tim, he was advised to look in the left hand pocket of his Australian blazer. 'I thought I'd lost mine about 12 months ago, and that's where it was,' Horan told him. 'I bet it's in your left breast pocket.' Sure enough, there it was.

But of all the quirky happenings Horan and Little have been involved in over the years, none would impact on Australian rugby quite like the one in South Africa in May 1994.

A perfect autumn day greeted the Queensland team, as they arrived in Durban to prepare for the Super 10 final against host side Natal at the magnificent Kings Park Stadium six days later.

The match represented the culmination of the six-week tournament incorporating the best 10 provincial teams from Australia, South Africa, New Zealand and the South Pacific.

The Queensland players who had been to the stylish east coast resort city the year before knew exactly what to expect. Those who hadn't were in for a pleasant surprise. As the team bus worked its way through the city streets and out onto the esplanade, the attractions of Durban were laid out before them: sparkling blue water and the wide white sandy beaches neatly drawn off from high rise hotels by a yawning promenade which stretches as far as the eye can see.

And peering down on it all at the northern end of the strip—the luxurious 22-storey Elangeni Hotel; its gentle s-shaped facade makes it one of Durban's most identifiable landmarks.

When the bus pulled up in the hotel's driveway, duty boy Matthew Pini read out the room list—Eales/Morgan, Carozza/Herbert, Smith/Pini, Horan/Little . . . *Perfect!* With Little having only just arrived back from his off-season with Italian club Milan, there was a lot of catching up to do—so many stories to be told over late night hot chocolates and toasted sandwiches.

The players clustered around the reception desk, like eager adolescents in the school tuckshop line. They were anxious to check into their rooms and get down to the beach for a surf. Horan was one of the first to emerge—sidling up beside his roommate with the key. 'How 'bout this?,' he said. 'Room No 1213. I guess that means I sleep on the inside bed.' The pair had roomed together dozens of times, but the room number—the amalgamation of their jersey numbers—was just a little bit spooky.

An hour later, as the Queenslanders lay by the pool, or wandered down the promenade, rubber-necking at the local attractions, they couldn't help sniggering at a New South Wales decision to cancel their trip to Durban.

A month before, NSW Rugby Union president Peter Crittle had declared his team would not be travelling to the troubled province of Natal, after a 'travel advisory' had been issued by the Australian Embassy in Johannesburg, recommending the postponement of all unnecessary travel to the region. However honourable his intentions in protecting the welfare of the New South Wales players, Crittle's decision appeared to be a little hasty. Any prior consultation with Natal Rugby Union officials would have told him the trouble spots were almost 200km out of Durban—and posed no threat to visitors to the coastal city. New South Wales Rugby Union executive director David Moffett made a fleeting visit to the republic to assess the situation first hand, but mysteriously never stopped in Durban. The NSW decision was final. They forfeited their match, and any chance they had of playing in the final of the prestige provincial championship.

However strange the Queenslanders initially thought the decision was, their views were a lot stronger after being in Durban for 12 hours. As team vice-captain Rod McCall said over dinner the first night: 'Warm water, blue skies, 23 degrees, good surf, friendly people . . . why wouldn't you want to come here? You'd swim across here if you couldn't get a plane.'

His Test second-row partner John Eales agreed: 'State of Emergency? They've got to be kidding. The biggest problem we've had since arriving is finding enough surfboards.'

It was Monday afternoon, the final wasn't until Saturday, but Queensland coach John Connolly had little work in store for the players over the ensuing week. In the past two months, the team had played six matches in Argentina, two in Port Elizabeth, flown across to New Zealand to meet Otago in a Super 10 game in Dunedin, then journeyed back across the Indian Ocean to Durban.

In between times, there had been home games against Northern Transvaal, Transvaal, and North Harbour—the third clinching the Reds' berth in the Super 10 final. On the plane to Durban, winger Paul Carozza tallied up the flights the team had boarded since March 1. It was 25 in all. Carozza in jest complained to assistant coach Andrew Slack that he couldn't sleep at home unless he was in a chair, while No 8 Sam Scott-Young confessed he was even toying with the idea of having his wife Donna serve him dinner on a tray, so as not to break his routine. There'd been a lot of travel. Clearly, rest was required.

The team had a light run daily and, on the last morning, took a stroll across to the awesome Kings Park Stadium, just to get the feel of the ground and rehearse a few moves. It was in the empty stadium Rod McCall can remember watching Horan—wraparound sunglasses, flowery hat, multi-coloured bike shorts—picking up passes from his toes, and just flicking them on. So quick, so calm, so composed. It was a casual 15 minute training session, and yet McCall could not ever remember seeing anyone more in control on a rugby field. Horan was not yet 24, and he'd already played 30-

something Tests. McCall wondered just how good he'd be when he reached his peak. It was an awesome proposition.

Crrrrrrrrunch (Uuuuuuummmmmmpfff)

Queensland coach John Connolly and the reserves bench, sitting 35m away on the sideline, could almost hear the creaking of bones and the compression of bodies as the first scrum packed down, the Super 10 final not more than a minute old.

There was an almighty roar from the locals. In the shadows of the grandstand, Queensland prop Adrian Skeggs was sent rocketing skywards—popped straight out of the scrum by Natal's man mountain prop, Guy Kebble, as the two front rows collided.

'Jesus, Skeggsie would almost have to qualify for bonus frequent flyer points with that trip, wouldn't he?' Anthony Herbert remarked to lighten the moment of tension. Connolly could hardly bare to watch as the scrum re-packed. If this was how the scrum was going to hold up, it had been a long way to come for nothing. However, the very next scrum, the fears were allayed. Skeggs gripped on for dear life, the Queensland scrum refused to budge, and skipper Peter Slattery cleared the ball comfortably for Lynagh.

The Wallaby flyhalf, ever the visionary on the field, noticed Natal's midfield was tightly bunched, so he calmly steered the ball across field with his right boot, almost straight into the arms of unmarked Queensland winger Barry Lea. Try time! Two minutes gone—Queensland ahead 5–0—and 48,000 people stunned. The silence was deafening. By half-time the Reds had opened up a 12–0 lead, and were looking very much in command. Out in the backs, Lynagh was dictating terms, while up front, the scrum and the lineout were more than holding their own. At tighthead, Skeggs had all but nailed himself to the Kings Park turf—not another frequent flyer point to be earned.

However, no crystal ball gazer could have anticipated the turmoil ahead. With just five minutes gone in the second half, and with Natal gathering momentum with every attacking phase, Horan lunged to his right attempting to halt the progress of Springbok flyhalf Henri Honiball.

CRRRRAAAAACK! His left knee collapsed under him, like a cheap deck chair. Play continued momentarily, while Horan lay on the ground, writhing in pain, his face buried in his hands. Queensland team physio Richard Dunn, having not seen the incident, ran out on the field suspecting he would be treating Horan for concussion.

'He had his hands over his face—I thought he'd got a bad knock in the head,' Dunn says. 'Then I saw his left leg—it was obviously something far more serious.' Team doctor Greg Smith arrived a minute later, pushing aside two local ambulance men who seemed genuinely bamboozled by both the seriousness and urgency of the occasion. Smith kneeled down, his eyes immediately fixing on Horan's kneecap, which was bulging out the left side of his leg—about 4cm from where it should be.

'He was in incredible pain. He kept wailing "what the f . . . is the matter with my knee, what the f . . . is the matter with my knee",' Smith recalls. 'I told him he'd dislocated his kneecap, but even then, seconds after the accident, he was convinced it was something much worse.'

As Horan was being stretchered from the field, his face still buried in his hands, the alarm bells were ringing across the Indian Ocean, and into the loungeroom of Bob Dwyer's seaside home at Coogee, in Sydney. The national coach was sitting alone, watching the game.

Wallaby team physio, Greg Craig, stretched out in front of the television in the study of his home in the northern beaches of Sydney, also bolted upright to watch the action replay. Horan had run, pivoted and changed direction all in the one movement. His ankle was almost parallel with the ground. It didn't look good.

In Toowoomba, Mike and Helen Horan sat glued to their television set, waiting for an update on Tim's condition. A trained nurse, Helen didn't hold any great hopes of a favourable report.

Meanwhile, Horan, lying in the Kings Park medical room, was struck by an uncomfortable feeling of deja vu. Just 12 months before, in his only other outing at Kings Park, he'd finished up lying on the same bed, as medical staff stitched a large gash in the back of his head. How he wished it was stitches again. Local orthopaedic surgeon, Dr Christopher Terreblanche, manipulated the kneecap back into its rightful place, before Horan was given a pethidine injection, and assisted into the changing room to shower.

Five minutes later, with Horan having just spread himself out on a physio table, a bag of ice on his knee, the tranquillity of the dressing shed was broken by the sound of a key in the door. He looked up to see Little—his best mate, his best man, his centre partner . . . the other half of Room 1213 . . . being carried into the shed.

At any other time, in any other place, under practically any other circumstance, there would have been a quick quip, a smart comment—at the very least, a smile. Instead the pair just looked at one another glumly, unable to juice one drop of humour from the moment.

The two had played together since they were 11, in all parts of the globe—from Bundaberg to Buenos Aires, from Cape Town to Calgary, from Dublin to Durban. Now, in the same half of the same game, they injure the same knees—tackling the same opponent, on the same part of the field.

'It was really strange—we just didn't have anything to say to each other,' Little recalls. 'We just lay there in silence, wondering what was going on out on the field. We could hear the cheering, but we didn't know the score or what was going on.'

Little's injury was almost as freakish as Horan's. Charging across field—like Horan in pursuit of the lithe Honiball—Little had collided with teammate Ilie Tabua, who had fallen to the ground immediately in front of him. Little's left knee flexed and buckled backwards. If he was an ostrich, he would have been fine. Ostrichs are bu lt for hyperextension exercises, but humans are not. Some sort of structural damage was inevitable.

He got to his feet with assistance from Dunn, and tried to hobble back into position, but the leg felt alarmingly flaccid. 'Can you strap it,' Little asked in one last vain hope. 'No mate you're off. Come on let's go.'

Little's departure from the field completed a miserable day for centres. By the 58th minute all four had retired with Natal having lost both Jeremy Thompson and Springbok Pieter Muller before halftime. Out on the field, Queensland were in disarray, their 12-point cushion at halftime now whittled away to just two points.

Test wingers Damian Smith and Paul Carozza were taking it in turns to play centre, tackling opponents on suspicion—just in case they got the ball. There were black and white jerseys appearing from everywhere, far more urgent, far more confident than they had been in the first half. Some 48,000 fans sensed the tide had turned. Perhaps with any other flyhalf in the world wearing the No 10 jersey, Queensland's situation might have been irretrievable. But master tactician Lynagh assumed control, the same way he had done in so many of his 67 Test matches for Australia. Two late penalty goals, and an angled field goal sealed the Reds' 21–10 victory.

Queensland skipper Peter Slattery accepted the spoils—but the elation which should have been derived from such an enormous achievement was conspicuously absent. Like hard-nosed businessmen, the players seemed more intent on finding out what price had been paid for the Super 10 trophy.

As they filed into the dressing shed, ballpark figures became apparent. Horan and Little were lying side by side, their tracksuit pants hacked from the knee down, to aid the icing process. Faces dropped, smiles disappeared.

'It was one of the quietest winning dressing rooms I can ever remember,' coach John Connolly says. 'I suppose it was a bit like Sir Edmund Hilary climbing up Mount Everest, and discovering a five-star hotel at the top. The whole thing was just a massive anticlimax. Nobody really knew the extent of the damage then, but everybody feared the worst. You don't often get a good knee injury.'

As the huge crowd filtered out into the parking lot to begin world rugby's largest post-match function—a massive carnival-style party extending the length and breadth of 10 football fields—Horan and Little were being lifted into the back of the best ambulance Durban had to offer at the time—a small mini-van with faulty transmission.

In a trip which might have been organised by television spy, Maxwell Smart, the driver, a visitor from nearby Pietermaritzburg, lost his way to the hospital. And, as fate would have it, the hospital was on top of a hill. Every time he stopped at an intersection, so did the engine of the spluttering little van.

'Seriously, it was like Keystone Cops,' says chaperon, Dr Greg Smith. 'These guys didn't know where they were going, and the ambulance wasn't keen to take them.' By the time the vehicle finally pulled up into the hospital driveway, Horan and Little were in agony, the effects of the pethidine having gradually subsided. While Smith argued about hiring crutches and wheelchairs, the players had their legs immobilised by cylindrical plaster casts. The FA Cup final, between Manchester United and Chelsea, flickered away on the TV in the background. Horan never liked watching soccer on television, but this game was particularly trying. So too were the endless stream of doctors and nurses who sheepishly requested autographs.

*To Julie, best wishes Tim Horan. To Christopher, all the best, Jason Little.*

'It's hard to imagine two people more obliging,' Smith recalls. 'Here they were, in great pain, scribbling notes on pieces of paper for orthopaedic surgeons.'

The novelty of the wheelchairs lifted spirits for a while. Leaving the hospital, Horan, ever the competitor, challenged Little to a race down the main thoroughfare, crashing him into a cold water fountain when the race track narrowed. Things were gradually returning to normal. The pair arrived back at the team hotel at 10pm, but not before another magical mystery tour around Durban—the driver's sense of direction no better on the way home than it was on the way to the hospital. Some 15 minutes later, they were sitting on their beds in Room 1213, matching shirts, matching plaster casts, matching despondent faces.

As the night grew longer, late night visitors filed through the door, playful props Dan Crowley and Cameron Lillicrap specifically to tickle their feet, which were poking out the end of the plaster casts. Others offered more traditional commiserations.

If the situation wasn't so serious, it would have been comical. Neither slept a wink, Horan in particular remembers it as the most uncomfortable night of his life.

*It's got be more than a dislocated kneecap,* he thought to himself.

By 8.30 the next morning, the team was on the bus, in readiness for the long flight home. A couple of late night revellers only just met the deadline, arriving back at the hotel in the nick of time, courtesy of a hair-raising ride along the beach in a speeding beach buggy. Early morning sunbakers had created an ideal slalom course for the driver, a surf lifesaver who'd been befriended by the desperate duo just 15 minutes earlier. Team celebrations had been dampened, but not entirely extinguished. Durban's resort-like atmosphere had made sure of that.

Up and off. Durban—Johannesburg. Out. Change planes. Wait two hours. Johannesburg—Perth. Out. Wait one hour. Get back on. Perth—Sydney. Out. Change planes. Wait another hour. The 24-hour journey was never going to be fun, even before throbbing knees and plaster casts were taken into account. There were obvious problems associated with flying Horan and Little economy class—the plaster casts simply wouldn't fit—so arrangements were made to have them upgraded to first class.

There's something special about travelling at the front end of a 747—the giant seat, all the gadgets, your own TV set, 144 videos to choose from—it tends to bring out the little boy in even the wealthiest of businessmen. But as Horan eased himself into the monstrous seat, three rows back from former PM Malcolm Fraser, who'd been in South Africa for the inauguration of the new Government, he couldn't stop thinking what he wouldn't give to be sitting in economy, seat 130D, wedged in between two smelly, chain-smoking fat blokes, if it meant he could walk off the plane at the other end.

*The pain. It's gotta be more than a dislocated kneecap.*

Down the back of the plane, Rod McCall was holding court, explaining about the team's audacious bet. A keen gambling man when the odds are right, McCall couldn't understand why nobody, least of all the South Africans, gave Queensland any chance of winning the game.

*Lynagh, Horan, Little, Slattery, Wilson, Tabua, Eales, Morgan—14 Wallabies . . . Hmmmmm, it wasn't a BAD side. We've got be some chance.* So on a quiet afternoon during the week, McCall had rung home to find out the odds being offered on the match by Darwin sports betting agency, Centrebet.

Natal 2–5, minus nine and a half points, Queensland 7–4 plus five and a half. SEVEN TO FOUR—you're kidding!

After consultation with a few, but not too many, senior players, the plunge was made—$10,000 to $28,750. He thought it through . . . when we win, everybody will be happy. If we lose . . . well . . . we won't lose.

'Excuse me miss, could we get some more champagne brought down the back of the plane.' The party moved up another gear.

Two rows further forward Lynagh, Queensland and Australia's goalkicking guru, gulped. *Thank God they didn't tell me. I wouldn't have been able to put the ball on the mound.*

The team landed in Brisbane at 1.30pm, almost 25 hours after setting off from Durban. The scenes at the domestic terminal were chaotic. Littered among the hundreds of well-wishers and relatives was the largest media contingent ever assembled in the history of rugby union in Queensland.

Camera shutters clicked, and cameramen jockeyed for position as the wounded warriors crutched their way up the gangway and into the arrival lounge . . . matching shirts, matching plaster casts, matching crutches, matching blank faces.

'You'd swear it was a giant con, wouldn't you?' one reporter observed. 'If I hadn't stayed up all night and watched the game, I would have been convinced it was all crap.'

No. Sometimes fact IS stranger than fiction.

Smith had already made arrangements for the pair to see celebrated Brisbane surgeon, Dr Peter Myers. By six o'clock that night Horan and Little were sitting in his Wickham Terrace surgery, waiting anxiously.

Horan was called in first. Little remembers sitting alone in the waiting room peering around the walls at the framed photographs of past patients—the Great White Shark, Greg Norman, rugby legends Tony Shaw and Mark Loane, and a few others who looked familiar, but he couldn't place. Meanwhile the clock ticked away loudly in the background. 6.30, 7 o'clock, 7.30, 8 o'clock. The longer Tim stayed in there, the worse Jason feared the news would be.

Finally, the door squeaked open. Two-year-old Lucy appeared, followed by Katrina. There were tears welling in her eyes. She struggled to get the words out. 'Peter thinks Tim's done the lot—everything,' she said, before bursting into tears.

There was nothing Jason could think of saying to help the situation. The pair of them sat there in silence, while Lucy dismantled the magazine rack. A couple of minutes later, Tim emerged, Myers by his side. Jason was surprised at the composure Tim showed. 'He didn't say much. He seemed quite calm—perhaps he was in shock.'

Myers was comparatively happy with the prognosis on Jason's knee. He had partially torn a couple of ligaments, and a cartilage. Myers needed to conduct further tests in the morning, and depending on the results, would probably operate that night, straight after he'd done Tim.

The next time Jason saw Tim was 11pm the following day. He was being wheeled out of the operating theatre just as Jason was going in. Tim was still heavily sedated and totally incoherent, but a couple of paces behind the trolley was a forlorn looking Greg Smith. He just shook his head. 'It's a mess,' was all he said as they passed one another in the corridor.

The following morning, when Jason came to, he was lying in a bed beside Tim on the fourth floor of the Holy Spirit Hospital. Jason felt well enough to try to coerce one of the nurses into ordering him a pizza. His knee might have been aching, but his stomach was rumbling. He hadn't eaten in 36 hours. Tim, however, was groaning audibly and obviously in great pain. Jason just wanted to get out of there. He found it depressing lying there listening to Tim in such obvious pain. Only when he got home to New Farm, and looked at the wall calendar next to the phone did he realise the significance of the date. May 18—Tim's birthday.

Katrina remembers the day too—like none other in their two and a half years of married life. Not so much because it was Tim's birthday, but because it was the first time she had ever seen her husband cry. She'd arrived at the hospital midway through the morning. The sight of Tim lying in bed in agony confirmed in her own mind what Peter Myers had intimated at midnight—that he couldn't guarantee Tim would ever play rugby again, particularly at the top level.

'I just burst into tears when I saw him. It was the first time I really appreciated just how serious the injury was. Rugby was Tim's life—to think he could be stripped of it so early in his career made me so sad. I guess it was a bit like Kieren Perkins suddenly developing an allergy to chlorine. It's one thing for a gifted sportsman to give up their career, but to have it taken away was something totally different.'

Later that day, Myers came into the ward to explain in medical terms the damage the dislocated knee had suffered, and even more importantly, the processes and time-frame required to correct it. He itemised the damage, the same way a militant unionist would a heavy log of claims:

- Anterior cruciate ligament ruptured
- Medial ligament ruptured
- Lateral and medial cartilages both torn and crushed
- Dislocated patella, resulting in a small fracture under the patella femoral joint
- Partially torn posterior cruciate ligament
- A piece of bone, the size of a 20c piece, chipped off the lateral condial.

In laymen terms, the knee was stuffed. To help Tim appreciate just how much damage he had done, Myers pointed out it was lucky the joint had skin over it or the lower bone—the tibia—may have detached altogether.

Myers explained the harsh realities. Just to sew back the cartilage, Tim was looking at a recovery period of three to six months. A dislocated patella, on its own, would take up to three months. The anterior cruciate reconstruction, six to eight months, and a medial ligament tear anywhere between six and 12 weeks.

None of the injuries on their own were uncommon, he said, but it was very rare to have all of them together. Horan clearly had two options. He could have the operation, and let time be the major player in the healing, or he could work like hell and try to accelerate the recovery process. But Myers wanted him to understand—even with the second option, as he'd told Katrina the previous night, there were no guarantees he would ever be able to play rugby again.

Guarantees or no guarantees, there was never any doubt in Horan's mind which he would choose. 'I had to give it a go. It would have been horrible, conceding defeat and then having to go through life wondering what would have happened if I'd given it a go. I owed it to myself to have a shot.'

As anxious as Horan was to 'get the show on the road', Myers estimated he would have to wait an additional four weeks for the massive swelling to subside. He was also not prepared to operate until the Wallaby centre could bend his knee to 90 degrees.

It became Horan's single priority over the next month. With assistance from Queensland team physio Richard Dunn, he stretched the leg to 60 degrees, then 65, back to 60, 65 again, then 70. After a month he'd reached 80—a mere four centimetres short of the required mark. Myers decided to put him under anaesthetic, to see if he could manipulate the joint that crucial extra 10 degrees. If he could, he would go ahead and operate. If he couldn't, he would have to delay the reconstruction a couple more weeks.

Horan was booked back into the Holy Spirit Hospital, and placed under heavy anaesthetic. When he finally came to, he had no idea what day it was, or whether Myers had performed the reconstructive surgery. And nobody it seemed was prepared to tell him. If his throbbing knee didn't kill him, the anxiety of not knowing would.

'That was the worst thing—waking up and not knowing whether it had been done. I kept on asking the nurses: 'Have I had the operation? Have I had the operation?' But none of them would tell me. They said I'd have to wait for the doctor. Then the anaesthetic started to wear off, and the knee started to throb like hell. I was dry retching for eight hours straight. I realised Peter must have operated.'

He certainly had. For almost two and a half hours—cleaning, drilling, grafting, screwing, stapling and sewing. The end result was the workings of a totally new knee.

It would probably be two months before Tim could even walk, but in another sense he had already taken the first—and most important—step on the steep slope to recovery.

He'd decided not to give in.

# Chapter Fifteen

## The White Moment

*'A champion is a guy who gets up when he can't.'*
BOXER JACK DEMPSEY

The sky to the east had a pinkish tinge, the sun still to emerge from the dark depths of the Pacific Ocean.

Wallaby team physio, Greg Craig, bounded down the stairs of his Palm Beach home to stir some life into his listless house guest. 'Let's go, let's go, up and at 'em!'

Tim Horan tried to focus his weary eyes on his watch. 'What time is it?'

'Time to get tortured.'

It was a Tuesday morning, in early July, 1994, but it could have been a Wednesday. Or a Saturday. It wouldn't have mattered. Every day was the same. Up at 5.45am, into the car, a 17km drive south to the Narrabeen Sports Medicine Clinic to commence the daily toil, right on the dot of 6.30am.

'Righto, let's go . . . come on, move it.'

That Horan was waking up in Sydney, in a house overlooking the city's northern beaches, underscored his total dedication and commitment to recovery. He had packed his bags, kissed his wife and young daughter goodbye, and moved

down there for three months, so he could have daily physio-
therapy on the knee.

Not that there was any shortage of good physios in Brisbane, but Tim had been treated by Craig since he'd first
appeared on the Wallaby scene back in 1989, and felt very
comfortable with his knowledge and experience. What's
more, Craig was working just three mornings a week—the
rest of the time he was prepared to devote to Horan's rehabilitation.

The Australian team physio knew from the first minute he
had a major project on his hands. He'd been watching the
game live on television. When Horan's knee collapsed the
way it did, he was anxious. Horan had called the same night
from South Africa, just to bring him up to speed with the
preliminary prognosis. 'It looks like Jas has gone, but they
reckon I've just dislocated my kneecap,' Horan had told him.
'Mate—I hate to tell you this, but from what I saw on television, it looks like Jason will be OK, but you're stuffed.' As
much as Horan hated to hear it, he knew deep down Craig
was right. 'The first night, I was probably trying to convince
myself that the injury wasn't that serious,' Horan admits. 'But
sitting on the plane, I remember saying to Jason: 'If I'm only
out for four months, I'll be as happy as Larry'.'

Greg Craig had seen some badly messed-up knees in his
20 years as a physio, but only one worse than Tim's. The
leg belonged to an Australian representative body-surfer, who
as Craig vividly recalls, was crunched onto a coral reef while
surfing the infamous 'Wedge' in Hawaii in 1987. The body-
surfer had suffered all of Tim's damage, but also ruptured a
nerve in the lower part of his leg. It took an eternity, but
Craig got the surfing fanatic back in the water competing at
a national level.

If Horan had been 29, and approaching the twilight of his
rugby career, Craig would have strongly advised he call it
quits, gradually get his leg back into shape, then take up a

more sedentary pursuit like golf or lawn bowls. But he wasn't. He knew as well as anyone in the Wallaby camp that Horan was in his prime, with five or six good seasons of football ahead of him. Craig was keen to be part of a miracle recovery mission—not just for Australian rugby's sake but also for Tim's own peace of mind. 'There are few things I find more frustrating than seeing an elite level sportsman have their career cut short by injury,' Craig says. 'They have to be given the opportunity to fulfil those dreams. It would be horrible to look back in 15 years time, and say: "I wonder if I could have played again, if I'd really done the work". He simply had to give it a go.'

Horan agrees: 'If I'd tried to come back and failed—OK. I could have lived with that. But not knowing would have driven me insane. I had to give it my best shot.'

So on July 3, just 18 days after the reconstruction, the rehabilitation process began. He flew to Sydney, and moved into the downstairs room of Craig's comfortable home, temporarily becoming Greg and Cathy Craig's third child, a badly restricted but nonetheless playful older brother to nine-year-old Jordan and seven-year-old Mitchell.

Seven days a week they worked, up each morning at dawn. Tim got to know every corner, every hill, every traffic light in the 17km drive to Narrabeen. He even knew when the lights were going to change, how fast he had to drive to catch the next green light.

The Narrabeen Sports Medicine Clinic is located inside the grounds of the New South Wales Academy of Sport, which meant the complex was a halfway house for elite athletes on the comeback trail from injury. Olympic 400m runner Darren Clark, Davis Cup tennis player Jason Stoltenberg, marathon swimmer Shelley Taylor-Smith, and Commonwealth Games sprinter Tim Jackson were just a few of the familiar faces Horan noticed stretching, strengthening and rebuilding muscles on the equipment in the centre. But there were dozens of others—car accident victims, skiers, netballers, soccer players, all striving to recapture their mobility, their livelihood. With everybody in the same situation, it made for a very positive, supportive environment, conducive to gut-busting exercise. It was also quite competitive. If the person on the adjacent table had undergone an operation around the same time, and was well in advance in terms of their recovery, there was just another incentive to push yourself harder.

Horan was starting from square one—slow stretches, moving onto very light exercises, trying to build muscle control in the knee, and range of motion. Six hours in the morning, back home for lunch, then back to the clinic. Or downstairs to Craig's personal gymnasium—'the meat locker' as he calls it—for another couple of hours of stretching in the afternoon. For two months, Horan measured his life, his achievements in degrees. 'That's good—85, we've got 85, now we want 90, let's try for 90,' Craig would say, sounding like an auctioneer trying to drum up bids for a fibro house in Sydney's outer west.

The pain Horan had to endure was incredible. He now finds himself at a loss to describe it. 'Probably only people who have been through a similar ordeal will be able to understand, but I guess it's a bit like grabbing a finger, bending it back as far as it will go—then taking it back just as far again.' Worst of all was 'the double'. Whenever Horan heard Craig call for assistance, he knew a 'double' was just moments away, and that alone was almost enough to send him into a cold sweat of panic. Craig would stabilise Horan's body—that is, sit on him—while an accomplice bent his left knee as far as he could. Lying face down on the table, Horan would use a pillow to muffle his piercing scream. Craig got to know the scream. He could tell by the pitch just how much pain Tim was experiencing. But that didn't mean he refrained, or relented. The pain was just part of the package Horan had bought into.

Craig was inspired by the resilience Horan showed through the difficult early stages of his recovery. As the honorary physiotherapist for the Wallabies since 1985, Craig had manipulated the muscles and limbs of some tough types in his time, but not too many tougher than Horan. 'He put up with incredible pain, but he had to. There are no short cuts to a recovery process like that.' The steely determination and the singlemindedness never wavered, the only discernible change in Horan, according to Craig, was the temporary loss of his playful sense of humour. No practical jokes, no gags, and a distinct shortage of the trademark one-liners.

After a couple of weeks, Craig sensed a gradual turnaround, an awakening from the comic coma. He decided to put his hunch to the test. He ducked off to a joke shop and bought an exploding pen. The next time Horan was asked to sign an autograph at the clinic, Craig lunged, like the consummate gentleman insisting on lighting his lady's cigarette: 'Here mate, I've got a pen'.

'Thanks Craigy.' Horan pulled off the cap: KABOOM! The writing implement detonated in his hand. No matter how childish the prank, it worked a treat. Almost within hours, Horan was transformed. The tomfoolery was back in full swing.

'Keeping Tim's spirits up was all part of it,' Craig says. 'The problem with serious knee injuries is the improvement is so gradual. When you're working on it eight hours a day, it's like watching hair grow. You don't notice the very gradual change. So a positive mental attitude is paramount.'

Tim was soon joined in Sydney by Katrina and daughter Lucy, who, by now, had learned that Daddy had 'a good knee and a sore knee'. She also knew through sheer weight of repetition, the meaning of the word careful. The Horans moved into a split-level waterfront home at Palm Beach, which had generously been made available by its owner, Rod James, a rugby enthusiast who was simply doing his little bit to help Horan along the road to recovery. Hearing of Horan's intention to move to Sydney for a few months, James had contacted Olympic bid chief Rod McGeoch, who in turn had passed on the offer of accommodation to Bob Dwyer.

The magnanimous gesture was another source of encouragement for Horan, who was already receiving magnificent support and understanding from his employers at Castlemaine Perkins.

'To think somebody was prepared to give up their holiday home for three months, just to help a footballer get fit again is very special. I know Rod has three daughters who used the house all the time, so it was a very big sacrifice to make. It was the sort of thing which really spurred me on.' (A framed Wallaby jersey, with an inscription: 'To the James family, thanks very much for your support. Best wishes. Tim Horan', now takes pride of place in the loungeroom of the house.)

As much as Horan knew the hard work would one day pay a dividend, the immediate return was painfully slow. To stay focussed, he set goals, to put progress within a time frame. He drew up a list, and stuck it on the refrigerator. It didn't need a heading.

1. Walk again properly.
2. Move well enough to play with Lucy on the swings.
3. Finish the treatment—and the intense pain.
4. To play rugby some time again.
5. To play for Queensland and Australia again.

It had been almost two full months since the damage had been done, and no sign of the first checkpoint. That didn't surprise him, but it served as a reminder of how little distance he had travelled, and what a long hard road he had ahead of him.

Sunday, July 10, Tim remembers the date because he wrote it on the fridge. Not exactly Checkpoint One, but worthy of notation all the same.

In the swimming pool that afternoon, he'd been doing the usual stretching exercises. All of a sudden, Craig disappeared under the water, bobbing up some 10m away: 'OK Tim, walk to me.'

'Yeah good one mate.'

'No—come on, seriously, walk to me. It's not that far.'

Horan didn't expect to be walking unaided for another two weeks. There was *no* way he was ready for this. He felt sick in the stomach just thinking about it.

'COME ON . . . STOP BEING A SOOK . . . WALK TO ME!'

Horan clenched his teeth, and ever so gingerly planted his right foot on the floor of the pool. Then the left, so quickly it hardly touched the bottom. Right, quick left. Right, quick left. A couple of pauses, but he made it to Craig, and back again.

Katrina remembers Tim coming home in the afternoon, absolutely delighted with himself. 'I'd ask him each day what he did, the answers were always much the same until that day. He was on cloud nine.'

For three days, that was practically all he did—wade up and down a pool—a bit further, a bit faster each day, teaching himself how to walk again. After he mastered the partial weight bearing, next step was terra firma. Convinced the time was right, Craig stripped him of his crutches, and put them down beside the pool, well out of Horan's reach.

Horan was petrified: 'It sounds pathetic, but you just don't trust the leg to take the weight, even in the pool, where the water carries a third of the load. You're sure it's going to collapse underneath you.' Step by step, one foot after the other, slowly, carefully, unsteadily. Tim couldn't ignore the irony of the situation—it wasn't so long ago he was watching his daughter Lucy mastering the same skill.

Amid all progress and self-gratification, there was the odd emotional setback. Like the afternoon he hobbled into a milk-bar at Avalon, to pick up a banana smoothie to toast the day's achievements.

The bearded proprietor recognised him immediately: 'Gidday Tim, how's the knee. Do you reckon you'll be right to play in the World Cup?' Something suddenly dawned on Tim. What sort of answer could he give the man?

'Here I was so proud of the fact that I was able to walk the length of a swimming pool without the use of crutches, and this guy's asking me about playing in the World Cup. What do I say to him? "Yeah, sure, just as long as it's played in a swimming pool".'

'You can't be rude. It's not his fault. He was just being friendly, and you appreciate their interest. But his question made me realise just how high public expectations were. It's never: "Hi Tim, how's the knee, when do you reckon you'll be able to walk properly again". It's always: "Do you reckon you'll play in the World Cup". It's understandable of course, but that doesn't make it any less frustrating. At the time, I hadn't even given a thought to playing football. All I wanted to do was get my life back—to be able to walk again, to be able to go down to the park with Katrina and Lucy, and to dive into the surf and swim.'

If that was the small down side of being in the public eye, it was more than counter-balanced by the up side—the astonishing support he received when he first suffered the injury. In the space of a month, more than 200 letters arrived at his home in Wilston, either sent direct or forwarded by the Queensland and Australian rugby unions.

They came from all over the world—France, England, Scotland, South Africa, Wales, Ireland, Papua New Guinea, Argentina, and New Zealand—dozens from New Zealand.

They had been penned by people of all ages, from all walks of life—doctors, housewives, six-year-old juniors, grand-mothers, priests, teenage girls, past players, rugby administra-tors and sponsors, journalists, politicians, old school mates, real estate agents, physiotherapists, carpenters . . . there seemed no end to the variety.

The messages enclosed were just as diverse. Some sought to encourage and inspire, others to console, quite a few to advise, but almost all wished to thank him for past deeds, and hoped he had the speediest of recoveries.

Horan has kept the lot, in two giant yellow envelopes underneath the desk in his study, and pulls them out every now and then to remind himself of the hopes he is carrying on his shoulders. The letters make uplifting and entertaining reading.

'There is one lady, a retired schoolteacher in Dalby, who has vowed not to watch another game of rugby on TV, until Jason and I are back in the centres,' Horan reveals. 'She used to be a rugby league fan, but one day, while flicking through the channels, she stumbled on a Test match. She found out we both grew up on the Downs, and has been a rugby fanatic ever since. I also got a great letter from a bloke in Victoria who described himself as a 63-year-old ex-average player. He used to run 10 miles on weekends to watch club games. He says his enthusiasm for life has been revitalised by the Wallabies' efforts over the past couple of years. It's great to hear those things. It's very easy to forget the people sitting at home watching the games on TV. You don't realise how much pleasure you give them.'

As much as Horan valued every letter he received, there were a few which carried such special significance he ironed them out and blue-tacked them to the wall in his home office. He looks straight at them whenever he sits at his desk.

One is a newspaper clipping—a story about Paul Azinger, the American golfer who returned to the professional circuit after surgery for cancer. A one line quote in the story has been highlighted with a pink pen: *It's not what you accomplish in life, it's how much you overcome to do it.*

The second is a letter he received from All Black flanker Michael Jones, one of numerous international players who contacted Tim to wish him well in his recovery. But Jones speaks from experience having suffered a similar career-threatening knee injury himself a couple of years earlier. In a three page handwritten note, the great All Black loose forward encouraged Tim not to ever give in:

*There'll be frustrations along the way, days when you think you're getting nowhere, but keep at it—if you do, I really believe you'll get back to your awesome best . . . If I can do it mate, so can you . . .*

But the excerpt which moved Horan most of all was included in a letter from David Lewis in Canberra: Lewis, the former executive director of the ACT Rugby Union wrote:

*Tim, the biggest challenge is yourself. If you can beat yourself, you can beat anybody. You will beat this injury . . . You may have heard of the Russian weightlifter Yuri Vlason. You may too have read what he wrote: 'At the peak of tremendous and victorious effort, while the blood is pounding in your head, all suddenly comes quiet within you. Everything seems clearer and whiter than ever before, as if great spotlights had been turned on. At that moment, you have the conviction that you contain all the power in the world, that you are capable of everything, that you have wings. There is no more precise moment in life than this, the WHITE MOMENT, and you will work hard for years, just to taste it again.'*

*Tim, you will experience the white moment again. Of that I'm sure.*

Horan must have read Vlason's words a hundred times. And every time he does, the heartbeat quickens. He gets a sudden urge to stop whatever he's doing and stretch the knee. Further than it will go.

In early September, 1994, that's exactly what happened. Having cycled the hilly 17km down to Narrabeen in the morning, Horan was determined to tackle the return journey. It was hot, it was windy, it was incredibly demanding. But with Craig a single rotation behind, yapping out words of encouragement, a distraught Horan finally made it home, wobbling into the Palm Beach driveway like a five-year-old novice without trainer-wheels. A couple of days later, a giant 'egg' had swelled up over the kneecap. Something was clearly wrong.

Craig's original suspicion was correct—the staple in the knee had dislodged, resulting in a low grade infection in the joint. No staple can be removed from a knee until three months after its insertion, which meant Horan had to sit around twiddling his thumbs for two weeks, before going back to Brisbane for further surgery. It was the one time since the injury he has contemplated tossing in the towel. 'I'd done all this work, and got to the stage where I was walking and riding really well—all of a sudden I'm back on crutches, unable to walk to the fridge to get a drink. I felt like I'd been through all that pain for nothing. I wanted to throw myself off the balcony.'

In the end, the setback proved to be only minor. Three weeks after Myers had removed the staple, and flushed out the joint Horan was back to where he was three weeks before. Two steps back to go four forward, but finally, he felt it was worthwhile.

Three days before the first World Cup camp at Hyatt Coolum on the Sunshine Coast, Horan went for his first light jog since the fateful afternoon in Natal. It was as far removed from Kings Park in Durban as could possibly be imagined. A man practising Tae Kwon Do, and a lady walking her dog, watched on as Greg Craig put the 1991 World Cup star through his paces in a small park around the corner from his house.

He was still light years away from a football field, but there were patches of blue sky starting to poke through the clouds which had hung over his football career since May 14.


It had taken more than 10 years, but finally they were apart. Tim in Sydney stretching, strengthening, rebuilding. Jason in Brisbane, worrying, deliberating, deciding . . . about rugby league.

The offer had to rank as one of the largest—if not *the largest*—in the history of the professional code, and it was being dangled before a young man who hadn't played the game since the Jandowae Under 12s in 1982. Some $1.2 million over four years, including assorted bonuses, all for playing football. He would be MAD not to take it. Surely . . .

The first phone call from the South Queensland Crushers came in August 1993, days after Little's match-winning two-try performance in the second Test against the Springboks at Ballymore. Darryl Van de Velde, the Chief Executive of the new Brisbane-based club, was merely sounding him out: 'Are you interested in having a chat with us?'

Little said he was, without really stopping to think. Like always, there was that little bit of intrigue . . . *I wonder what I'm worth now . . . I'd be unwise not to at least hear them out . . . I've got to keep my options open.*

A few days later, the pair of them sat down over breakfast at the Sheraton Hotel, where Van de Velde explained about the Crushers philosophy. The club was not scheduled to enter the Winfield Cup until 1995, so plans and objectives were really all he could talk about. Nonetheless, Little was quite impressed by both the man and what he had to say. Little explained he had already committed himself to playing the off-season with Italian club Milan at the end of 1993, but wouldn't mind having another chat after that.

The follow-up call came some 10 months later, in early June, while Little was still sidelined by the knee injury he'd suffered in Natal. He sat down with Geoffrey Schuhkraft, a Crushers consultant, in Schuhkraft's office in Surfers Paradise. The tone of the second meeting was a little bit more up-tempo: 'We want you! You're not getting enough ball in rugby union, you'll have a lot more opportunity to show your skills if you play league, you're not the athlete you could be . . . blah blah blah.' It was the type of talk that had previously deterred him from even contemplating switching codes, but this time it was backed up with statistical information to support the claims . . . how many times on average he touched the ball during a game of rugby, how many times he could expect to receive it in a game of league—the approximate number of defenders waiting for him in both instances.

'They had really done their homework,' Little says. 'It was hard not to be impressed. They were very professional in their outlook, unlike other clubs I'd spoken to, who would spend 10 minutes at a time bagging rugby.'

But there was still no talk of money or contracts. That came a couple of weeks later, when he met Schuhkraft again, this time at the Caxton Hotel in Petrie Terrace, on the fringe of the Brisbane CBD. It was there Schuhkraft started mentioning ballpark figures, estimating that Little could earn around $1.5 million if he played rugby league for five years. Little was simply flabbergasted. He remembers pushing what was left of his steak around in the mushroom sauce on his plate, while he thought about the figure over and over again. It was more money than he'd ever imagined could be made out of football.

Three or four days later, there was another meeting, this time on the back deck of Jason's house, overlooking the river at New Farm. The discussion seemed to be retracing old steps, so to get the ball rolling Little asked that something be put in writing—a contract drawn up for him to consider. He requested the document be faxed down to Fraser Perrin, his former Souths and Queensland rugby teammate who was working as a solicitor on the Gold Coast.

Driving back down to Bond University on the Gold Coast that afternoon, his mind was spinning. *What should I do? Should I give up rugby? I love rugby. But the money. It's an incredible amount of money. I'd never be offered that sort of money again, surely. But really, how important is the money? Would I even enjoy playing rugby league? I couldn't turn back if I didn't. Jesus . . . what if I'm no good at it—what if I'm a dud. What do I do then? I'll have nothing. No. I wouldn't be a dud. I'd be fine. But what about all my rugby friends. Would I get to see them if I played league.*

All the issues kept swirling around in his head. He felt like he was in a giant tumble-dryer. Round and round and round. It just wouldn't stop. He tried to get the league discussions out of his mind. He had mid-term exams. He had to study.

But the issue wouldn't go away. Nor would the Crushers. Why would they? They'd already lured Garrick Morgan and Anthony Herbert, two of Little's Queensland and Australian teammates to the club. Now they'd written out a legally binding contract to pay a 23-year-old $260,000 for some 20-odd games of football. The pressure had to be maintained. They called, again and again. They called so frequently Little wasn't game to turn his mobile phone on. Every time he did, it rang. He needed more time to think. *What do I do? What do I do?*

'They were the worst couple of weeks of my life,' Little says. 'There were so many things running through my mind. The Crushers had asked me not to say anything to anybody, but with a decision of that magnitude, it was impossible. You have to bounce it around with people.'

Jason spoke to his parents. Pat was not particularly keen for him to play rugby league, Ray looked at it a little more clinically and commercially. The offer was, after all, an excellent opportunity for Jason to establish himself financially. But neither advised him to do one thing or the other. Ultimately, they said, it was a decision 'that only you can make'.

He sought the opinion of a couple of close friends, in their late 30s and early 40s, who advised him on business matters from time to time. But the exercise was riddled with shortfalls. One, because they were dyed-in-the-wool rugby supporters and two, because they were quite financial themselves. The money would not have appealed to them nearly as much as it did to Jason.

He also spoke to a few teammates—Damian Smith, David Wilson and Tim. All said much the same thing. It was a good offer, a *great* offer. Naturally they would miss him if he went, but at the end of the day: 'You have to do what's right for Jason Little'.

Tim, in particular, could appreciate the mental anguish Jason was going through. He had been in exactly the same situation three or four times himself, so purposely butted out. 'Ultimately the decision has got to come from within,' Horan says. 'There's nobody else who can make it for you. But I sympathised with Jason. I can honestly say I'd never seen him the way he was in late September, early October. For weeks you could hardly talk to him. Every time you did it was like he was on another planet—even more than normal. I don't think people realise just how much pressure is involved in a decision like that. Clearly it was the toughest one Jas had ever had to make.'

To complicate matters further, while the deliberations were going on and on, the Crushers' offer was going up and up. From $260,000 a season, to $270,000, to $280,000—more and more bonuses tossed in. It was all a bit embarrassing—$260,000 or $280,000—it didn't really matter. The money wasn't the reason Jason was holding out. But he was hardly going to tell the Crushers that.

Meanwhile, the phone calls kept coming. One day in the second week of October, Little came home to his Gold Coast apartment just after lunchtime to find 22 messages on the answering machine, most of them related in some way to the Crushers' offer. The club wanted an answer—two deadlines had already been broken. They were running out of time and patience. Their big launch was just around the corner. On the off-chance Little didn't sign, they needed to leave themselves time for negotiations with a suitable alternative.

Little wasn't trying to be difficult. He honestly didn't know. One morning he would wake up and say to himself: 'Right that's it. I'm going.' By dinner that night, there would be lingering doubt. The next morning: 'No. I'm staying.' It went on for weeks.

Two nights before his final deadline, October 21, Little was sitting in the library at Bond University, almost buried in a pile of text books he'd been reading but in no way digesting. He pushed them aside, pulled out a block of foolscap, drew a line down the middle of the page and started tallying the 'Pros and Cons' of his current dilemma. In the 'Pro' column he listed the following: *Money, Security, Brisbane* (that he didn't have to move to Sydney to play league appealed enormously), *Challenge, Change*. Across the other side: *Give up freedom, Lifestyle, Rugby friends, Study, No turning back*. They were not listed in any order, but clearly, there were two factors weighing more heavily than the others. It was a battle between money and lifestyle.

Less than 24 hours before 'D-day', he had no idea which way he would lean.

At 7.15am on Friday, October 21, Darryl Van de Velde was already in his car on the way to work. He had a huge day ahead. The Crushers were assembling their team publicly for the first time at a lavish launch for more than 350 VIP guests. Amid all the pomp and ceremony would come the big announcement. The Crushers had finally signed up rugby union's hottest property, Jason Little.

Mere kilometres from the clubhouse, Van de Velde's car phone rang. It was Little. Suddenly, the Crushers party was short on pizzazz, the food would taste a little stale, the beer a little flat.

'I'm really sorry, Darryl, I've decided to stay with rugby.'

Van de Velde had heard a whisper the night before that the deal was off, but was nonetheless disappointed. 'Was there anything we could have done?' he asked forlornly.

'No. You did everything you could. I've just decided I want to play rugby union.'

When Van de Velde arrived at work, he immediately made his way into the dining room and removed the 'JASON LITTLE' name tag from one of the sponsor's tables already set up in readiness for the function. In the office downstairs, there was a Crushers kit bag, complete with personalised jersey, which would have to be unpacked. The room list for a team training camp at Caloundra's Oasis resort that weekend would also have to be altered. Anthony Herbert would now have a room to himself.

It was an extremely close call. The big one had wriggled off the line, just as Van de Velde was hauling it into the boat.

The news was to sweep the sporting world. Sydney reporter Peter Jenkins managed to get through to Little on his mobile phone, only 15 minutes after he had delivered his final verdict to the Crushers. Some 20 minutes after Jenkins put the story to air on radio 2UE, he had 37 phone calls from people trying to find out more.

Later that morning, the Queensland Rugby Union issued a press statement from Little, explaining his reasons for turning down the Crushers' offer. The media release stipulated that Little had study commitments all day, and could not be contacted. But that didn't stop three television crews and two newspapers turning up at Bond University, and hauling him out of lectures for interviews.

When his flatmate Annie McIntyre appeared at the door of his Marketing tutorial at 2.30pm, a frustrated Little presumed there was yet another urgent media enquiry. But he was wrong. She had driven to the campus to deliver a phone message. His mother and father had been involved in a car accident while driving down from Dalby to talk to him about his big decision.

Both were in the Toowoomba Base Hospital, Ray with 70 stitches in his right arm and Pat with a dislocated shoulder. Neither injury was particularly serious, but the news couldn't have come at a worse time. Having finally poked his head through the clouds, he now had another major concern to handle.

'It was definitely one of the more eventful days in my life,' Little recalls. 'It felt like it lasted 80 hours.'

Horan admits being very surprised when Jason rang him that morning, and told him he'd decided to stay with rugby. 'Initially I thought there's no way he'll go (to league). But the further down the track he went, the more convinced I was he'd switch. I reckon if the Crushers could have given him another two weeks to think about it, Jason would have switched for sure. But when forced, he made the only safe decision available to him.'

Little isn't so sure. 'Maybe, but in the end my mind kept coming back to a day I'd spent after a Bledisloe Cup Test in Sydney. There were about 12 of us—players plus wives and girlfriends—cruising around the Harbour on a giant yacht, eating seafood and drinking champagne. It was just the perfect day. I didn't want it to end. I feared I might have to sacrifice those type of occasions if I switched to rugby league.'

What Jason did find staggering—and heartening—was all the letters of public support he received when he declared his allegiance to rugby union. There were dozens and dozens from people he'd never heard of, congratulating him on the decision, and saying how important it was for the game. On the flip side, he realises there are probably twice as many again, who think he's either mad, or the beneficiary of a major counter offer from rugby union administrators.

Neither is true. 'It's hard to explain to people your rationale for staying with rugby,' Little says. 'On the surface, it would seem financially unwise, but it's impossible to put a monetary value on the enjoyment I get from being involved with the Wallabies. The lifestyle, the places you go, the fun you have—days like the harbour cruise—I rate as more important than the money. As far as the counter offer is concerned, the Queensland and Australian Rugby Unions simply looked more at the big picture, piecing together a package that would allow me to pursue my University degree. Rugby league may have been very lucrative in the short term, but a University degree will be a lot more beneficial in 10 years time.'

Monetary awards aside, Little has mixed feelings about the game of rugby league itself. Yes, he believes it would provide more opportunity to show individual attacking skills, but at the same time, he is uninspired by the monotony of the play. 'From an outsider's point of view, rugby league looks to have become very structured,' he says. 'Three hits up the middle, a couple out wide, then a kick on the sixth tackle. It seems most matches are decided on error rate. The team that forces their opponents into mistakes—particularly dropped balls—usually wins. I like to think in rugby, there's greater reward for creativity, although I'm the first to admit that there's nothing worse to watch than a really static game of rugby.'

As much as the league talent scouts, and the league fans, would like to see it happen . . . they may just be left wondering how Little and Horan would fare in the professional ranks. Years would not seem to be a barrier given that 30 is a more than respectable age for footballing retirement. But there remain other more significant obstacles.

Little, at the time of turning down the Crushers' record offer, hinted it was 'now or never' as far as rugby league was concerned. He acquiesced slightly as time wore on, but league remains a distant challenge—if a challenge at all. Of far more immediate concern was the Wallabies' defence of the World Cup in May-June 1995.

And as Bob Dwyer and the Wallabies began the intense six-month period that would take them to South Africa, Horan was not entertaining any serious thought of playing rugby—let alone rugby league. He was concentrating on nothing more challenging than walking without a limp. Quite literally, he was taking it one step at a time.

As the New Year ticked over, and a new chapter of contrasting challenges began, Horan and Little were together again, sailing a 47-foot yacht around the Great Barrier Reef with football chums Garrick Morgan, Brett Johnstone and Damian Smith. Dangling a line over the bow of the boat, cold beer at the ready, Johannesburg seemed a blue moon away.

If they could look into the future, they would see themselves together still, in 10, 20, even 40 years time. They'll still be playing golf—Horan insisting on countless side wagers while dreaming up different and more elaborate ways of trapping his prize bunny. The vegetables may still be mysteriously disappearing from his plate, but the public speaking will be impeccably polished, and the outings of the Culture Club more varied and interesting than ever.

Little will have mastered the art of changing the tap washers, and cooking the perfect pizza. But he will still be warding off would-be ear touchers, and will be no less wary of the nab waiting around the next corner.

There will, of course, be many more quiet dinners for three, unless a brave young maiden can put the sort of tackle on Little that he has executed so many times himself. If so, Horan will reciprocate the best man duties Little performed at his wedding. And then, perhaps, the children of these two great mates will grow up with that same eternal and indefinable bond.

The crystal ball, too, would show the pair together again in South Africa for the 1995 World Cup. But what joys and challenges the pair will share is beyond prediction, except to say they might steer clear of Room 1213.

Little, his knee fully recovered from that diabolical May afternoon on their last visit to the republic, seems destined to play a key role in the Wallabies' bid for back-to-back triumphs. And how sweet it will be if his best mate is standing beside him, in the proud line of gold jerseys, belting out the words of 'Advance Australia Fair' before each game.

Yet, for all the experiences they have shared, all the parallels they have walked, and all the memories still to be collected, what they wouldn't give to make that trek back out to Goondiwindi, the World Cup in hand, to see 'Woody' wear that tie just one more time.

# Statistics

## Jason Sidney Little
### AUSTRALIA

### 1989
| | | |
|---|---|---|
| v **France** (Strasbourg) | W | 32-15 |
| v **France** (Lille) | L | 25-19 |

### 1990
| | | |
|---|---|---|
| v **France** (SFS) | W | 21-9 |
| v **France** (Ballymore) | W | 48-31 |
| v **France** (SFS) | L | 28-19 |
| v **USA** (Ballymore) | W | 67-9 |

### 1991
| | | |
|---|---|---|
| v **Wales** (Ballymore) | W | 63-6 |
| v **England** (SFS) | W | 40-15 |
| v **New Zealand** (SFS) | W | 21-12 |
| v **New Zealand** (Auckland) | L | 6-3 |

### World Cup
| | | |
|---|---|---|
| v **Argentina** (Llanelli) | W | 32-19 |
| v **Wales** (Cardiff) | W | 38-3 |
| v **Ireland** (Dublin) | W | 19-18 |
| v **New Zealand** (Dublin) | W | 16-6 |

### Final
| | | |
|---|---|---|
| v **England** (Twickenham) | W | 12-6 |

## 1992

| | | |
|---|---|---|
| v **New Zealand** (SFS) | W | 17-16 |
| v **New Zealand** (Ballymore) | W | 19-17 |
| v **New Zealand** (SFS) | L | 26-23 |
| v **South Africa** (Capetown) | W | 26-3 |
| v **Ireland** (Dublin) | W | 42-17 |
| v **Wales** (Cardiff) | W | 23-6 |

## 1993

| | | |
|---|---|---|
| v **Tonga** (Ballymore) | W | 52-14 |
| v **New Zealand** (Dunedin) | L | 25-10 |
| v **South Africa** (SFS) | L | 19-12 |
| v **South Africa** (Ballymore) | W | 28-20 |
| v **South Africa** (SFS) | W | 19-12 |
| v **Canada** (Calgary) | W | 43-16 |
| v **France** (Bordeaux) | L | 16-13 |
| v **France** (Paris) | W | 24-3 |

## 1994

| | | |
|---|---|---|
| v **Western Samoa** (SFS) | W | 73-6 |
| v **New Zealand** (SFS) | W | 19-18 |

Debut v France aged 19 years 71 days
31 Tests (1989-94)
10 Tries (Total points—47)

## Additional National Honours

Australian Under 17 1987
Australian Schoolboys 1987
Australian Under 21 1989

## Queensland

Schoolboys 1987
Under 21 1988

Open grade debut v Cuyo (Argentina),
March 1989
Youngest player ever to play 50 games
(v Otago), April 1993
Total games – 61 (1989-94)
Total points – 63 (15 tries)

## Club
First grade debut v University, March 1988
Brisbane Club Premiers 1991-93
Grand finalists 1988-89

## TIM JAMES HORAN
## AUSTRALIA

### 1989
| | | |
|---|---|---|
| v **New Zealand** (Auckland) | L | 24-12 |
| v **France** (Strasbourg) | W | 32-15 |
| v **France** (Lille) | L | 25-19 |

### 1990
| | | |
|---|---|---|
| v **France** (SFS) | W | 21-9 |
| v **New Zealand** (Christchurch) | L | 21-6 |
| v **New Zealand** (Auckland) | L | 27-17 |
| v **New Zealand** (Wellington) | W | 21-9 |

### 1991
| | | |
|---|---|---|
| v **Wales** (Ballymore) | W | 63-6 |
| v **England** (SFS) | W | 40-15 |
| v **New Zealand** (SFS) | W | 21-12 |
| v **New Zealand** (Auckland) | L | 6-3 |

## World Cup

| | | |
|---|---|---|
| v **Argentina** (Llanelli) | W | 32-19 |
| v **Western Samoa** (Pontypool) | W | 9-3 |
| v **Wales** (Cardiff) | W | 38-3 |
| v **Ireland** (Dublin) | W | 19-18 |
| v **New Zealand** (Dublin) | W | 16-6 |

## Final

| | | |
|---|---|---|
| v **England** (Twickenham) | W | 12-6 |

## 1992

| | | |
|---|---|---|
| v **Scotland** (SFS) | W | 27-12 |
| v **Scotland** (Ballymore) | W | 37-13 |
| v **New Zealand** (SFS) | W | 17-16 |
| v **New Zealand** (Ballymore) | W | 19-17 |
| v **New Zealand** (SFS) | L | 26-23 |
| v **South Africa** (Capetown) | W | 26-3 |
| v **Ireland** (Dublin) | W | 42-17 |
| v **Wales** (Cardiff) | W | 23-6 |

## 1993

| | | |
|---|---|---|
| v **Tonga** (Ballymore) | W | 52-14 |
| v **New Zealand** (Dunedin) | L | 25-10 |
| v **South Africa** (SFS) | L | 19-12 |
| v **South Africa** (Ballymore) | W | 28-20 |
| v **South Africa** (SFS) | W | 19-12 |
| v **Canada** (Calgary) | W | 43-16 |
| v **France** (Bordeaux) | L | 16-13 |
| v **France** (Paris) | W | 24-3 |

Debut v New Zealand aged 19 years 70 days
33 Tests (1989-93)
16 Tries (Total points – 70)

## Additional National Honours
Australian Under 17 1987
Australian Schoolboys 1987
Australian Under 19 1989

## Queensland
Schoolboys 1987
Under 19 1988

Open grade debut v Western Samoa
(Apia, March 1990)
Celebrated 50 games for Queensland (v Northern
Transvaal, Ballymore, March 1994)
Total games – 56 (1989-94)
Total points – 111 (27 tries)

## Club
First grade debut v Wests, March 1989
Brisbane Club Premiers 1991-93
Grand finalist 1989

# Index